PASCAL IN PRACTICE
Using the Language

ELLIS HORWOOD BOOKS IN COMPUTING SCIENCE

General Editors: Professor JOHN CAMPBELL, University College London, and BRIAN L. MEEK, King's College London (KQC), University of London

Series in Computers and Their Applications

Series Editor: BRIAN L. MEEK, Computer Centre, King's College London (KQC), University of London

Atherton, R.	**Structured Programming with COMAL**
Bailey, R.	**Functional Programming with HOPE**
Barrett, R., Ramsay, A. & Sloman, A.	**POP-11: A Practical Language for Artificial Intelligence**
Berry, R.E.	**Programming Language Translation**
Bishop, P.	**Fifth Generation Computers: Concepts, Implementations and Uses**
Brailsford, D.F. & Walker, A.N.	**Introductory ALGOL 68 Programming**
Bull, G.M.	**The Dartmouth Time Sharing System**
Burns, A.	**New Information Technology**
Burns, A.	**The Microchip: Appropriate or Inappropriate Technology**
Carberry, J.C.	**COBOL: A Practical Approach**
Chivers, I.D.	**A Practical Introduction to Standard PASCAL**
Chivers, I.D. & Clark, M.W.	**Interactive FORTRAN 77: A Hands-on Approach**
Clark, M.W.	**pc-Portable FORTRAN**
Cleal, D.M. & Heaton, N.O.	**Intelligent Systems: A User Perspective**
Cope, T.	**Computing using BASIC: An Interactive Approach**
Dahlstrand, I.	**Software Portability and Standards**
Davie, A.J.T. & Morrison, R.	**Recursive Descent Compiling**
de Saram, H.	**Programming in micro-PROLOG**
Deasington, R.J.	**A Practical Guide to Computer Communications and Networking, 2nd Edition**
Deasington, R.J.	**X.25 Explained: Protocols for Packet Switching Networks, 2nd Edition**
Eastlake, J.	**A Structured Approach to Computer Strategy**
Eisenbach, S.	**Functional Programming: Languages, Tools and Architectures**
Ellis, D.	**Medical Computing in Practice**
Ennals, J.R.	**Artificial Intelligence: Applications to Logical Reasoning and Historical Research**
Fernando, C.	**Cluster Analysis on Microcomputers**
Fossum, E. *et al.*	**Computerization of Working Life**
Gray, P.M.D.	**Logic, Algebra and Databases**
Harland, D.M.	**Concurrency and Programming Languages**
Harland, D.M.	**Polymorphic Programming Languages**
Hill, I.D. & Meek, B.L.	**Programming Language Standardisation**
Hogger, C.J. & Hogger, E.I.	**PROLOG for Scientists and Engineers**
Hutchins, W.J.	**Machine Translation: Past, Present, Future**
Hutchison, D.	**Fundamentals of Computer Logic**
Hutchison, D. & Silvester, P.	**Computer Logic: Principles and Technology**
Lester, C.	**Advanced Programming in PASCAL**
McKenzie, J., Elton, L. & Lewis, R.	**Interactive Computer Graphics in Science Teaching**
Matthews, J.	**FORTH**
Meek, B.L., Heath, P. & Rushby, N.	**Guide to Good Programming Practice, 2nd Edition**
Millington, D.	**Systems Analysis and Design for Computer Applications**
Moore, L.	**Foundations of Programming with PASCAL**
Moseley, L.G., Sharp, J.A. & Salenieks, P.	**PASCAL in Practice: Using the Language**
Moylan, P.	**Assembly Language for Engineers**
Narayanan, A. & Sharkey, N.E.	**An Introduction to LISP**
Paterson, A.	**Office Systems: Planning, Procurement and Implementation**
Pemberton, S. & Daniels, M.C.	**PASCAL Implementation**
Pesaran, M.H. & Slater, L.J.	**Dynamic Regression: Theory and Algorithms**
Peter, R.	**Recursive Functions in Computer Theory**
Phillips, C. & Cornelius, B.J.	**Computational Numerical Methods**
Ramsden, E.	**Microcomputers in Education 2**
Schirmer, C.	**Programming in C for UNIX**
Sharp, J.A.	**Data Flow Computing**
Smith, I.C.H.	**Microcomputers in Education**
Späth, H.	**Cluster Analysis Algorithms**
Späth, H.	**Cluster Dissection and Analysis**
Stratford-Collins, M.J.	**ADA: A Programmer's Conversion Course**
Teskey, F.N.	**Principles of Text Processing**
Tizzard, K.	**C for Professional Programmers**
Turner, S.J.	**An Introduction to Compiler Design**
Whiddett, R.J., *et al.*	**UNIX: A Practical Introduction for Users**
Whiddett, R.J.	**Concurrent Programming: Techniques and Implementations**
Yannakoudakis, E. & Hutton, P.	**Speech Synthesis and Recognition Systems**
Young, S.J.	**An Introduction to ADA, 2nd (Revised) Edition**
Young, S.J.	**Real Time Languages**

PASCAL IN PRACTICE
Using the Language

L. G. MOSELEY, M.A., Dip.Soc.Ad.
Senior Lecturer
J. A. SHARP, B.Sc.(1st Class Hons.), Ph.D.
Lecturer
P. SALENIEKS, B.Sc.(1st Class Hons.)
Temporary Lecturer
all of Department of Mathematics and Computer Science
University College of Swansea

ELLIS HORWOOD LIMITED
Publishers · Chichester

Halsted Press: a division of
JOHN WILEY & SONS
New York · Chichester · Brisbane · Toronto

First published in 1987 by
ELLIS HORWOOD LIMITED
Market Cross House, Cooper Street,
Chichester, West Sussex, PO19 1EB, England
The publisher's colophon is reproduced from James Gillison's drawing of the ancient Market Cross, Chichester.

Distributors:
Australia and New Zealand:
JACARANDA WILEY LIMITED
GPO Box 859, Brisbane, Queensland 4001, Australia
Canada:
JOHN WILEY & SONS CANADA LIMITED
22 Worcester Road, Rexdale, Ontario, Canada
Europe and Africa:
JOHN WILEY & SONS LIMITED
Baffins Lane, Chichester, West Sussex, England
North and South America and the rest of the world:
Halsted Press: a division of
JOHN WILEY & SONS
605 Third Avenue, New York, NY 10158, USA

British Library Cataloguing in Publication Data
Moseley, L.G.
Pascal in practice: using the language. —
(Ellis Horwood series in computers and their applications)
1. PASCAL (Computer program language)
I. Title II. Sharp, J.A. (John Anthony) *1955–*
III. Salenieks, P.
005.13'3 QA76.73.P2

Library of Congress Card No. 86–27875

ISBN 0–7458–0064–5 (Ellis Horwood Limited — Library Edn.)
ISBN 0–7458–0170–6 (Ellis Horwood Limited — Student Edn.)
ISBN 0–470–20779–5 (Halsted Press)

Phototypeset in Times by Ellis Horwood Limited
Printed in Great Britain by Butler & Tanner, Frome, Somerset

Table of contents

To the chaste huntress *sui generis*

L.M.

To my wife Pam, our son Richard,
and our daughter Rosslyn

J.S.

To my parents, Christine and Fred,
and to my sister, Anne

P.S.

Introduction

This is not a textbook on the programming language Pascal in the conventional sense. The reader cannot just take this book away in the expectation of finding a detailed explanation of the syntax of the language. It is definitely a book about USING the language. It assumes that the reader is already learning the language, either in some formal class at school, university or elsewhere, or else from one of the many good textbooks which are currently available (or even from some of the dreadful ones which are also available).

All three authors are actively involved in teaching computer science, including Pascal, and are concerned about some of the difficulties which beginners face when they are confronted with realistic programming problems and have only a conventional textbook and some lecture notes to help them. A conventional textbook has to explain accurately what the constructs of a language are and to introduce examples of its use which are appropriate to the learning level of the student. It is our experience that such an approach leaves a great deal of confusion, and means that students often have to struggle for unnecessarily long and frustrating hours to solve programming problems with which they are confronted.

SOME PROBLEMS

For complete beginners the problems are obvious. They have to learn something about the art of programming as well as learning the details of Pascal. However, many people, especially many young people, today learn the BASIC computer programming language at an early stage in their education. It is not uncommon for applicants to universities or polytechnics to have contributed articles to popular computer magazines, or to have sold some software to a local commercial organisation. One would expect that, with such a background, learning another programming language would be simple. After all, they should know about assignment, loops, conditional statements, and (if they have been fortunate enough to use a structured BASIC) something about breaking a program into smaller, more manageable sections. However, it is a frequent observation that even these experienced students have difficulty when they transfer to a rich and structured high-level language like Pascal. Among these problems are :

the use of meaningful identifiers (i.e. giving objects names which mean something to other people)

the use of procedures and functions (i.e. breaking a large problem up into a series of smaller ones — which frequently recur in different programs)

varying loop structures (usually of the kind ''when do you want to do something 1000 times and when do you want to do it an unknown number of times'')

conditionals

file-handling

records

pointers and recursion

and especially the use of parameters (how to get different parts of a large program — perhaps written by different members of a team — to communicate reliably with each other).

Above all, the greatest problem for beginners in a high-level language is learning to design an overall solution to the task which faces them. Far too often they get bogged down in trivial details and their overall solution becomes a messy tangle which is virtually impossible for them to understand, and actually impossible for anyone else to understand !

It appears that knowing about the individual concepts in the language is not sufficient to get people started in writing serious programs. One needs something more than this. Obviously one needs practice and experience. There is, however, all the difference in the world between having 20 years' experience and having 1 year's experience, repeated 20 times. Beginners normally need some sort of examples to work with, some sort of starting point. In our experience, they will initially develop a programming style which reflects that of those who teach them (if those who teach them in fact have a recognisable style). However, as they successfully tackle more and more demanding problems, they start to find their own solutions both to the substantive problems and to the technical details which they must master. They start to develop their own consistent series of type and variable names. They have stored on disk a large number of procedures and functions for handling strings, sorting, searching, performing mathematical operations, and so on.

Pascal is in principle a simple, rather stripped-down language. It does have within it, though, the seeds of growth. From it one can build structures and operations which are useful and often beautiful as well. As beginners develop experience, they should start to develop their own extensions to the language. In this book we deal with standard Pascal, without frills or extensions. However, we would expect that after 10 or 12 weeks, the typical student will have built up a stock of commonly used operations which are sufficiently distinctive that one will be able to talk about programming, not in standard Pascal, but in ''Smith Pascal'' or ''Jones Pascal''.

In this book we have tried to provide a series of such examples. Many of them are simple. Most of them are of a kind which cause difficulties to at least a substantial minority of students. We have tried to start off with small sections, the bricks as it were. Later we have tried to put some of the ideas, and even some of the code, together to make what, to continue the analogy, might be regarded as a wall. Towards the end we have tried to make a house, or at the very least a garden shed.

The authors have tried to divide the work between them according to their particular experience. Moseley and Salenieks, who are involved in teaching a large first-year class, have taken the smaller scale examples — the bricks and the walls, as it were. The larger examples are contributed by Sharp. This has in turn meant that the smaller scale examples, being direct exemplars for use, or even for copying, have received a more detailed discussion than have the large ones. However, the large ones deserve detailed study. At some point in the student's learning, he or she will have to look at someone else's code and try to make sense of it.

We hope that by the usual method of breaking a program down into subproblems (expressed as procedures and functions), using meaningful identifiers, having a clear layout, and reasonable comments, we have made these examples comprehensible to beginners. The student should try to demonstrate to himself that he has understood the concepts by translating them into his own code, with his own variable names, his own functions and so on. Reading a book may help, but it must be supplemented with hours at a computer terminal. If this book encourages students to spend fewer but more productive hours at the terminal, we shall be well satisfied.

1

Some first steps: variables and values

PROBLEM STATEMENT 1 MILEAGE CALCULATION 1

TOPICS COVERED Identifiers
Program layout and indentation
Comments and self-documentation
Reading/Writing and Formatting
Constants

Let us take a simple problem, which later we will develop to make it more complex. In this, its first, form it is a problem which could more easily be solved using a pocket calculator, as long as the solver knew how to use the calculator. However, in later chapters the added dimensions of the problem will make it clearly not suitable for such a solution.

A company employs a large number of travelling salesmen. After each journey, each one submits a form stating:

a. the mileage on the speedometer at the start of the journey
b. the mileage on the speedometer at the end of the journey
c. how many gallons of petrol were consumed
d. the cost of petrol per gallon.

For each such form the company wishes to know:

e. the total number of miles driven
f. the total cost of the petrol used
g. the miles-per-gallon obtained on the journey

As these calculations are to be done routinely by one of the clerical staff in their spare time, it is decided that a small program should be produced to do the calculation. You have to design it, bearing in mind that there is a good chance that something grander will probably be wanted if this simple system proves successful. A program such as the following might do the trick.

PROGRAM

```
{A program to calculate mileage for a single travelling salesmen. }
{Note that it contains no provision for repeating the process without }
{re-running the program, and that it saves no information for later use. For }
{example, one cannot work out the average mileage of all salesmen
combined. }
program simplempg(input, output);
const  maximumlimit=2000;
var    startreading, finishreading, milesdriven : integer;
       gallonsused, costpergallon, totalcost, mpg : real;

begin   { THERE MAY BE AN INSERTION HERE LATER }
       write('What was the speedo reading at the start of the journey ? ');
       readln(startreading);
       write('And the reading at the finish of it ?                    ');
       readln(finishreading);
       {CHECK THAT THE DATA ARE NOT IMPOSSIBLE}
       if startreading>finishreading then
       begin
           writeln ('!!!!!!!!!!!!!!!!!!!!!!!!!!!!!!!!!!!!!!!!!!!!!!!!!!');
           writeln ('That is impossible. The reading at the start of');
           writeln ('the journey must be less than that at the end !!');
           writeln ('Try again');
           writeln ('!!!!!!!!!!!!!!!!!!!!!!!!!!!!!!!!!!!!!!!!!!!!!!!!!!')
       end else  { AT LEAST THE MILEAGE IS NOT CRAZY }
       begin          { GET THE PETROL DATA }
           write ('how many gallons were used ?                ');
           readln (gallonsused);
           write ('And how much per gallon did they pay ?      ');
           readln (costpergallon);
           { DO THE CALCULATIONS }
           totalcost := gallonsused * costpergallon;
           milesdriven := finishreading-startreading;
           mpg := milesdriven/gallonsused;
           { FINALLY PRINT THE RESULTS }
           page(output);
           writeln ('++++++++++++++++++++++++++++');
           write ('On this journey a total of ',milesdriven:5,' miles ');
           writeln ('were covered, at a total cost of £',totalcost:6:2);
           writeln;
           writeln ('The driver averaged', mpg:5:1,' m.p.g');
           if milesdriven>maximumlimit then
           begin
             writeln ('!!!!!!!!!!!!!!!!!!!!!!!!!!!!!!!!!!!!!!!!!!!!!!');
             writeln ('!EXCEEDS COMPANY LIMIT—REFER TO MANAGER!
             writeln ('!!!!!!!!!!!!!!!!!!!!!!!!!!!!!!!!!!!!!!!!!!!!!!')
           end;
           writeln ('++++++++++++++++++++++++++++')
```

```
                    end
end.
{-----------------------------------------------------------------}
```

RESULTS

The results below come from three runs of the program. The first gives a "normal" run, the second gives invalid data, and the third gives an implausibly large number of miles driven.

```
What was the speedo reading at the start of the journey? 1200
And the reading at the finish of it?                     1400
How many gallons were used?                              6.0
And how much per gallon did they pay?                    1.96
++++++++++++++++++++++++++++++++++++++++
On this journey a total of 200 miles were covered, at a total cost of £11.76

The driver averaged 33.3 m.p.g
++++++++++++++++++++++++++++++++++++++++
What was the speedo reading at the start of the journey? 1503
And the reading at the finish of it?                     1211
!!!!!!!!!!!!!!!!!!!!!!!!!!!!!!!!!!!!!!!!!!!!!!!!!!!!!!!!
That is impossible. The reading at the start of the journey must be less than
that at the end !!
Try again
!!!!!!!!!!!!!!!!!!!!!!!!!!!!!!!!!!!!!!!!!!!!!!!!!!!!!!!!
What was the speedo reading at the start of the journey?  1503
And the reading at the finish of it?                     15487
How many gallons were used?                                340
And how much per gallon did they pay?                          1.96
++++++++++++++++++++++++++++++++++++++
On this journey a total of 13984 miles were covered, at a total cost of £666.40
The driver averaged 41.1 m.p.g
!!!!!!!!!!!!!!!!!!!!!!!!!!!!!!!!!!!!!!!!!!!!!!!!!!!!!! !
EXCEEDS COMPANY LIMIT—REFER TO MANAGER!
!!!!!!!!!!!!!!!!!!!!!!!!!!!!!!!!!!!!!!!!!!!!!!!!!!!!!
+++++++++++++++++++++++++++++++++++++++
```

DISCUSSION

Clearly this program has several shortcomings. Firstly, each time a new calculation is to be performed the program must be run again. We shall overcome this in the second version later. For more substantial problems, for example, if we wish to amalgamate information about several salesmen, the structure is inadequate. Even as a simple program, though, it will probably save time for routine work.

What points should we note about it?

1. The structure should be clear. In this case, the structure is:

a. Get the speedometer data
b. Check them
c. Get the petrol data
d. Do the calculations
e. Print the results

Get the overall structure of the program clear

2. Even if this was not clear from the layout of the structure, it should be so from the comments, which essentially follow this structure. In a sense, the comments are the skeleton of the program. Once they are clearly in place, the actual coding is trivial.

Overall comments help more than detailed ones

3. The variable names reflect the objects which they represent, e.g. startreading, finishreading, milesdriven. This is more important than may be apparent at first sight, even in a short program. It is very important in more substantial ones. Try replacing the variable names used here with simpler ones. For example, use ***a*** instead of ***startreading***, ***b*** instead of ***finishreading***, and so on. Introduce a few random syntax errors, or even logical ones, and give both versions (one with ***a***, ***b***, etc., the other with ***startreading*** etc.) to a friend to debug to see which is the easier to understand and modify.

For many beginners a discussion of identifiers seems elementary and unprofitable. However, even VERY simple matters, such as which characters or letters you use, can make a difference. Someone who calls a procedure ***readin*** is inviting the typing error ***readln***, when one tries to use that standard procedure. This sort of slip is often very difficult to trace, because one does not see it. You may have typed ***readln***, and when you spot it, it is obviously wrong. However, you may well look at it 10 or 20 times, and each time what you will see is ***readin***. Often it is only when a friend comes to look over your shoulder (presumably with fresh eyes for the problem) that they (or you) spot the typing error. A more sensible choice of identifier would have removed the problem before it had arisen.

We had a student who included in her program at various points the statement:

```
i := i + 1;
```

and the program produced mysterious results. In particular, it produced a lot of people whose surnames always consisted of exactly two characters, no more, no less. Eventually, when we traced the error we found a very simple typing slip.

```
i := 1 + 1;
```

It does not look very different, but it means that ***i*** never becomes larger than 2 (after all most of us know that 1 + 1 = 2, and it is independent of the original value of the variable ***i***). This problem would have been less likely to occur had she used a statement such as:

```
index := index + 1;
```

Choose identifiers to be meaningful and unambiguous

4. The indentation shows, one hopes, how the program is structured. For example, if the starting mileage is higher than the finishing mileage, the program goes into an indented ***begin*****.....*****end*** block to inform the user of this fact. If it is not, and the readings are possible, it goes into a separate block.

Indentation, especially when it is consistent, makes a program easier to read—and more reliable

5. Note that, even though we could have declared all the quantities to be real numbers, we have reserved that type for the gallons, cost and miles-per-gallon variables. The speedometer readings and the miles driven are declared to be integers. On a simple example it might not make a great difference, but there are two major reasons for this apparently pedantic differentiation. Firstly, it reflects our own psychology. When asked the price of petrol, we usually reply £1.96, or £1.93. We do not usually round it to £2 exactly, and certainly do not truncate it to £1 exactly. The pence matter. Similarly, most people think of the amount of petrol they have consumed as being, say, three and a half gallons. One would not normally say ''exactly 3'' or ''exactly 4''. If we did so, the choice of truncation or rounding might make a big difference to the mileage figure which resulted. If you have driven 100 miles and have used 3.5 gallons of petrol, your mileage is 28.6. Using a truncated gallonage would increase this to 33 (100/3); using a rounded gallonage would reduce it to 25. In the case of the number of miles driven, the situation is different. If someone asks you how far it is to London, you would probably reply ''190 miles'', or ''225 miles'', not ''134.7''. You would be very unlikely to reply ''1.347169 e2''.

So the first reason is to make the type fit our natural way of thinking about an object, which will minimise the risk of our making an error in the first place.

Secondly, if we do make logical mistakes, there is at least a chance that the compiler will detect them. Suppose that we wish to categorise a sample of people in a survey as male or female. We could choose to do this as, say 1=female 2=male. We could similarly choose 'F'=female 'M'=male. Is there any real difference brought about by our choice ? The answer is

''Yes''. It is possible that someone may do something crazy like trying to work out the average sex of the sample. If we had defined the variable to be of type integer (i.e. 1 or 2), the machine will happily perform the requested calculation and inform us that the average sex of the sample is 1.87 or whatever. If, on the other hand, the variable was defined as a character one, the machine would diagnose a type conflict since one cannot logically add 'F' and 'M' together and divide by 2. It is clearly nonsense to say that the average sex of a group of people is halfway between 'J' and 'K', say. By choosing to make our variable of type character, we remove this possible source of error.

Make your identifiers fit the objects which they represent — in both name and type

6. We have done a limited amount of data-checking, i.e. we have ensured that the program will not work if people type in their start and finish readings in the wrong order (since that would give a negative number of miles driven, and you cannot do that — even in reverse gear!). However, the data-checking is limited. We have tried to safeguard against a less than honest salesman putting in an improbably high claim (say thousands of miles a week) and hoping that the machine will give him a large expenses cheque without question. In this case we have merely checked that the number of miles driven is not greater than a predetermined maximum limit. If it is, a warning is printed to refer the matter to a manager. Note that the maximum limit is declared as a constant, called (obviously, one hopes) ***maximum limit***. This is the usual way to declare such quantities since if later we wish to raise or lower the limit, say to 5000 miles, we have to alter only one object in the program. It especially important that we do not have to search through for every occurrence of the number 2000 and alter each one. We might be tempted in that case to do it using a global search and replace command. All well and good if the only occurrence of the number 2000 is when it refers to the maximum limit. If we use the number 5000 (or even 1235000) for other purposes, there is a strong likelihood that we shall inadvertently (and incorrectly) alter those too. The resulting errors are often very hard to trace ! It is not the most sophisticated form of checking, but it does remove, very simply, two possible sources of real-world error.

Of course, if the user typed in 'Fred' for the starting mileage, the program would fail. We can guard against this — but that requires rather more knowledge of number representation than one can at the moment assume.

It is commonly the case that the actual calculations which the program performs makes up only a small proportion of the total code. A larger proportion is often taken up with data-checking and tidy formatting of input and output.

Let the program check your data — it will not get bored

7. Note that we have used field-widths to format the output. This is, of course, to try to ensure tidiness. A miles-per-gallon figure of 53.7 is quite respectable. How good is one of 0.537+e2, 5.37+e1, or even 5.37+e2? We can certainly work it out. However, it is not our natural way of thinking, and thus is a likely source of error even for someone who can think in scientific notation. Perhaps just as important is the fact that the output will probably be used by someone for whom the scientific exponential notation is not a natural way of thinking, and who may make a mistake because of it, or at least waste some time working out what it means. That is not to say that one should never use scientific notation. There are many problems in which it IS the natural way of thinking — for example in a program to study the speed of internal computer operations where the size of the exponent may be the most important single piece of information and where one would prefer to have 1.45-e6 rather than trying to count a lot of zeroes in a small number.

Remember that someone has to read your output

8. We have noted that the program has to be re-run for each salesman and that it is not suitable for a more extended analysis amalgamating all the journeys to give total costs and average mileages. To do this properly would need a certain amount of program redesign.To do the former, to overcome the problem of having to re-run it for each salesman, is simple, and an example of how a program can grow naturally. We simply put the whole program (apart from the ***begin*** ...***end***.) inside a loop controlled by the answer to a question. Of course we would have to declare another variable, e.g. ***answer***, of type character. Then the program would look like this:

```
begin
        repeat { COPY MAIN PROGRAM INTO HERE }
                write ('Any more to do ? Answer Y for Yes, N for No');
                readln (answer)
        until (answer='N') or (answer='n')
end.
```

It is commonly the case that a program can be developed in stages by quite simple means such as this. If the program is properly designed, and is made modular, being divided into meaningful procedures and functions, such a development is usually freer of stress. Note that we talk of a program being "developed", not "written". It is unusual for a program to be written down in its entirety and to work first time. More commonly one writes sections and tests them independently; then one tries to amalgamate them.

Do it step-by-step—it will be quicker than one long jump

PROBLEM STATEMENT 2 SIMPLE INCOME TAX

TOPICS COVERED Reinforcement of concepts in Mileage 1
Introductory initialisation
Arithmetic operators

Write a program that reads data about an employee's weekly earnings, calculates the amount of income tax payable and prints the results.

For an employee the input consists of:

Employee Code Number: An integer in the range 1 to 99 inclusive.
Gross Weeks Wage: A real number greater than 0.0.
Tax Code: An integer in the range 200 to 450 inclusive.

The output for an employee consists of the input and the amount of income tax payable.

The tax code multiplied by an integer scale factor (equal to ten in 1985/6) gives the yearly tax free allowance. This must be converted to give the weekly tax free allowance truncated to a whole number of pounds. Any income above this allowance is taxed at the standard rate (equal to 30% in 1985/6).

PROGRAM

```
program taxexample1 (input, output);
{ calculate and print the weekly amount of income tax payable by an
employee according to problem statement 2 without any input data chec-
king. }

const weeksinyear = 52;
      taxyear = 1985;
      scalefactor = 10;
      taxrate = 30.0;
var   employeeid, taxcode, weeksallowance:  integer;
      weekspay,weekstax,taxablepay:         real;

begin { MAIN }
      { initialise variables }
      employeeid := 0; taxcode := 0; weeksallowance := 0;
      weekspay := 0.0; weekstax := 0.0; taxablepay := 0.0;
      { input data }
      write('Enter employee code number :');
      readln(employeeid);
      write('Enter gross weeks wage      :');
      readln(weekspay);
      write('Enter tax code for ', taxyear:4, '      :');
```

```
    readln(taxcode);
    writeln;
    { calculate the weekly tax free allowance and deduct standard
      rate tax from any pay in excess of the allowance, without rounding
      or truncating any fractions of pence in the taxable pay or the weeks
      tax }
    weeksallowance := (taxcode * scalefactor) div weeksinyear;
    taxablepay := weekspay-weeksallowance;
    weekstax := (taxablepay / 100.0) * taxrate;
    { output results }
    writeln('Employee code number      : ', employeeid:3);
    writeln('Tax code for ', taxyear:4, ' : ', taxcode:3);
    writeln('Income tax payable        : ', weekstax:6:2)
end.
```

RESULTS

```
Enter employee code number   :  18
Enter gross weeks wage       :  161.77
Enter tax code for 1985      :  220
Employee code number         :  18
Gross weeks wage             :  161.77
Tax code for 1985            :  220
Income tax payable           :  35.93
```

DISCUSSION

1. To find out how much tax an employee has to pay, we must write a program that prompts the user for information about an employee, processes it and prints the results. As well as these three tasks, it will also need to do some "house keeping". There are many different ways such a program could be written. Our goal is to make the program easy to read and easy to modify. It is tolerably compact and efficient, but we do not sacrifice clarity for minor savings of memory or execution speed.

Make sure that the overall structure is clear

2. The house keeping entails declaring all identifiers used in the program and setting each constant and identifier to a sensible initial value. Integer variables are initialised to whole numbers and real variables to numbers that include a part after the decimal point. This shows that we are aware of what each variable is being used for, as well as giving marginally more efficient code. (However many compilers and interpreters would do such optimisation automatically.) Most of the constants are only used once, but they are still declared globally at the start of the program. This makes the program easier to read, since the purpose of

weeksallowance := (taxcode * scalefactor) / weeksinyear

is clearer than

weeksallowance := (taxcode * 10) / 52

Parentheses are used to show that we mean (taxcode * 10) / 52 and not taxcode * (10 / 52). The names of all constants and variables are chosen to be as significant as possible, without being unduly long. All identifiers must differ in their first 8 characters. Ours will be written in lower case letters although ISO standard Pascal also allows upper case to be used and this can enhance readability (e.g. ***weeksallowance*** and ***WeeksAllowance***). Most systems will not let ***week*** and ***Week*** be used as two different variables. All values that could change (like the tax rate) are declared as global constants so that they can be updated easily. Then only the constant definitions have to be changed. It is not necessary to search through the whole program and alter every occurrence of the constant.

Use meaningful identifiers, even for constants

3. When the program is run, the user is prompted to enter each piece of information. Although each prompt shows what is required, no attempt is made to check that the input data are valid or plausible and the program cannot recover from bad input. The program 'works' so long as it receives exactly what is expected. But it will fail when given non-numeric data, for example a string of characters when a number was expected. Even when it does not fail, the results may still be wrong. If the gross week's wage was entered as 9400 instead of 94.00, the tax bill will be unduly large! At this stage it is enough to be aware of the pitfalls of bad input data. Later we will look at some techniques that can be used in programs to detect and often correct bad data.

A few disastrous calculations make one concentrate on data-checking. A little thought makes it less painful

4. Comments are included to give an outline description of the calculations and to emphasise details that would otherwise be missed on a cursory reading. For instance, how should the fractional part of taxable pay be treated? Is it ignored, or is it rounded up to the nearest penny (using the standard function ***round***) before the weekly tax is calculated? This small detail could add several hundred pounds a year to a large company's tax bill. The output is intended to be reasonably self-explanatory, so that it is clear what each number means. Field-width specifications are used to print each number to the required accuracy. It is meaningless to print the gross weekly wage to more than the nearest penny, since this is the smallest unit of currency. All the input data are echoed to make the results self contained.

The user can also see exactly what input data were used to produce the results. The numeric values are lined up to make it easier to read the output. This program is not our last word on tax calculation; the topic will be developed later.

If you make it comprehensible to others you will probably understand it yourself

2

Making decisions and structuring data

PROBLEM STATEMENT 3	**MILEAGE CALCULATION WITH COMMENTS**
TOPICS COVERED	Conditional statements IF .. THEN v. IF .. THEN .. ELSE Formatting constant string output Testing for equality and inequality

In the example of the salesmen's mileages we merely printed out the mileage obtained, without comment. What, though, would we need to do if we wished to have printed some comment to the effect that on each journey the mileage was, say, Good, Average or Poor ? Firstly, we would have to define what we meant by the words ''Good'', ''Average'' and ''Poor''. Would we do it simply, for example:

Good	over 40 miles per gallon
Average	over 30 but less than or equal to 40 miles per gallon
Poor	30 miles per gallon or less

or would we do it in a more complex and dynamic fashion ? For example:

Good	20% or more above the average for all salesmen in the last month
Poor	20% or more below the average for all salesmen in the last month
Average	Those in between

We pose the question merely to show that a problem statement must be defined. There are usually many ways of defining concretely the meaning of words like ''Good'' or ''Average'', which are the words which we use in a commonsense specification of a problem. It is important that we are aware that these words can have more than one interpretation, and that we spend some time exercising our imagination to devise several definitions. It may be that at the end of the day we shall actually use the first, simple one which came to mind on the spur of the moment. If we have not tried to think of alternatives, though, we cannot be confident that we have covered all the possibilities, or even the obvious ones. It does make a difference. For example, in studies of the extent of poverty, the figures which appear in the results depend very much upon how one defines poverty. For the moment we draw your attention to the need to think carefully about turning commonsense specifications into concrete operational measures. In the present example, this is not our main concern, so we shall illustrate our points using only the first, simple, definition.

PROGRAM FRAGMENTS

```
{-----------------------------------------------------------------}
            roughmpg:=round(mpg);
            {SECTION TO SHOW A POOR USE OF CONDITIONAL
            TESTS }
            if roughmpg > 40 then writeln ('GOOD':10);
            if roughmpg > 30 then writeln ('AVERAGE':10);
            if roughmpg < 30 then writeln ('POOR':10);
            {SECTION TO SHOW A BETTER USE OF CONDITIONAL
            TESTS}
            if roughmpg > 40 then writeln ('Good':10)
            else
                      if roughmpg > 30 then writeln ('Average':10)
                      else writeln ('Poor':10);
            {-----------------------------------------------------------------}
```

RESULTS

```
What was the speedo reading at the start of the journey?  100
And the reading at the finish of it?                      200
How many gallons were used?                                 5.2
And how much per gallon did they pay?                       1.60
+++++++++++++++++++++++++++++++++++++
On this journey a total of 100 miles were covered, at a total cost of £8.32
The driver averaged 19.2 m.p.g
+++++++++++++++++++++++++++++++++++++
POOR
   Poor

What was the speedo reading at the start of the journey?  500
And the reading at the finish of it?                      600
How many gallons were used?                                 3
And how much per gallon did they pay?                       1.9
+++++++++++++++++++++++++++++++++++++
On this journey a total of 100 miles were covered, at a total cost of £5.70
The driver averaged 33.3 m.p.g
+++++++++++++++++++++++++++++++++++++
AVERAGE
     Average
```

```
What was the speedo reading at the start of the journey?  1000
And the reading at the finish of it?                       1100
How many gallons were used?                                 2.1
And how much per gallon did they pay?                       1.62
++++++++++++++++++++++++++++++++++++++++
On this journey a total of 100 miles were covered, at a total cost of £3.40
The driver averaged 47.6 m.p.g
+++++++++++++++++++++++++++++++++++++++++
   GOOD
AVERAGE
    Good
```

DISCUSSION

We have shown two attempted solutions to the problem (both are obviously only code fragments which would be inserted at the appropriate point in the original program — probably using a text editor). Both are real code, taken from programs written by beginning students. The output of the two should be distinguishable — one is in upper case, the other in lower case. What are the similarities and differences between these two attempted solutions?

1. In both cases the annotation to the results is given a field-width. The action to be taken is:

```
writeln ('Some comment' : field-width);
```

not

```
writeln ('Some comment');
```

This ensures that the comments are aligned on the right-hand side, i.e. the final letters below each other in the same column on the printout or screen display. Had the field-width's specifications been omitted, the comments would have been left-justified (not right-justified), i.e. the 'G' of Good, the 'A' of Average, would have been above each other (rather than the 'd' of Good and the second 'e' of Average. The reasons for preferring right-justification of field-widths in most (but not all) applications are:

(a) we think that it looks neater — but that is purely a matter of personal aesthetic judgment, and there is no reason for anyone else to agree with us on such a matter.

(b) if later we wish to add additional comments on the same line, e.g.

```
21.2        Poor  Refer car for servicing
34.6     Average  No further action required
48.9        Good  Give "Salesman of the month" award
```

such additional comments will also be neatly aligned, since they will all start in the same column.

If, in the example above, we had not used field-width specification, they would have started wherever the previous word happened to finish. The printing of that previous word might have taken place 500 lines earlier in the program, or in some deeply nested procedure. There would have been guesswork about what our output would look like; it would be dependent upon unpredictable factors. By specifying how we want it to look, we can safeguard ourselves to a large extent against such unpredictable fluctuations.

The larger the difference in the length of words in a printed message, the more untidy becomes the effect of omitting field-width specifications. If our comments had been:

Really Outstandingly Good
About Average
Bad

and we had omitted field-width specifications, any subsequent printing later on the same line would have been really untidy and unpleasant.

Of course, you may be absolutely certain that your program will never be modified, that it is such a perfect jewel that no on would dare touch it (not even you), or that the problem has been so completely solved that no one would ever re-formulate it in a slightly different form. In that case, either method of formatting the output will do. However, it is very rare for a real-life program in a high-level language to continue unmodified to the end of its days. Anything which you can do to make such possible later modifications easier is to be welcomed.

Finally we would stress that the layout of results matters. Remember — someone has to use your program. If the format of your output is poor, they will not use it as effectively as you hope. Indeed, they may not use it at all. Worse still, they may not even buy it.

Think about formats — for the user and for your successors who will have to maintain the program

2. The first version will quite simply fail, i.e. it will perform wrongly, in at least two ways. The first way is shown by asking the question ''What will happen if a salesman averages exactly 30 m.p.g ?'' The most likely outcome is that no comment at all will be printed. Of course what should be printed is the comment ''POOR''. The point is one of logic, not of programming. When using a conditional test of the kind ''IF.....THEN'', a common mistake is, at the same time, to make both too many and not enough tests. Here we have an example where not enough tests are being made. The programmer tested for the condition of ***roughmpg*** $<$ 30 and that of ***roughmpg*** $>$ 30, but he failed to specify (or, apparently, even consider)

what would happen in the condition ***roughmpg*** = 30. This is very common, even though it appears obvious. It is less apparent here than it might otherwise be, since the tests come in different statements.

Don't forget to test for equality

3. The other way in which the first version will fail is that it will print comments when it should in fact not do so. However, it will not exhibit this silly behaviour under all circumstances. Let us take as examples three salesmen who obtain mileages of 24.6, 33.2, and 46.7 m.p.g. respectively.In the case of ***roughmpg*** = 24.6 the machine will first check whether that is greater than 40. It is not, so nothing will happen as a result of this test. Similarly, it will go on and check that 24.6 is not greater than 30. Again nothing will happen as a result of this test. Finally, it will check whether 24.6 is less than 30. This time the test evaluates to TRUE and it will accordingly print the word "POOR". In this case, the code produces the result which we expect. A small but in fact premature sigh of relief is often heard at this point.

In the second case, the machine will check whether 33.2 is greater than 40 and, finding that it is not, will pass silently on to check whether it is greater than 30. It finds that this is TRUE and, quite properly, prints the word "AVERAGE". Rather superfluously, it will then go on and none the less check whether 33.2 is less than 30. That is plainly FALSE so it does nothing more. The result of the 3 statements is to print the word "AVERAGE" and nothing else. Once again, it has produced what we expected. Apparently the code is working correctly. Let us just check the third example to be certain.

In this final case it checks whether 46.7 is greater than 40. It is, so this TRUE evaluation leads to the word "GOOD" being printed. All correct so far. It then goes on to check whether it is greater than 30. (Why not, since that is the next statement?) Unfortunately, this also is TRUE — 46.7 is > 30 — so it will print "AVERAGE". Finally, it will plough remorselessly on to make the final test of whether 46.7 is less than 30. Fortunately that is FALSE and it will do nothing more. In this case it should have printed out one comment — "GOOD". In fact, it has printed out two comments — "GOOD" and "AVERAGE", which is of course a logical nonsense.

What has happened is that the programmer has made too many tests. What he should have realised is that once one of the tests evaluates to TRUE (for example the mileage is over 40) we do not need to make the other tests at all. They should automatically be FALSE, and if they are not there is something wrong with our logic.

Ensure that your IF is not really an ELSE IF

4. In the second version this is taken care of. The use of the ELSE clauses ensures that unnecessary tests are not being made. With the 46.7 example, once the machine has printed "Good", the subsequent ELSE forces it to ignore the rest of the conditional statement. It therefore by-passes the

subsequent unnecessary tests and ''drops through'' to whatever follows. After all, the second version is only one statement, whereas the first version is clearly three separate statements.

In the 33.2 example it would check whether that is greater than 40. The test evaluates to FALSE so it would follow the ELSE branch, testing for 33.2 > 30. That succeeds, so having printed the appropriate message it will ignore the next ELSE, since it knows that 33.2 cannot be less than 30. If either of the first two tests had been true it would never have got to this point. However, by the same logic if it does get to this point, it does not have to make any more tests. It is not necessary to test whether 24.6 is less than 30. It must be. Any salesman who gets to the second ELSE must, with no further testing, merit the description ''Poor''.

ELSEs minimise your testing

5. This raises the question of efficiency. We saw that in the second version a ''Good'' mileage figure generates one, and only one, test; it does not bother to test for ''Average'' or ''Poor''. Similarly an ''Average'' figure will generate only two tests. Rather less obviously a ''Poor'' figure generates only two tests, as well. The first version, though, is not only wrong, it is inefficient as well. It ALWAYS generates three tests no matter what data we feed it. It does unnecessary and unproductive work. Even in the worst case (a data set with no ''Good'' mileages at all in it) the second version has two tests per salesman, while version one has three, i.e. 50 % worse. In the best case (where all the mileages are ''Good'') the second version performs only one test per case, while the first version stolidly ploughs on with its three tests. This time it would be 200 % worse. With a large set of data, this would waste a fair amount of machine time.

ELSEs are usually more efficient

6. Of course, if you get large numbers of IF..THEN..ELSEs in a single statement, there can be two unfortunate results:

(a) the program starts to straggle across the page (and sometimes even off it altogether)

(b) the code becomes increasingly confusing to read.

The CASE statement can in most instances prevent these two outcomes. It is dealt with later in the book.

There is always something more to learn

7. In this case we have converted the value of the variable ***mpg*** (which is a real) to that of ***roughmpg*** (which will have been declared as an integer). The reason for this was to demonstrate the problems involved in using conditional statements without bringing in the complications of testing

for the equality of two real numbers. We shall not deal with this in detail here, but you should be aware that real numbers are stored with a limited degree of precision, i.e. they are accurate to only a certain number of decimal places. Thus, after a certain amount of calculation which should produce the number 30.0 exactly, a real number may be stored as, say, 29.999999999999 or 30.000000000001, neither of which is equal to 30.0. This means that two real numbers which, after some calculation, should be exactly equal are frequently almost but not exactly equal, and the machine will think that they are in fact unequal.

The normal method of avoiding this problem is to define a constant (frequently called ***epsilon***, although you might care to call it ***verytinynumber***) with a small value such as 0.0000001 and then instead of asking whether ***x*** and ***y*** are equal, ask whether the difference between them is less than the value of that tiny constant.

Instead of:

```
if x = y then .........
```

we would use a statement such as:

```
if (abs(x-y)< verytinynumber) then ......
```

However, considerations such as these are important particularly in numerical applications. They may not occur too frequently in the beginning programmer's experience. You should be aware that there are problems of accuracy when handling real numbers, and that it is possible to devise techniques to overcome such problems of accuracy. However, unless one does take precautions, testing for the equality of reals is dangerous. Objects which should be equal often are not quite so.

Beware of testing reals for equality

PROBLEM STATEMENT 4 DAYS IN THE MONTH

TOPICS COVERED: Simple arrays; Data-checking; Simple use of boolean variables; Modifying a program

Write a program that reads in a date and calculates and prints the number of days in the month. The date is to be given as three whole numbers on one line in the order of : day (1 or 2 digits), month (1 or 2 digits), year (always 4 digits) with each number separated from the next by at least one blank space. Each date must be checked to ensure that the input is in the following ranges:

Date : An integer>= 1 and <= the last day in the month, not taking leap years into account
Month : An integer >= 1 and <= 12
Year : An integer >= 1753 and <= 2000

If the date is valid then the number of days in the month must be printed, otherwise the date and an error message warning that the date is invalid are to be printed. When the program is working satisfactorily, extend it to take leap years into account.

PROGRAM

```
program dateexample1a (input, output);
{ calculate and print the number of days in a month, reading the date as three
whole numbers on one line, in the order dd mm yyyy. The year must be given
as 4 digits and leap years are not taken into account. }

const  firstyear = 1753;{ first full year of the gregorian calendar }
       lastyear = 2000;
var    daysinmonth          : array[1..12] of integer;
       date, month, year : integer;    validdate       : boolean;
begin  { MAIN }
       { initialise the number of days in each month during a non-leap year }
       daysinmonth[1] := 31; daysinmonth[2] := 28; daysinmonth[3] := 31;
       daysinmonth[4] := 30; daysinmonth[5] := 31; daysinmonth[6] := 30;
       daysinmonth[7] := 31; daysinmonth[8] := 31; daysinmonth[9] := 30;
       daysinmonth[10] := 31; daysinmonth[11] := 30; daysinmonth[12] := 31;
       write('Enter date (dd mm yyyy) : '); { input and validate the date }
       readln(date, month, year);
       writeln;
       if (year < firstyear) or (year > lastyear) then validdate := false
       else
              if (month < 1) or (month > 12) then validdate := false
       else if (date < 1)or(date > daysinmonth[month]) then
       validdate := false
                     else validdate := true;
       if validdate then { output the results or an error message }
       begin
              write('There are ',daysinmonth[month]:2,' days in month ');
              writeln(month:2,' of the year ',year:4,'.');
              writeln('Leap years have not been taken into account.')
       end else
```

```
    begin
        write('The date ',date:2,' / ',month:2,' / ',year:4,' is invalid.');
        writeln('Please try running the program again.')
    end
end.
```

RESULTS

Sample run one.

Enter date (dd mm yyyy) : 28 02 1984.
There are 28 days in month 2 of the year 1984.
Leap years have not been taken into account.

Sample run two

Enter date (dd mm yyyy) : 29 2 1984
The date 29/ 2/1984 is invalid. Please try running the program again.

DISCUSSION

1. The problem of finding out how many days there are in a given month can be broken down into several smaller tasks. First the user must be prompted to enter the date on a single line in the order of day, month, year, just as it is required in the problem specification. If each number is separated by at least one blank space, but not any other character, the

readln(date, month, year)

statement will cause each number to be read and stored in a separate variable starting with the date and finishing with the year. Then we must check that the data are valid, rejecting any obviously incorrect values like 32nd May and finally printing the results for dates that are possible. We cannot verify that the user has typed what they intended to, but we can check that what is given is plausible.

Break the problem into smaller, more easily-solvable steps

2. A date is valid if each number is an integer within the range given in the problem specification. Since the date, month and year have all been declared as variables of the type integer, we do not have to test whether they are whole numbers. This is done automatically as they are input and if any non-integers are entered an error message will be printed and the program will stop. To test that each number is within range, a compound IF statement is used. This consists of several simple if...then...else statements joined together. The first 'simple if' checks whether the year falls before the first year or after the last year that we want the program to work for. 1753 is declared as the first year because it is the first full year when the Gregorian calendar (named after Pope Gregory XIII) was used, replacing the less accurate Julian calendar. Both 'boundary' years are declared as constants at the beginning of the program so that they can easily be changed if necessary.

If the year lies outside that range then the date cannot be correct and we record this fact by setting the ***validdate*** variable to be false. Otherwise we go on to check whether the month number is between 1 and 12 inclusive, setting ***validdate*** to be false if it isn't and continuing to check the date if it is. Finally, the date is checked and ***validdate*** is set to false if it is outside the correct range and true if it isn't.

The same boolean variable can be set by several independent tests

3. Each month does not contain the same number of days, so a table is used to test if a date is after the last day of the month. At the start of the program each of the twelve entries in the table is initialised to the correct number of days in the month. Then the month number is used as an index into the table to find out how many days there are in it. An alternative to using a table would be to replace the 'simple if' with a compound one that tested each month explicitly, or a case statement as described in the first menu-driven library system example (problem 5). This has the disadvantages of making the test longer and less clear as well as being slightly slower because it performs tests that are not strictly necessary.

Table look-up is a simple but powerful data-checking technique

4. The results will be printed out if the date was plausible and an error message will be printed if it was invalid in any way. To make the output self explanatory, input values are printed in both cases.

The benefit of using 'compound if' statements in place of the equivalent set of 'simple ifs' is that they make the program more efficient and easier to read. When they are used correctly, only the minimum number of tests are made. In this example, if the year is found to be invalid then ***validdate*** is set to false and the remainder of the 'compound if' is ignored. Since the date cannot possibly be valid any more, we do not waste time testing whether the month and date are in range. A set of 'simple ifs' would all be executed regardless of the outcome of the first one. Testing will always begin at the start of a 'compound if' so it is good practice to test for things that are most commonly wrong first when this kind of statement is being used to filter out invalid data. The same applies to the ordering of conditions within a single if test.

The ordering of conditional tests can sometimes save time

5. Whilst this program works, it does not take leap years into account. Recall that a year is leap if it is exactly divisible by 4 and not the first one in a century. The first year in a century is only leap if it is exactly divisible by 400. So 1900 is not a leap year, but 2000 is one. Whenever one whole number is exactly divisible by another, there will be no remainder and the easiest way to test this is with ***'mod'***— the standard Pascal function to find the modulus. Therefore,

year mod 400 = 0 for a leap century...and

(year mod 4 = 0 & year mod 100 <> 0) for any other leap year.

By incorporating this into a 'simple if' test, February can be given 29 days if it is a leap year and 28 days otherwise. It is not essential to reset February to 28 days if the test fails because it has already been initialised at the start of the program. However it is a good idea to program 'defensively' by setting the date in both parts of the IF test, since this can make the program more robust. The 'simple if' test is kept separate from the one which checks the date for the sake of clarity.

Should you wish to take care of leap years you can do so as follows:

```
{---------------------------------------------------------------------------}
{ set the number of days in february to 29 on a leap year & 28 otherwise }
if ((year mod 4 = 0) and (year mod 100 < > 0)) or (year mod 400 = 0) then
daysinmonth[2] := 29 else daysinmonth[2] := 28;
{---------------------------------------------------------------------------}
```

Refining and modifying programs is easy — if they are structured

6. In passing, it should be noted that the 'compound if' could have been rewritten to correct a common misuse of the IF statement. The first example read:-

```
else if (date < 1) or (date > daysinmonth[month]) then validdate:= false
                                                  else validdate := true;
```

Although this is correct, it is better to replace it with

```
else validdate := (date >= 1) and (date <= daysinmonth[month])
```

which is simpler and equally correct. Observe that the relational operators ('<' and '>') had to be changed (to '>=' and '<=' respectively) and the 'or' replaced by an 'and' to achieve the correct result. The part that tests the year and month has also been changed. It is logically equivalent to the first alternative, but shows a different balance between brevity and clarity.

Modifying boolean expressions requires care, a knowledge of boolean algebra, or preferably both

PROBLEM STATEMENT 5 LIBRARY PROGRAM (INITIAL DESIGN)

TOPICS COVERED
- Designing an outline program
- Breaking a program into procedures
- Procedure stubs
- Menus and CASE statements
- A Boolean function

Most of the exercises in this book are independent, but a few will be extended as more features of Pascal are discussed. One such example concerns the computerisation of a library. For the moment we are concerned with the user interface with such a system. We require a menu procedure which will select the appropriate action depending upon a single letter entered. The action to be carried out will be a simple procedure stub which just identifies the fact that it has been called. The actions we are going to allow the system to perform are:

1) Allow a user to borrow a book.
2) Allow a user to return a book.
3) Allow a book to be either added to or deleted from the stock of the library.
4) Allow a borrower to be added to or deleted from the membership list.
5) Print out a list of books borrowed by a given person.
6) Print who (if anybody) has borrowed a certain book.

PROGRAM

```
program library(input,output);
{---------------------------------------------------------------------------------}
procedure borrow;
begin
        writeln('borrowing book')
end;
{---------------------------------------------------------------------------------}
procedure return;
begin
        writeln('returning a book')
end;
{---------------------------------------------------------------------------------}
procedure addbook;
begin
        writeln('adding a book to the library')
end;
{---------------------------------------------------------------------------------}
```

```
procedure deletebook;
begin
        writeln('deleting book from library')
end;
{-----------------------------------------------------------------------------------}
procedure join;
begin
        writeln('joining library')
end;
{-----------------------------------------------------------------------------------}
procedure leave;
begin
        writeln('leaving library')
end;
{-----------------------------------------------------------------------------------}
procedure printloaned;
begin
        writeln('print books loaned to borrower')
end;
{-----------------------------------------------------------------------------------}
procedure findborrower;
begin
        writeln('find who has borrowed a book')
end;
{-----------------------------------------------------------------------------------}
function terminate: boolean;
begin
        terminate := true;
        writeln('thank you for using the library — bye')
end;
{-----------------------------------------------------------------------------------}

function menu: boolean;
var             ch : char;
begin
                writeln('Welcome to the library — what facility do you
                wish to use?');
                writeln; writeln('Borrow a book —              type b');
                writeln('Return a book —                       type r');
                writeln('Add a book to the library —           type a');
                writeln('Delete a book from the library —      type d');
                writeln('Join the library —                    type j');
                writeln('Leave the library —                   type l');
                writeln('Print out books on loan —             type p');
                writeln('Find who has a borrowed a book —      type f');
                writeln('Terminate using the library —         type t');
                readln(ch);
                menu:=false
```

```
        case ch of
              'b','B' : borrow;
              'r','R' : return;
              'a','A' : addbook;
              'd','D' : deletebook;
              'j','J' : join;
              'l','L' : leave;
              'p','P' : printloaned;
              'f','F' : findborrower;
              't','T' : menu := terminate
        end
end; {menu}
{---------------------------------------------------------------}
begin          {MAIN PROGRAM !!}
               while not menu do
end.
{---------------------------------------------------------------}
{Yes, that is the entire main program}
```

DISCUSSION

1. Note the general structure of the solution. It is a common one in the solution of real-world problems. We present a menu of choices (borrowing a book, returning one and so on) and permit the user to make a choice. That choice is then referred to in a case statement with different actions being taken upon the arrival of different choices.

A menu is a common and useful structure for many problems

2. One rather unusual feature of this program is the WHILE loop. This merely reads:

```
while not menu  do
```

In this casc thc loop has no body. Nothing follows the DO. At first sight this may seem illogical. However, all the work is done inside the function ***menu***. This is a boolean function and therefore has the value TRUE or FALSE. As long as it has the value FALSE the function will continue to execute. Its value changes to true only when the ***terminate*** option is selected. Note that even here the function ***menu*** is itself always initialised — in this case to the value FALSE.

The main program body can sometimes be very brief indeed !

3. We could have done the job with a lot of IF..THEN.. ELSEs. This would have looked like:

```
if (answer='a') or (answer='A') then addbook else
if (answer='b') or (answer'B') then borrow else
... and so on ad nauseam.
```

Pascal provides a conditional structure to obviate the need for such a convoluted and cumbersome way of making decisions. This is the CASE statement. It takes the form:

```
case variable of
            valuelist1 : action1;
            valuelist2: action2;
                 etc.
end;      {case}
```

Note that it has an END with no associated BEGIN. This is unusual, and is found elsewhere only in the definition of records. It is sufficiently unusual for it to be a common source of errors for beginners, so watch out for it. The case statement is a much tidier way of representing multi-way decisions than is a series of IF... THENs. This makes the program easier to read, to understand, and to debug. It also minimizes the risk of errors in the first place.

Case statements are useful. They are often associated with menus

4. We have for the first time introduced procedures. These sub-programs usually do most of the work of the program. Using procedures, as you will see later, and as you will come to realise in your own work, is the single most important factor in breaking a problem down into its constituent sub-problems. Solving a problem usually consists of defining it as a series of smaller problems (which may in turn be defined as a series of smaller problems... and so on) and then putting those solutions back together again. It is important to try to keep going until you have a sub-problem which you can solve easily. Many people claim that a procedure should ideally be no longer than a page long. Anything longer is thought to be hard to understand in its entirety.

Procedures represent the solutions to sub-problems — use them

5. In our present case, the program is only under development, so the procedures are not worked out in any detail. What we have here is a general solution to the overall problem of the library. We know that we need to make provision for borrowing etc. At the moment we have not specified how this will be done, merely THAT it will be done.

The procedures used here are well below the minimum length needed to avoid confusion. Indeed, they consist of only one statement each. These statements are merely ***writeln***s saying what the procedure will (eventually) do. We recommend structuring a program in this way. Such simple procedures at an early stage of development are often called procedure *stubs*.

Use procedure stubs at an early stage of developing a program

6. Later, of course, these procedures will become much larger and may well in turn have procedures within themselves to solve sub-sub-problems. However, having got the overall structure correct, we can take care of the details later. Indeed, it is quite possible that different procedures may be written by different programmers in a programming team.

The details can usually be worked out later

3

Loops and initialisation

PROBLEM STATEMENT 6 CALCULATING MEANS AND STANDARD DEVIATIONS

TOPICS COVERED

- Meaningful identifiers
- Initialisation and incrementing/summation
- Text-files
- Arrays and FOR loops
- Efficient array access

You work for a survey analysis company and the organisation often wishes to calculate the mean and standard deviation of a list of integers, e.g. the ages of people in a commercial sample. The output which is required consists of the original data (i.e. a list of numbers), the arithmetic mean (commonly called "the average", although it is only one way of measuring averages), and the standard deviation. The program needs to store the input data values since it is possible that later you will wish to modify the program to sort them so that you can calculate the median as well as the mean.

We obviously have to read the data and store — so that we can print them out later when we print the results. The other two quantities are calculated by simple formulae. We shall use the abbreviations:

x	one value (data item or observation)
Σx	sum of the x values
Σx2	sum of the squares of the x values

Using this notation, the formulae are:

$$\text{Arithmetic mean} = \Sigma x/n$$

$$\text{Standard deviation} = \sqrt{}(n.\Sigma x^2 - (\Sigma x)^2)/n$$

So we need to calculate as we read the data, the following quantities, since we shall need them in the final computations:

n — the number of items read in
Σx — the sum of the individual items read in
$\Sigma x2$ — the sum of the squares of the individual items.

We know that we will rarely, if ever, have more than 500 items in one set of data, but we do not know how many items there will be in any particular set. It is a common situation in which data sets vary markedly in size, but always within some maximum limit. We do, however, know that the data will be stored in a file called ***datafile***, one item on each line of the file. The data have been through the rigorous data verification procedures which should be (and very often are) employed in such organisations.

PROGRAM

```
{------------------------------------------------------------------}
program meanandsd (input, output, datafile);
const  maxitems = 500;
type   listtype = array [1..maxitems] of integer;
var    n, sumofx, sumofxsquared, item, index : integer;
       mean, sd                              : real;
       list                                  : listtype;
       datafile                              : text;
begin  { INITIALISE VARIABLES TO BE SUMMED OR
            INCREMENTED }
       n := 0;
       sumofx := 0;
       sumofxsquared := 0;
       reset (datafile);
       { READ DATA FROM FILE. SUM X AND X-SQUARED }
       while (not eof (datafile)) and ( n < maxitems) do
       begin
              readln (datafile, item);
              n := n + 1;
              list [n] := item;
              sumofx := sumofx + item;
              sumofxsquared := sumofxsquared + sqr (item)
       end;
       {DO CALCULATIONS OF MEAN AND STANDARD
       DEVIATION}
       mean := sumofx / n;
       sd := ( sqrt (sumofxsquared * n — sqr (sumofx))) / n;
       { PRINT LIST OF DATA AND THE COMPUTED
       RESULTS }
       for index := 1 to n do writeln ( list [index] );
       writeln ('Mean':10, 'Standard deviation':20);
       writeln;
```

```
        writeln ( mean:9:1, sd:12:1)
end
{------------------------------------------------------------------}
```

DISCUSSION

1. We are using an array to store the items read in. We have to store them so that we can print out the list at the end of the program. It would be silly to have 500 separate single-valued variables when we can have one array variable with a simple integer index. In Pascal an array must have a size so that the compiler can allocate an appropriate amount of space to it in memory. We have set the size of the array to 500, since we know that is the maximum which is likely to occur in normal practice.

In fact, we set it to be ***maxitems*** long, where ***maxitems*** has previously been declared as a CONSTANT with a value of 500. This means that we can, for the moment, use ***maxitems*** in the program, knowing that it means 500. If we wish later to change the program to allow it to analyse data sets up to, say, 2000 items, we merely need to alter the CONST declaration to:

```
maxitems = 2000;
```

All the references to ***maxitems*** in the program will be left unchanged. It will merely have a different value. This is a simple way to minimise the amount of work needed to modify the program, and, more importantly, to reduce the possibility of errors creeping in when modifying it. As we have noted before, in a large program it is very easy to fail to notice one 500 which should be altered to 2000, or, worse still, to alter one 500 which refers to something entirely different.

Constants save labour and reduce unnecessary errors

2. We have declared a user-defined type for our array. This type (***listtype***) is not strictly necessary for the present crude first draft of the program. However, as you are probably aware by now, programs do grow. One way in which real-life programs grow is by the writing of procedures to perform various operations. Indeed, most large programs can be seen as a structured collection of procedures — which are often written by different people. Procedures communicate with each other and with the main program by passing objects as parameters. We might well wish to pass our array, the list of data items, as a parameter to a procedure at a later date. In that case we MUST (not merely MAY) have a type ready for the parameter, since a parameter list can be specified only using existing type names — not type declarations.

Think ahead

3. We have declared several integers. We hope that ***sumofx*** and ***sumofxsquared*** are self-explanatory from their names. (This is sometimes called ''self-documenting''.) The variable ***item*** is used to hold the value of each data item as it is read in. There is a reason for having this variable, which is after all a temporary one which changes its value each time a new item is read. We could have read our data items directly into ***list [index]***, but there are advantages to using a temporary single-valued variable like ***item***. These advantages are explained in point 6 below.

We have no idea what values these 3 variables may take, except that they must be integers. They will work, unless we get into the unlikely situation of an integer cropping up which is too large for the machine to represent (a condition called ''integer overflow''). We shall ignore that possibility for the present.

Two other variables — ***n*** and ***index*** — are also declared as integers. They are different from the other three, however. They do not HAVE to be declared as integers since we have some knowledge of how big they can be. Variable ***index***, the loop control variable in printing the results can never be larger than ***n***, since we explicitly say:

```
for index := 1 to n do ......
```

Variable ***n***, in turn, can never be larger than ***maxitems*** (although it may, and usually will, be smaller). Indeed, we should be at pains to ensure that a situation can never arise in which the number of items which we try to read into an array is larger than the number of items which we have said it can hold at the maximum. The relation ***n***> maxitems indicates an error somewhere.

Since we have this natural limitation on the range of values which these 2 variables can take, we could have declared them to be not integers, but sub-ranges of integer. For example, our ***var*** declaration could have included:

```
var          index, n : 1..maxitems;
```

This would give us the advantage that the compiler would automatically check the bounds of these variables and would signal an error if we tried to assign to either of them a value greater than ***maxitems*** (or less than one, for that matter). In most serious programs one would take advantage of this characteristic of the compiler. In our present program we have left them as integers mainly because sub-ranges have not yet been covered. In fact, most references to them in this program will in any case be checked automatically since many references are to them as array indices and the compiler checks those anyway. This covers most (but not all) sources of error. In order to minimise run-time errors we have built in one simple example check to ensure that the array will not be over-filled. The last clause of:

```
while (not eof (datafile)) and ( n < maxitems) do
```

does this. It is a crude check, but it does show that checks are possible.

It's not always obvious what type a variable should have

4. There is an initialisation section in the program. The three variables ***n***, ***sumofx***, and ***sumofxsquared*** are explicitly given the value 0 before anything is done with them. Why do this? Why do it for these 3 variables and not, say, for ***index*** and ***item*** as well?

The variable ***index*** can never go wrong or get a false value, since it is used only as a FOR loop control variable, i.e.

```
for index := 1 to n do .......
```

Therefore it will automatically be given the value 1 at the start of the loop and that value will replace whatever happened to be there beforehand. Remember, something will be in the memory locations where ***index*** physically is stored. It might be the number 0, since some compilers automatically set integers to 0 (but not all — we know of one which starts with all the integer variables having a value of over 10 million). It might, however, be something left there by the last user whose program happened to wander into that part of the machine's memory — say the last two letters of a surname, or the middle two digits of someone's telephone number. In the case of ***index*** this does not matter since the first thing which the FOR loop will do is to wipe out the garbage which is there and replace it with the integer 1.

Similarly for ***item***, although the reason is slightly different. It always gets its values by means of a READLN (not by starting a FOR loop as was the case for ***index***). Whenever a READLN (***variablename***) occurs, the existing garbage stored in ***variablename*** is wiped out and overwritten. When used, ***item*** will always contain the value of the last item (age, income, or whatever) which has been read in.

We have also not initialised the 2 real numbers — ***mean*** and ***sd***. Their first use is on the left-hand side of an assignment statement, so whatever garbage they initially contain will be overwritten on this first use. They are not in any serious danger of being abused. At least it would require some very tortuous logic so to abuse them.

The other 3 variables — ***n***, ***sumofx***, and ***sumofxsquared*** — are used in a quite different and potentially more dangerous manner. They do not have their old values replaced entirely by some new independent values coming in from the outside. Instead they are incremented in some way, i.e. they have something ADDED to them. This means that their new values each time they are calculated depend upon what their old values were. For all of them we see the standard way of incrementing or summing in Pascal in the form:

```
newvalue := oldvalue + something;
```

e.g.

```
n := n + 1;
sumofx := sumofx + item;
```

In such a usage the variable name appears not merely on the left-hand side of an assignment statement, but on the right-hand side as well. We are not merely REPLACING a value; we are ADDING to it. Thus the new value depends on the old value.

Once it has achieved an appropriate value, any further additions should be safe. However, it has to get to an appropriate value the first time, since the danger lies in the first addition of all. The first time that we perform an addition involving the variable we want to be sure that the old value is correct. In the present program the correct initial ''old values'' are all 0. Some compilers will automatically ensure that these are so arranged. However, if we wish to be sure that a variable has a correct initial value (0 in the present case), we can only be certain of it if we consciously and explicitly give that value ourselves. Most programs contain at least a short initialisation section; some have quite long sections. If we fail to do this job properly the resulting errors can be quite mysterious and hard to trace, wasting hours of debugging time, and thinning the hair excessively.

Initialisation matters — if in doubt, do it

5. Since we do not know how many items there are to be read in each case, we have done the data reading in a ***while not eof*** loop with the addition of a small crude check to stop filling past the end of the array.

Choose a loop structure appropriate to the problem

6. Each datum read in is used in 3 ways:

(a) it is stored in the list to be printed back later
(b) it is added to ***sumofx***
(c) it is squared and added to ***sumofxsquared***.

We could perform task (a) first, reading directly into the array with:

```
n := n + 1; readln (datafile, list [n]);
```

and then use its value by referring to it as ***list [n]***. Instead of doing that we have read the datum into what is in effect a temporary variable, called ***item***. Why is this?

It is partly for the usual psychological reason of keeping clear in our minds what we are doing. In this case it is a 4-step process:

(a) read an item;
(b) store the item in the array;
(c) add the item to ***sumofx***;
(d) square the item and add the result to ***sumofxsquared***.

Our program logic follows this 4-step process.

There is also another question, this time one of efficiency, which applies very frequently when one is reading, storing into one or more arrays, and doing other calculations with the item read. How many operations does the machine have to perform to undertake these tasks? In particular, how many steps does it have to take to look up a value which you wish to use several times?

Getting the content of a simple, single-valued variable such as ***item*** involves the following steps:

(1) Look up the name ***item*** in a symbol table.
(2) Note the machine address at which that variable is stored.
(3) Go to that machine address and get the contents.

(There may actually be more steps, especially in multi-user paged systems, but this is the minimum which is logically needed. Clearly, the type of the variable matters since, for example, an integer takes up more bytes than a character, the machine has to know not only where to start reading, but where to stop as well!) In the case of references to an array, in our case to ***list [n]***, more steps are needed:

(1) Look up ***list*** in the symbol table.
(2) Note the machine address at which this array starts.
(3) Look up ***n*** in the symbol table.
(4) Note the address at which it, too, starts.
(5) Go to the address of ***n*** and read the value which is stored there.
(6) Add that value to the address obtained in step 2, thus obtaining the address at which ***list [n]*** starts.
(7) Go to that new address and read the value which is stored there.

So, whenever we want the value of ***item***, the machine has to go through at least 3 steps. Whenever we want the value of ***list [n]***, it has to go through at least 7 similar steps. So, if we wish to use this value several times, it is worth while storing it in ***item*** rather than (as we are tempted to do) reading it directly into ***list [n]***. By using ***item*** as a temporary variable and only putting the value INTO ***list [n]*** (not TAKING it out again), we are halving the amount of work which the machine has to do to look things up. It is worth our while using ***item*** even in the simple program which we are currently discussing. In larger programs, especially those which use multi-dimensional arrays, there can be a great gain in efficiency by using a temporary single-valued variable like ***item*** instead of reading directly into an array cell like ***list [n]***.

Simple variables are easier to access than are arrays

7. When we come to print out the data, we use a FOR loop, not a WHILE or REPEAT loop. This is because we wish to do something (in this case WRITELNing a value) a fixed or predictable number of times. After all, the machine knows how many items were read in; it counted them using ***n := n+ 1***. So in deciding when to stop printing we do not need to make any test more complicated than "is ***index*** bigger than ***n***?". Hence a simple FOR loop is perfectly adequate.

Use the simplest loop structure appropriate to your problem

PROBLEM STATEMENT 7 ELECTION RESULTS (INITIAL DESIGN)

TOPICS COVERED More on arrays

A simple program is required in order to calculate the results of an election. A maximum of ten candidates may be standing in the election and we are going to refer to them as candidates 1 to 10. Results will be received from a number of different polling stations. The format for the input is as follows:

On the first line the number of candidates standing. On subsequent lines (until end-of-file) we shall input two integers, the first being the number of the candidate, and the second the number of votes for that candidate at a particular polling station. No record is kept of the results at a particular polling station.

The output should list the winning candidate (the one with the most votes) and the complete set of results showing votes cast, and the percentage vote obtained by each candidate.

PROGRAM

```
program election(input,output);
{program to calculate winner in election the output will consist of the
winner, the number of votes cast per candidate, and the percentage vote for
each candidate }
const   maxcand = 10;
type    indexer = 1..maxcand;
        ballot = array[indexer] of integer;
        percents = array[indexer] of real;

var     votes    : ballot;
        portion  : percents;
        poll, winvotes, total   : integer;
        nocand, cand, i         : indexer;
begin   writeln('how many candidates?');
        readln(nocand);
        {should test that answer <= 10}
```

```
    for i := 1 to nocand do
    begin
        votes[i] := 0;
        portion[i] := 0
    end;
    total := 0;
    writeln('type in voting in form ''cand no. votes cast'' ');
    writeln('one per line — terminate with ctrl-d (eof)');
    while not eof do
    begin
        readln(cand,poll);
        votes[cand] := votes[cand] + poll;
        total := total + poll
    end;
    winvotes := votes[1];
    {potentially the first candidate may have won}
    portion[1] := votes[1] * 100 / total;
    cand := 1;
    for i := 2 to nocand do
    begin
        if votes[i] > winvotes then
        begin
            cand := i;
            winvotes := votes[i]
        end;
        portion[i] := votes[i] * 100 / total
    end;
    writeln('winner is candidate',cand:3,' with',votes–cand],'
    votes');
    writeln;
    writeln('summary of results');
    writeln('candidate votes cast percentage vote');
    for i := 1 to nocand do
    writeln(i:5,votes[i]:14,portion[i]:18:2)
end.
```

RESULTS

```
how many candidates?
5
type in voting in form ''cand no. votes cast''
one per line — terminate with ctrl-d (eof)
1 34
3 67
2 78
1 45
4 45
5 45
```

```
4 98
3 54
3 67
2 65
5 43
1 2
winner is candidate 3 with      188 votes
summary of results
candidate                 votes cast   percentage vote
1                         81           12.60
2                         143          22.24
3                         188          29.24
4                         143          22.24
5                         88           13.69
```

DISCUSSION

This problem is fairly straightforward. Reading in the data is accomplished by using a simple loop. At the same time as inputting the data we can calculate the total votes cast. This makes calculating the percentage vote cast easier later. An important point to note is the way we use simple variables to contain values that are used repeatedly rather than having repeated array accesses. The final point worth mentioning is the calculation of the percentage vote. We use the calculation ***votes * 100 / totalvote***. This ensures that we use integer arithmetic for the multiplication rather than floating point. This is usually faster and more accurate. It could be argued, however, that we should calculate the value ***100 / totalvote*** only once.

One loop can do a great deal of work

PROBLEM STATEMENT 8 SORTING (AND DEBUGGING AN ALGORITHMIC IMPLEMENTATION)

TOPICS COVERED
- Implementing an algorithm from a book
- Sorting and questions which it raises
- Debugging and the use of trace statements
- Appropriate loop structures
- Comments and documentation

Write a program that reads a fixed number of integers into an array, sorts them into ascending order and prints the sorted array. You should decide how many numbers the program will sort and declare this value as a global constant. The user should be told how many numbers to type and each one should be read from a new line. Begin each line with the prompt ''Number n : '' where ''n'' is the number of the integer about to be entered. Any internal sorting algorithm that sorts the numbers in place may be used. Print one blank line, the heading ''Numbers in ascending order:'' and a second blank line. Then print the numbers in ascending order with one space between each number. If no numbers were read, print the message ''No numbers to sort'' instead of the above. Assume that all the numbers are small enough to be stored as integers.

PROGRAM

```
program insertionsort (input, output);
{Sort <nmax> integers according to problem statement 8 -linear sorting
algorithm}
const   nmax = 5;
var     i, j, searchkey, n  : integer;
        found               : boolean;
        table               : array [1..nmax] of integer;

begin
        { MAIN }
        {read <nmax> numbers into an array called <table>}
        writeln('Enter ', nmax:1, ' whole numbers.');
        writeln('They will be sorted into ascending order.');
        writeln;
        for n := 1 to nmax do
        begin
                write('Number ', n:1, ' : ');
                readln(table[n]);
        end;
        {Sort the array in place, working from left to right.Each time the
        for loop is executed, take one element and insert it in the correct
        place among the sorted elements at the left end of the array}
        for i := 2 to n do
        begin
                {select a new element to be inserted}
                searchkey := table[i];
                j := i − 1;
                found := false;
                {Move each sorted element > searchkey one place to the
                right until the correct place is vacant.}
                while (j > 0) and not found do
                if searchkey < table[j] then
                begin
                        table[j+1] := table[j];
                        j := j − 1
                end else found := true;
                {insert the new element in the vacant place}
                table[j+1] := searchkey
        end;
        {print the sorted table}
        if n > 0 then
```

```
        begin
            writeln;
            writeln('Numbers in ascending order:');
            writeln;
            {n holds the number of numbers read}
            for i := 1 to n do write(table[i]:1, ' ');
            writeln
        end else writeln('No numbers to sort')
end.
```

RESULTS

Enter 5 whole numbers.
They will be sorted into ascending order.

Number 1 : 42
Number 2 : 13
Number 3 : 22
Number 4 : 57
Number 5 : 8
Numbers in ascending order:
8 13 22 42 57

DISCUSSION

1. Sorting is the process of arranging items –in order–. It is often done to speed up a later search for members of the sorted set. The items are usually records in a file or elements in an array. They must be rearranged so that their keys are ordered in some way. (Numeric and alphabetic order are the most common.) Keys uniquely identify each element. For simple elements like numbers, the key is the number itself. For more complicated elements, like records containing information about people, the key might be the national insurance number. Then it would be faster to sort using the keys. This is because the keys are small compared to whole records, so they can be compared more quickly.

A sorting utility is provided by many computer systems. Often it is easier and quicker to use it than to write a sorting routine. But if a utility is not provided, or is not suitable, you will have to write your own routine. There are many different sorting algorithms, each with its own advantages and disadvantages. Sort methods are traditionally classified as

1) Internal. — These are used when the computer's main memory is big enough to store all the elements that are being sorted.

2) External. — They are used when there are too many elements to fit into main memory at once. While some are being sorted, the rest are kept on backing storage devices (like floppy disk drives). The rate of data transfer

between primary and secondary memory is usually what governs the speed of these sorting algorithms. We deal with one method of external sorting in problem 27, chapter 9.

Sorting is a complex topic — there are whole books on the subject

2. Some factors that must be considered when deciding what algorithm to use are

1) Speed. The simplest algorithms take time proportional to the number of elements (N) squared. Advanced ones take time proportional to N times the base two logarithm of N (written N log N). No sorting algorithm that works by comparing pairs of keys can make less than N log N comparisons and still guarantee to sort every possible combination of elements.

2) Storage requirements. — Algorithms that sort in place are the best, needing an amount of memory proportional to the number of elements to be sorted. Those using linked lists to store the data need an extra N words of memory for pointers.

3) Simplicity. — The simple algorithms are often easiest to implement and can be faster than advanced algorithms for small numbers of elements.

4) Stability. — Stable algorithms preserve the relative order of records with equal keys. For example, if an alphabetical list of candidate names is sorted in order of exam mark then only a stable sorting method will leave candidates with the same mark in alphabetical order. Even if an algorithm is not stable, it is possible to enforce stability by lengthening the keys so that there are no equal ones.

Choosing an algorithm is often a compromise between conflicting factors

3. This example shows you how to write a program that uses a simple algorithm to sort whole numbers stored in an array. A faster algorithm is then described and the performance of both methods is compared. The simple method is called linear insertion sort and the faster one is called Shell sort. Both use nested loops to do the sorting. FOR loops are chosen when the number of iterations is known in advance. WHILE loops are used when the number of iterations is not known until the program is running. Their advantage over REPEAT–UNTIL loops is that the test to decide whether they should be executed is made at the start. If it fails, the statements inside the loop body are not executed at all. With a REPEAT–UNTIL, the statements inside the body have to be executed at least once. Insertion sort works by considering one element at a time. It is the method often used by people to arrange a hand of playing cards. Each new element (or playing card) is put in its rightful place among the already sorted items. The insertion

is done by moving larger elements one position along in the sorted part of the array. Then the new element is put in the vacated position.

Choose a loop structure which is appropriate to the task in hand

4. Our sorting program starts by reading integers, one per line, into an array in the order that they are typed by the user. At each stage, prompts are printed so that the user knows what to type. The number of numbers that can be sorted is fixed when the program is written and cannot be changed while the program is running. This simple method was chosen because, in this example, the workings of the sorting algorithm are more important than the mechanics of reading the data. You might like to modify the input routine so that the user is asked to say how many numbers there are to sort. Remember to check that your array is large enough to hold them all before you read any of them.

5.Once all the numbers have been read in, the linear insertion algorithm sorts them into ascending order. If you would like them sorted into descending order, change the test from

```
if key < table[j]
```

to

```
if key > table[j]
```

Reversing a decent sort is normally simple

6. Linear insertion sort uses a WHILE loop to do a sequential search that finds the final location of each element. The first unsorted element becomes the key and is compared with each of the already sorted elements in turn, starting with the largest. If the key is smaller, the larger element is moved one place to the right. Then the key is compared with the next largest element and so on, until the right place is found. When the key has been put in the right place, the next unsorted becomes the key and the whole process is repeated. To help you understand how this happens, try working through the following, 22, 57 and 8, typed in that order. Remember that each time the program goes round the FOR loop, it puts one more number into the sorted part of the array. You can easily produces traces like this yourself by adding ***writeln*** statements to the program in appropriate places.

```
Times round for loop = 1
table order = 42 13 22 57 8
new key is table[2] = 13
compare key with table[1]
moving table[1] to table[2]
insert 13 at table[1]
```

new order = 13 42 22 57 8
now the first 2 elements of the array are sorted
Times round for loop = 2
table order = 13 42 22 57 8
new key is table[3] = 22
compare key with table[2]
moving table[2] to table[3]
compare key with table[1]
insert 22 at table[2]
new order = 13 22 42 57 8
now the first 3 elements of the array are sorted
Times round for loop = 3
table order = 13 22 42 57 8
new key is table[4] = 57
compare key with table[3]
insert 57 at table[4]
new order = 13 22 42 57 8
now the first 4 elements of the array are sorted
Times round for loop = 4
table order = 13 22 42 57 8
new key is table[5] = 8
compare key with table[4]
moving table[4] to table[5]
compare key with table[3]
moving table[3] to table[4]
compare key with table[2]
moving table[2] to table[3]
compare key with table[1]
moving table[1] to table[2]
insert 8 at table[1]
new order = 8 13 22 42 57
now the first 5 elements of the array are sorted.

Many compilers provide debugging aids such as tracers and profilers to try to lighten the process of program development. If your program is not doing what you expect it to do (even if it is doing something) you need to find out where the problem is. One of the simplest ways of doing this is to "trace" what is going on. For example, you may not be certain that a particular procedure is actually being called when it should. So put two WRITELN statements into the body of the procedure, one at the start, the other at the finish, which merely print out a message such as "I am now entering procedure ***dosomething***" and "I am now leaving procedure ***dosomething***".

If it is entering all the procedures which it should enter, perhaps it is setting the value of one or more variables incorrectly, so trace those, too. Messages such as "At start of procedure ***addemup***, x has the value 21" and at "At the end of procedure ***addemup***, x has the value 123456" help a great deal in locating the source of the errors.

Trace statements are a simple but very useful aid to debugging

7. However, when using procedures be careful to ensure that you print out the values of both the actual and the formal parameter. The problem may be that you are using a value parameter where you should be using a ***var*** one.

Test the parameter passing if the results are mysterious

8. The program is straightforward and the method stable. For sorting small numbers of elements, it can be faster than advanced algorithms. It is slowest when the elements are already sorted in reverse order, taking time proportional to N squared. The closer the elements are to being sorted, the more efficient the algorithm becomes. When the elements are already sorted, only one comparison is needed on each pass. Then the running time is proportional to N. Using a faster searching method, like binary search, would reduce the number of comparisons needed to find the insertion point for each element. But it would not reduce the number of moves needed to make space for the inserted element.

The efficiency of sorts often depends upon the pre-existing order of the data presented to them

9. Insertion sort is easy to understand and implement, but is not fast enough for many applications. What makes it slow is that elements that are out of place only move one position at a time. So if the smallest element occurs last, it will take N moves to get to the right place.Shell sort is a refinement of straight insertion sort which overcomes this difficulty by allowing elements to be exchanged that are far apart. It was proposed by Donald L. Shell in 1959 and is also known as diminishing increment sort or merge-exchange sort. An implementation of it is given below. To make it work, put this code in the sorting program in place of the code for insertion sort. Then alter the integer variable declarations from:

```
var i, j, key, n : integer;
```

to

```
var i, j, increment, temp, n : integer;
```

```
{-------------------------------------------------------------}
```

```
increment := n div 2;
while increment > 0 do
begin    {divide the elements into <increment> groups }
         for i := increment+1 to n do
         begin  j := i − increment;
                {sort each group of elements with linear insertion sort}
                while j > 0 do    { compare pairs of elements in each
                group }
                if table[j] table[j+increment] then
                begin  {swap the j-th and (j+increment)-th elements}
                       temp := table[j];
                       table[j] := table[j+increment];
                       table[j+increment] := temp;
                       j := j − increment
                end else j:=0
                {the groups are sorted, so set j=0 to exit from
                the while loop}
         end;
         increment := increment div 2 {start again with a
         smaller increment }
end
{------------------------------------------------------------}
```

10. The method can be viewed as a repeated application of linear insertion sort to separate subarrays of the original array. Although several passes are made through the whole array, it is faster than insertion sort because it makes fewer moves. (In our example, it makes four moves, compared with six by insertion sort.) Furthermore, each sorting step involves either few elements or elements that are already reasonably well sorted. To see how it works, here is a trace of Shell sort being used to sort the same five integers that were used with linear insertion sort.

```
Times round while loop = 1,
increment = 2
table order = 42 13 22 57 8
Times round for loop = 1
compare table[1] and table [3]
swap table[1] and table [3]
Times round for loop = 2
compare table[2] and table [4]
Times round for loop = 3
compare table[3] and table [5]
swap table[3] and table [5]
compare table[1] and table [3]
swap table[1] and table [3]
new order = 8 13 22 57 42
Times round while loop = 2,
```

increment = 1
table order = 8 13 22 57 42
Times round for loop = 1
compare table[1] and table [2]
Times round for loop = 2
compare table[2] and table [3]
Times round for loop = 3
compare table[3] and table [4]
Times round for loop = 4
compare table[4] and table [5]
swap table[4] and table [5]
compare table[3] and table [4]
new order = 8 13 22 42 57

Different methods may have analogous sequences

11. On the first pass the increment is two, and the elements are divided into two groups. Every second element goes into one group and the remaining elements go into the other group. The inner WHILE loop sorts both groups using insertion sort. Compare it with the WHILE loop used by the insertion sort program. On the second pass, an increment of one is chosen and the whole array is sorted. In general, if the increment is k, then the elements will be divided into k groups for sorting. The larger the increment is, the further elements that are out of place will be moved in each swap.

Different sequences of increments can be chosen; some work much better than others.Nobody has yet determined which is the best possible one for sorting large numbers of elements, if indeed there is one.

An apparently simple change often makes a very large difference

12. Here are some results that were obtained for these two algorithms using a DEC 11/750 minicomputer. They are the times taken to sort a collection of random integers and exclude the time taken to read the numbers and print the results. Each time is given in milliseconds and is the average of fifty runs.

number of elements	10	25	50	100	250	500	1000	2500	5000
insertion sort	1.7	9.7	26.8	132	765	3046	11859	75630	302437
Shell sort	3.0	9.1	21.4	55	201	411	974	2774	7660

Insertion sort starts quicker than Shell sort, but its advantage is soon overcome. By the time there are fifty elements, Shell sort has taken the lead. After that insertion sort becomes slower and slower in comparison. It takes five minutes to sort five thousand numbers, while Shell sort takes less than eight seconds.

The choice of method heavily depends upon the size of the problems. Thousands and millions do make a difference

13. Here is a second table looking at the differential effect of pre-existing order in the data.

N =1000	Shell sort	Insertion sort
random integers	974	11859
descending order	746	23586
ascending order	382	78
almost sorted	620	613

This second table compares the two methods with random and non- random data. One thousand integers are used for each test and the times are the averages for fifty runs, given in milliseconds. Shell sort is reasonably consistent, although it prefers data that are ordered. Insertion sort is inconsistent; it performs well when the numbers are in ascending order (already sorted!) and badly when they are in reverse order. To conclude, Shell sort is not the fastest algorithm known. However, it is better than insertion sort and a reasonable choice for medium sized files of data. This exercise has shown you how to sort integers. Try modifying the program to sort real numbers. When you have learned about records, you will be able to turn this program into a flexible sorting utility.

What works well in one context may not do so in another

14. When writing sort procedures the type of loop structure may make a difference. In particular, a FOR and a WHILE loop may differ very much in their efficiency. FOR loops must execute a fixed number of times no matter what may happen within them. Suppose that you are sorting an array of 1000 numbers and it may be obvious that you should terminate a loop after case number 5 (out of the 1000). A FOR loop will continue remorselessly to process the other 995 steps, even though it is an unnecessary waste of time. A WHILE loop controlled by some boolean condition (often an actual boolean variable) can, by contrast, terminate itself at any stage in the loop. So if a loop termination conditions arises on case 5, it can ignore the other 995. This can lead to a significant saving on large sorts.

Don't reach automatically for a FOR loop. It may be inefficient

4

Building bricks — procedures

PROBLEM STATEMENT 9	**PROCEDURES — GENERAL INTRODUCTION**
TOPICS COVERED	The design of procedures Parameters Differences between var and value parameters Local variables Layout and labelling of procedures

When we print out results, be they words or numbers, we often wish to have blank lines to make the output more readable or more pleasing to the eye. This can be done using WRITELN, e.g.

```
    { THIS PRODUCES TWO BLANK LINES ON THE OUTPUT }
        writeln;
        writeln;

{ THIS PRODUCES FIVE BLANK LINES ON THE OUTPUT }

        for index := 1 to 5 do writeln;
```

However, it is rather tedious to have to put in a lot of WRITELNs purely for the purposes of formatting. After all, one does not have to do anything very special to get nicely formatted output ACROSS the page. Pascal provides a standard facility, field-width specifications, to do that. It would be convenient if it provided a similar standard facility for spacing DOWN the page. It would be useful if one could say, for example:

```
        blanks( 5 );
        or
        blanks ( lengthofpage div 2 );
```

to get the required number of blank lines.

Of course, Pascal does not in fact provide any such facility. The language does, however, provide the facility for users to define their own procedures.

So we can in principle define our own procedure for printing an indeterminate number of blank lines. Obviously we wish to make it as flexible as possible so that when we call the procedure (i.e. USE it in a program — or even in another procedure) we can pass to it the number of lines which we wish to be left blank. We may wish to pass this quantity — the number of lines:

(i) an actual number — e.g. 10, which in Pascal is technically a constant;
(ii) a variable name which, obviously, will have been given a previous value by the program;
(iii) an expression.

For example:

(i) blanks (24);
(ii) blanks (sizeoftable);
(iii) blanks (pagelength − linessofar + 2);

We can ensure this by declaring our procedure to have a formal VALUE parameter since this can be replaced (as we have seen above) by an actual parameter which is a constant, a variable, or an expression. This threefold substitution possibility is true only of value parameters; it is not true of var parameters.

PROCEDURE

```
{--------------------------------------------------------------------}
{Procedure to display blank lines on the output for tidy layout }
procedure blanks ( howmany : integer );
var    index : integer;
begin
                    for index := 1 to howmany do writeln
end; {blanks}
{--------------------------------------------------------------------}
```

DISCUSSION

1. The procedure heading is fairly standard. It consists of the word ***procedure*** the procedure name (***blanks***), and, in brackets, one or more formal parameters. In this case there is one formal parameter — ***howmany*** — and it is declared to be able to accept as an actual parameter (when the procedure is actually used) constants, variables or expressions of type integer. Note that the parameter declaration is of the form:

parametername : parametertype

where ***parametertype*** is an identifier, i.e. a single word. In the case of an integer this has no special implications. If, however, we had been passing an array to the procedure we would have had to have available a user-defined type with a name. We could not declare the type in this parameter list at the head of a procedure. Thus we could use:

```
thislist   :   intarray;
```

but not

```
thislist   :   array [1..maxitems] of integer;
```

2. Procedures can be written without any parameters at all, i.e. we can have just the word ***procedure***, the name and then a semi-colon, with no bracketed list of parameters. To do so is, however, unusual and is normally dangerous. If one wishes to communicate information to a procedure or to pass information back from a procedure to the main program or to another procedure one should do it via parameters. To omit them leads one to manipulate from inside the procedure variables which do not belong to it, which are global. That is dangerous enough in small programs, since one often does things unintentionally to a global variable without realising that it will have side effects on another procedure later in the program. In large programs, written by many people, the omission of parameters is a recipe for disaster and potential bankruptcy.

Look with suspicion on parameter-less procedures

3. There is a local variable declared — ***index***. Note that it is declared inside the procedure. It therefore has no existence outside the procedure. It comes into existence when the procedure is used and disappears as soon as the call has finished executing. Indeed, if you declare a procedure but never use it (yes, people do sometimes do things like that, indeed some compilers inform you when you have done something so apparently illogical), the local variable will never come into existence. If you have another variable called ***index***, in the main program or in another procedure, it will be quite distinct from this local ***index***. You can do what you like with this local one (in our example we vary it from 1 to ***howmany*** and then leave its value undefined) and it will have no effect on any other ***index*** which may be lurking around.

Had we forgotten to declare it locally inside the procedure and a global variable ***index*** had existed, when we call our procedure with ***blanks (24);***, it would have, unintentionally, altered the value of that global variable and when we came to use it later its value would have been undefined. This would probably produce quite a mysterious situation since one would probably not look for the problem in something so innocuous as a procedure for displaying blank lines on the screen.

If you need variables only locally — declare them locally

4. Note that we have surrounded the whole procedure with a comment

consisting only of a line of dashes — {------------------------}. The reason for this is purely psychological. One wants the program to be readable and it is our experience that dashes are more visible, and a better way of dividing up a program, than is just blank space. A blank line in a program is not always easy to spot — a dashed line is nearly always visible.

Make your procedures stand out on the printed page

5. Note that after the ***end;*** of the procedure, and on the same line, we have put the name of the procedure inside comment brackets. This is not essential, but we recommend it since it makes the process of editing and debugging simpler. One can, for example, display, copy, delete, or otherwise manipulate the whole procedure using a line editor by asking it to perform the display, etc. from the ***blanks*** in the procedure heading up to and including the *{**blanks**}* at the end. This is not a rule, but it is a useful hint. It is certainly our standard practice.

Make your later editing easier by labelling the end of a procedure

PROBLEM STATEMENT 10 MORE ON PROCEDURES

TOPICS COVERED
- String-handling
- Packed arrays
- String initialisation
- Flexibility with parameters and constants
- EOLN and EOF

We often wish to read and write strings of characters, i.e. text. For example, we shall, in most computing environments, wish to read peoples' names, addresses, titles of books, and so on. One might think that this is such a common operation that there would be built into the standard language procedures to perform such operations. Strangely enough, although some dialects of Pascal, for example UCSD Pascal, enable one to use READ, READLN, WRITE and WRITELN to write out strings of characters of the kind mentioned above, such provision is not part of the standard language. One can use these built-in procedures to read or write integers, real numbers, characters and booleans, but one cannot use them to read user-defined strings (although one can write strings). In UCSD Pascal, a STRING (i.e. a string of characters) is a built-in type. In standard Pascal it is not; it has to be defined by the user. Therefore, we cannot use the built-in procedures to do everything we would wish with this user-defined type; one has to have purpose-built user-defined procedures for the purpose of reading strings. We shall also show how one can use such procedures for writing them as well.

In deciding how to define a type for storing strings of characters, several questions pose themselves.

1. How long do we wish our maximum string to be — 20 characters, 80 characters, or what?

2. Will we wish to compare strings at any point in the program ? For example, if we are going to sort names into alphabetical order, we normally do this by comparing one string with another to see which one is ''bigger'' in the same way that we compare numbers to see which one is bigger when we are sorting them. This affects how we define the string.

3. What will happen if we do not explicitly put something into the string? Here we come up against the question of initialisation. One compiler we know initialises all characters, both individually and as part of a string, to the character '?'. If one does not take corrective action one can have lots of names or addresses reading '????????????????????'

Similarly, in declaring the procedures for reading and writing, we have to ask ourselves questions like:

1. Will we wish to read only from the keyboard or might we wish sometime to read data from a text-file ? The latter is, after all, the commonest way of getting data in the real world. Similarly, do we wish to write only to the screen, or might we wish to write our output on a text-file for later use?

2. When we have finished writing a name, or a book title, do we want the next thing to be printed (say, the next book title) to appear on the same line, or on the next one? Or perhaps we want the flexibility to do either.

Thus, what is apparently a simple operation in fact involves quite a large number of considerations. We shall tackle these considerations by looking at a program which reads from a file containing three lines on each person in the file. Line 1 contains the name, line 2 the sex ('F' or 'M'), and line 3 contains the name of the university at which they are studying. We shall then create two files (***men*** and ***women***) each containing merely the name and university (on the same line), but not the sex. Obviously we shall put the males in one file and the females in another.

PROGRAM

```
{------------------------------------------------------------------}
{Program to read from one text-file and to create two separate text-files}

program procs (input, output, oldfile, men, women );
const         stringlength = 30;
type          string = packed array [1..stringlength] of char;
var           name, university : string;
              sex : char;
              oldfile, men, women : text;
{------------------------------------------------------------------}
```

```
procedure readstring     ( var subfile : text; var substring : string);
var                 index : integer;
begin
                    for index:= 1 to stringlength do substring [index] := ' ';
                    index := 0;
                    while not eoln ( subfile ) and ( index < stringlength ) do
                    begin
                              index := index + 1;
                              read ( subfile, substring [index] )
                    end;
                    readln ( subfile )
end; {readstring}
{----------------------------------------------------------------}
procedure writestring    (var subfile : text; substring : string; newline :
boolean);
var                 index : integer;
begin               for index := 1 to stringlength do
                    write ( subfile, substring [index]);
                    if newline then writeln ( subfile )
end; {writestring}
{----------------------------------------------------------------}


begin               {MAIN}
                    reset ( oldfile ); rewrite ( men ); rewrite ( women );
                    while not eof ( oldfile ) do
                    begin
                              readstring ( oldfile, name ); readln ( oldfile, sex );
                              readstring ( oldfile, university );
                              if sex = 'F' then
                              begin  writestring ( women, name, false );
                                     writestring ( women, university, true)
                              end else
                              begin
                                     writestring ( men, name, false );
                                     writestring ( men, university, true)
                              end
                    end;
                    writeln ('Program terminates satisfactorily')
end.
```

DISCUSSION

1. We are here using not just one text-file to read the data from, but one to read them from, and two more to write them to, suitably transformed. As always with text-files, we have to do 3 things before we can use them for reading or writing:

(1) Mention them in the program heading.
(2) Declare them as objects of type ***text***.
(3) RESET them (for reading) or REWRITE them (for writing).

Text-files are widely used; get acquainted with them early

2. We have declared a constant ***stringlength***. Once again the reason is one of good practice. We use it in both our reading and our writing procedures. In the case of reading we use it to ensure that we do not read anything which is too long for the array which will hold the names or universities. In writing, we use it as the terminating value for a FOR loop, to ensure that we write out the complete string of characters, including trailing blanks, so that our output will be neatly formatted. All the references in the active part of the program are to ***stringlength***; none are to the number 30. So if we wish to change the maximum length of our strings, we have to change only the CONST declaration. Similarly if we wish to use the procedures ***readstring*** and ***writestring*** in other programs all we have to do is to ensure that an appropriate constant is declared at the head of the new program. We can just copy the procedures using the editor.

Constants save a lot of wasted effort later

3. We have declared a user-defined type — ***string***. There are 2 points to be borne in mind about this declaration:

(1) We have to declare this type. In the program we are going to pass the ***name*** and ***university*** to and from the procedure ***readstring*** and to (but not from) the procedure ***writestring***. Therefore, there will need to be parameters — in this case they are both called ***substring*** — to those procedures. Parameters must have a type name, so we need the type ***string*** at the very least to enable this to happen.

(2) Note that we have declared the string to be a packed array of characters. The reason for the components being characters should be obvious. The reason for the array being packed is more technical. Suffice it to say for the moment that using a packed array, rather than an array, enables one to undertake comparisons if we need to. In this program we do not need to, but it is quite likely that we might wish to add to it, for example to sort the names into alphabetical order, and it is worth while being prepared.

Strings are normally represented as packed arrays of char

4. The new type is used immediately in the ***var*** declaration, as well as lower down in the parameter lists.

5. Compare the parameter lists in ***readstring*** and ***writestring***, especially the way in which the two parameters called ***substring*** have been specified. Note that, although they have the same name, they are quite distinct objects, and will not be confused with each other by the compiler.

In ***readstring*** the string parameter is declared as being a VAR parameter, i.e. it has the word ***var*** before it. In ***writestring*** this is omitted.

This is because in ***writestring*** we do not wish to CHANGE the contents of ***substring***. After all, when you write someone's name, you do not wish thereby to change their name, and that procedure does merely write out a string. That is why we leave the parameter ***substring*** as a value parameter. Indeed, even if we made a mistake in the procedure and changed the value of ***substring*** unintentionally this would not in any way corrupt what was stored in the actual parameters — in this case in ***name*** and ***university***. So it is also a protection of sorts.

In ***readstring*** on the other hand we DO wish to change the value. If the value of ***name*** is 'Jones, Bill' before we read the next name from file we want it to be 'Smith, Fred' or 'Jordan, Amanda' or whatever after we have done the reading. If we used a value parameter for this procedure, the protection we mentioned above would work against us. The parameter ***substring*** would change inside the procedure, but that new value would never be passed back to the main program and the actual parameter ***name*** would remain forever unchanged. Therefore, for this procedure we have to make it a VAR parameter. It's not a question of may, it is a question of must.

Of course, having made it a var parameter we have to ensure that the actual parameters which we pass to it are only variables. With a value parameter we could pass constants, variables and expressions. With var parameters we can pass only variables. In this program that is all we do.

Var and value parameters are dramatically different
The difference matters

6. The choice of names for the parameters merits some comment. In the case of substring, we have tried to make it obvious what the parameter is for: it is a SUBstitute for a STRING variable, hence SUBSTRING. It is not essential to do it this way, but using something mnemonic like this is one way of protecting ourselves against silly and mysterious errors. We recommend you to try to develop your own consistent form of nomenclature for parameters. With our file parameter we have adopted the same principle. The parameter ***subfile*** is a SUBstitute for a FILE. You do not need to use this particular convention. It will save you a lot of time and stress, though, if you adopt *A* consistent convention.

In the case of ***writestring*** we have called the third parameter NEWLINE. It is a boolean parameter which controls the way in which a string is printed and the preparation for what will be printed after it. If we pass the constant FALSE to it (and we can pass constants, since it is a value parameter), when the string has been printed, the printing head will remain on the same line so that whatever comes next will also be printed on the same line. If, on the other hand, we call the procedure with a third actual parameter of TRUE, it will proceed to the next line. Effectively this parameter controls the insertion of a newline character: hence our choice of name.

Choose mnemonic names for your parameters

7. We have tried to make the procedures flexible. In the case of ***writestring*** the boolean parameter makes it flexible enough to throw newlines or not depending on our choice of actual parameters. If we want to use it to print four things on one line we can call it three times with the final parameter FALSE and a fourth time with the final parameter TRUE. It is very simple. In the procedure all that happens is that the statement:

```
if newline then writeln ( subfile );
```

is executed. The words ***if newline*** are equivalent to ***if newline=true***. So, if we have passed the value TRUE it writes a newline character on the specified file. If the value passed is FALSE it does nothing, which means that it stays on the same line.

Similarly, the inclusion in both procedures of the parameter ***subfile*** makes the procedures flexible. The procedure ***readstring*** can read from any file of type text, e.g

```
readstring ( surveydata, party );
readstring ( addresses, town );
readstring ( diary, appointment);
```

Similarly ***writestring*** can write to any such file, e.g.

```
writestring ( results, address, false);
writestring ( results, subject, true);
```

What, though, if we wish to read from the keyboard, or write to the screen? That is taken care of. The keyboard, or the standard input, is in Pascal a file of type TEXT. It does not appear that way to the human, but as far as the machine is concerned it is such a file. Similarly the standard output, or screen, is a file of type TEXT. So we can specify these as a source of reading data or as a destination for writing data, e.g.

```
readstring ( input, nextaddress );
writestring ( output, personfound, true );
writestring ( output, listofnames [index], false );
```

Thus, simply by including an appropriate parameter we have made the procedure capable of reading from any text-file, including the keyboard, and writing to any text-file, including the screen. All we have to do to use these procedures properly is to ensure that when we call the procedure we specify the correct source or destination.

Make your procedures flexible

8. In each procedure we have a local variable which serves as an array index. Not surprisingly we have called it ***index***, and have done so in both procedures. In both it is used to control a FOR loop, while in ***readstring*** it is also used inside a WHILE loop. The fact that a variable with the same name appears in each procedure is not a source of possible confusion or error since, as they are both declared locally, they come into existence only when the procedure is called, and die as soon as its execution is terminated. This happens very frequently. We use each procedure twice for every name read — to read the name and university and to write those two quantities. Thus ***readstring***'s local variable ***index*** will be created and will die twice as many times as there are names in the file of data, and so will ***writestring***'s. With a large set of data, this could involve a large amount of birth and mortality.

Local variables exist only locally — and avoid confusion

9. Note that inside ***readstring***, apart from the check to ensure that we do not read more than ***stringlength*** characters (and thus do not overflow the string), the main check is to ensure that we do not read past the end of the line in the file of data. There is one important point to note about reading characters in particular from a text-file. The machine reads a character and checks to see if it has reached the end of the line. As long as it has not reached the end of the line there is no problem; it just goes on to read the next character. What, though, happens when it has read the last character on the line and the boolean variable ***eoln*** has been automatically set to TRUE? What will it read when it is next called ? Where is the reading head logically positioned?

In fact, the next thing to be read will be the end-of-line marker, which in Pascal is interpreted as a blank space. This means that we have to be careful. If we blithely go on reading, the next string to be read will begin with a blank space, quite wrongly. So we have somehow to "gobble up" the end-of-line marker, or read over it. The simplest way to do this is by a single READLN on the appropriate file, to move the printing head on to the next character after the end-of-line marker.

In fact, it is worth while to think about common operations as being in some regular form. In the case of reading characters from a text-file the general structure is:

```
{------------------------------------------------------------------------}
{while not eof (subfile) do
begin  while not eoln (subfile) do
          begin  read ( subfile, character); <---------- on one line
                 process if necessary
          end;
          readln ( subfile )         <---------- crucial step
end;
```

In the present program the WHILE NOT EOF loop is in the main program, and the WHILE NOT EOLN loop is in the reading procedure. The structure, though, is identical. The most important thing to remember, though, is that one must "gobble up" the end-of-line marker.

Don't forget the end-of-line marker

10. Inside the reading procedure we read the character directly into the string, i.e. into an array location. We do not, as we have done in other programs, store the data in a temporary variable such as ***item***. Recall that we did so in other cases to improve efficiency. In the present case, once we have read the item and stored it we do not do anything else with it, so there is no scope for a gain in efficiency. Therefore it would be less efficient to waste time putting it into a temporary variable only to transfer it immediately to the array.

11. There can be an initialisation section inside a procedure, just as there is in a main program. In fact, the ***readstring*** procedure has one, albeit a simple one. The line:

```
for index := 1 to stringlength do substring [index] := ' ';
```

is in fact a sort of initialisation. It ensures that all the characters in the array are set to be blank spaces before we read anything into it. We have, you will recall, specified that a string is 30 characters long. It is unlikely that most names and universities will be as long as that. Suppose we have the ***university*** being 'Oxford'. That is only 6 characters. What will happen to the other 24 locations ? Some compilers will set them to blanks automatically. The one mentioned earlier would, however, store this string — and print it — as

Oxford????????????????????????

If we read 'Newcastle-upon-Tyne' and then read 'Oxford', what would we get if we did not initialise the string to blanks before each reading operation? Obviously, the first 6 characters of 'Newcastle-upon- Tyne' would be overwritten and replaced. What of the rest, though? We have not told the machine to do anything with them, so they will remain unchanged. So reading the word 'Oxford' would result in a university with the name:

Oxfordtle-upon-Tyne???????????

If, as we have done, one initialises to blanks every time we can be sure that, before we read a new name or a new university, there are blank spaces in the array, and we will not get such nonsense. There are, of course, other ways round the problem (put in a marker and print only till you come to the marker, for example), but this is a simple solution which enables one to have clearly formatted output.

Be careful about initialisation — even inside procedures

12. At the beginning of the main program we have put in the comment:

{MAIN}

This is to help us find it with a string search using the editor when we come to debug programs. It is surprising how often one wishes to do this. The larger the program becomes the more useful a simple "marker" like this is. When you start programming, your programs will look like this:
Declarations

Main Body

Later, as you become more experienced, they will start to look more like this:

Declarations

Main Body

and in that case, it may take you some time to find the start of the main body simply by browsing.

Make it easy for you to edit your programs — use markers

PROBLEM STATEMENT 11 ELECTIONS AND ENUMERATED TYPES

TOPICS COVERED
- Enumerated types
- Arrays indexed by enumerated types
- Printing enumerated type values
- More on case statements
- Strings may not be case labels
- Accumulating results

In the last chapter we developed a simple program which calculated the results of an election. We referred to the candidates by number. Now we wish to refer to them by party. The following abbreviations will be used:

lab	Labour
con	Conservative
lib	Liberal
sdp	Social Democrats
cym	Plaid Cymru
mrl	Monster Raving Looney
rat	Ratepayers

As before, results will be received from a number of different polling stations. The format for the input is as follows:

On each line (until end-of-file) we will input the abbreviation for the party of the candidate, followed by the number of votes cast for that candidate at a particular polling station. No record is kept of the results at a particular polling station.

The output should list the winning party, and the complete set of results showing votes cast, and the percentage vote obtained by each party. The full name of the party should be printed, not just the abbreviation.

PROGRAM

```
program election(input,output);
{program to calculate winner in election. The output will consist of the
winner, the number of votes cast per party, and the percentage vote for each
party.
Lines that have been changed from the previous version are marked    *
additions are marked                                                  +
deletions are marked                                                 – }
                                                                   {–}
Declarations
type  party = (lab,con,lib,sdp,cym,mrl,rat);                       {*}
      ballot = array[party] of integer;                            {*}
      percents = array[party] of real;                             {*}
var   votes : ballot;
      newline; portion : percents;
      cnt, poll, winvotes, total : integer;                        {*}
      cand, i : party;                                             {*}
      rdparty : packed array[1..3]of char;                         {+}
{------------------------------------------------------------------}

procedure writeparty(pty: party);
{to write out value of enumerated type party +}                    {*}
begin    case pty of
              lab : write('Labour                 ');              {+}
              con : write('Conservative           ');              {+}
              lib : write('Liberals               ');              {+}
              sdp : write('Social Democrats       ');              {+}
              cym : write('Plaid Cymru            ');              {+}
              mrl : write('Monster Raving Looney');                {+}
              rat : write('Ratepayers             ')
                                                                   {+}
      end
end;
{------------------------------------------------------------------}
```

```
begin
{-}  for i := lab to rat do
     begin
{*}     votes[i] := 0;
        portion[i] := 0
     end;
     total := 0;
     writeln('type in voting in form ''party, votes cast'' ');
{*}  writeln( 'one per line — terminate with ctrl-d (eof)');
     while not eof do
     begin     for cnt := 1 to 3 do
               {+} read(rdparty[cnt]);
               {+}        if rdparty = 'lab' then
               {+}                cand := lab
               {+}        else if rdparty = 'con' then
               {+}                cand := con
               {+}        else if rdparty = 'lib' then
               {+}                cand := lib
               {+}        else if rdparty = 'sdp' then
               {+}                cand := sdp
               {+}        else if rdparty = 'cym' then
               {+}                cand := cym
               {+}        else if rdparty = 'mrl' then
               {+}                cand := mrl
               {+}        else if rdparty = 'rat' then
               {+}                cand := rat
               {+}        else writeln('invalid party');
               {+} readln(poll);
               {*} votes[cand] := votes[cand] + poll;
                   total := total + poll
     end;
     winvotes := votes[lab];
{*}  {potentially the first candidate may have won}
     portion[lab] := votes[lab] * 100 / total;
{*}  cand := lab;
{*}  for i := con to rat do
{*}  begin
           if votes[i] winvotes then
           begin
                   cand := i;
                  winvotes := votes[i] end;
           portion[i] := votes[i] * 100 / total
     end;
     {Display the results}
     write('the winner with ',winvotes,' votes was ');
{*}  writeparty(cand);
{+}  writeln;
{+}  writeln;
```

```
     writeln('summary of results');
     writeln('party          votes cast          percentage vote');
{*}  for i := lab to rat do
{*}  begin writeparty(i);
{5}          writeln(votes[i]:14,portion[i]:18:2)
     end
{+}
end.
```

RESULTS

```
type in voting in form ''party, votes cast''
one per line
— terminate with ctrl-d (eof)
lab 456
con 654
lib 456
sdp 987
cym 43
mrl 78
rat 678
con 672
lab 349
lib 234
rat 567
lab 786
mrl 987
rat 456
cym 65
mrl 987

the winner with 2052 votes was Monster Raving Looney

summary of results
party                     votes cast    percentage vote
Labour                          1591          18.82
Conservative                    1326          15.68
Liberals                         690           8.16
Social Democrats                 987          11.67
Plaid Cymru                      108           1.28
Monster Raving Looney           2052          24.27
Ratepayers                      1701          20.12
```

DISCUSSION

1. Although there is considerable flexibility for the programmer in the general concept of user-defined types, one does have to create these types by some combination (often an ingenious combination) of the existing standard

types built into the language. Although this is a powerful aid to developing clear and comprehensible programs, and makes the language almost infinitely extensible, it can sometimes leave one in as poor a situation as in other languages. For example, one may have a list of cars (or political parties) and refer to them as 1,2,3 instead of as ford, volvo, saab. The enumerated type allows you to define not only the name of a type but also the values which it can take on. In the present program we have adopted this method for indexing the array of votes. The array index is of enumerated type, with values such a ***lab***, ***con***, ***sdp*** and so on. This should make the purpose of the program more obvious.

Enumerated types can make programs much more readable

2. However, it should be noted that a variable of an enumerated type is not the same as a string of characters. Many beginners confuse the two. In the example above ***lib*** may look similar to ***'lib'***, but it is conceptually and practically vastly different. Under the standard language one cannot read or write ***lib***. One can at least write ***'lib'***. This means that one needs at least one procedure for transforming the enumerated type into its string equivalent. This is usually done by making the procedure a large case statement, as in the procedure ***writeparty*** above.

Writing enumerated types needs its own procedure

3. Reading them is impossible under the standard language. One has to read in the string representation and then do some transformation. In the program above this is done by a series of IF statements. One has to do it in this cumbersome way, because strings of characters cannot be used as values for a case statement. Thus one cannot say:

```
case stringvariable of
        'ford' : someaction;
```

but one can say:

```
case enumeratedvariable of
        ford : someaction;
```

Thus, the IF statements make it possible to transform the strings which are input into the enumerated types which are used for the actual indexing. That is how we normally 'read' enumerated type values. Similarly, the case statement in the procedure ***writeparty*** is used for the reverse process of turning the enumerated index values into strings of characters which can be printed. Again, this is normally how we 'write' enumerated types.

Special action is needed to distinguish strings and enumerated types

5

Sets and their uses

PROBLEM STATEMENT 12 COURSE CHOICES, SETS, AND DATA-CHECKING

TOPICS COVERED
Sets
Union and accumulation
IN and its use for data-checking
Structures — an array of sets

You are the administrator of an educational department which has a varying number of students, but never more than 200. They can take one or more courses from a list of 20 which are offered. The list of courses taken by each student is stored in a file called ***studentchoices***. Unfortunately, the administration is not very tidy and the courses are added to the list in no particular order. Each student's courses take up one line of the file, but when he or she registers for a new course, its code number (in the range 1 to 20) is added at the end, irrespective of its numerical order. In addition, you know that there are quite a lot of errors, and, although the largest real code number possible is 20, some entries like 44 or 76 find their way into the file. These have to be picked up in some way. Thus, a student's entry should read, say:

1 5 8 10 14 19

but may well read:

19 1 5 88 14 100

Once we have a method for storing the information about the students in some readily accessible form, we shall be able to devise methods for looking for particular items of information, e.g. the record numbers of students who are taking a particular combination of courses, say 1, 5 and 8. However, we have to develop the basic idea, so the first version of the program given below merely reads the students' choices from file and prints them out in a sensible order.

PROGRAM

```
{------------------------------------------------------------------------}
{Program to demonstrate the use of sets — describing course choices     }
{------------------------------------------------------------------------}
program coursechoice   (input, output, studentchoices);
const                 maxcourses = 20;
                      maxstudents = 200;
type                  coursedescriptor = 1..maxcourses;
                      setofcourses = set of coursedescriptor;
                      listtype = array [1..maxstudents] of setofcourses;
var
          list : listtype;
          oneset, checkset : setofcourses ;
          onecourse, index, total :integer;
          studentchoices : text;
begin     {MAIN}
          reset ( studentchoices );
          {INITIALISE ARRAY INDEX & THE SET FOR
          DATA-CHECKING }

          index := 0 ;
          checkset := [1..maxcourses];
          {READ DATA, CONSTRUCT SETS & STORE
          THEM IN THE LIST}
          while (not eof (studentchoices)) and (index < maxstudents) do
          begin
                index := index + 1;
                {INITIALISE THIS STUDENT'S SET OF
                COURSE CHOICES}
                oneset := [];
                { READ IN THIS STUDENT'S SET OF
                COURSE CHOICES }
                while not eoln (studentchoices) do
                begin
                      read (studentchoices, onecourse);
                      { CHECK IF THIS IS A VALID COURSE
                      CODE }
```

```
                if not ( onecourse in checkset ) then
                begin
                        write ('Error in Student #',index:3 );
                        writeln (' Erroneous entry: ', onecourse:3)
                end else
            {   ADD   IT   TO   THIS   STUDENT'S
            COURSE CHOICES }
                oneset := oneset + [onecourse]
            end;    {While not eoln}
            readln ( studentchoices );
            { STORE THIS SET IN THE LIST OF ALL
            STUDENTS }
            list [index] := oneset
        end; {While not eof}
        total := index;
        { PRINT THE RESULTS }
        writeln ('Student ','              Courses taken');
        writeln;
        for index := 1 to total do
        begin
            write ( index : 4,' ':5);
            oneset := list [index];
            for onecourse := 1 to maxcourses do
            if onecourse in oneset then write (onecourse : 3 );
            writeln
        end;
        writeln;
        writeln ('Program now terminates')
end.
{-------------------------------------------------------------------}
```

RESULTS

Error in Student # 5 Erroneous entry: 21
Error in Student # 5 Erroneous entry: 33

Student	Courses taken
1	1 2 3
2	9 10 12 20
3	1 5 7 9 11 13 15
4	1 2 3 4 5 6 7
5	6 7 8 9
6	1 2 3 6 9 20

DISCUSSION

1. We are using a new data-type in this program — the SET. This is useful for a wide variety of purposes. In this program we are using it to simplify:

(a) checking that input data are within acceptable ranges.

(b) avoiding double counting — so that no student will be recorded as doing the same course twice at the same time.

(c) building up, as a single object, a description of a student's choices.

(d) putting the courses into numerical order on the output, even though they may not be ordered on the input.

Sets may use 4 operators:

Union (+)
Difference (−)
Intersection (*)
IN

This program makes use of only two of these — Union and IN. The others are valuable, but we do not wish to introduce too much new material at one time.

Look at sets — they are more useful than you may think

2. Note that we have again defined several non-standard types. In this first version of the program we have no procedures, but in the second version we shall have, and we shall want to pass to and from those procedures several objects, including complete sets, and even a whole array. Note that ***coursedescriptor*** is a sub-range of integer, and ***setofcourses*** is a set of ***coursedescriptor***. Every programming language construct has to be implemented on a machine, and one cannot have a set of INTEGER (where would it finish, how much storage would need to be allocated to it ?). So we have explicitly made our set fit the range of courses available.

Sets are of finite size — ensure that yours are

3. The array ***list*** is an array of sets. That is, every "cell" in the array will contain a set. Thus, one can use statements which assign sets to an element of the array, such as:

```
list [index] := oneset;
```

One might visualise the array rather like:

Index	Contents	
1	[5, 7, 8, 19]	
2	[1, 2, 3, 5]	
3	[2, 3, 8, 19]	
4	[5, 6, 7, 8, 10, 12, 15, 18]	— a real swot
5	[]	— hasn't registered yet
143	[5, 7]	

4. One major use of sets is for checking certain sorts of input data in a simple way. The procedure is very straightforward. One initialises a set to contain all the valid values which may be accepted. Then, when data are being input, one checks to see if the datum which has just been read is IN the set used for checking. One can initialise the checking set in one of two ways:

One can enumerate the possible acceptable values. A common use is when the program asks a question (e.g. ''Do you want to do it again (Y/N)?'') to which the acceptable answers are actually only Yes or No. To simplify matters we accept the characters 'Y' or 'N'. Now, we know that people often forget to press the shift key to get uppercase characters, so to be on the safe side, we also include 'y' and 'n'. So there are four possible answers 'Y', 'y', 'N', 'n', and if any other answer is given, there is a good chance that the key was pressed by mistake. These possible answers are in no particular order, either in the alphabet or in the ASCII character representation. So, we simply initialise by enumeration, by listing which characters can be accepted as valid, using a statement such as:

```
possibleanswers := ['Y','y','N','n'];
```

If, on the other hand, the acceptable values form a consecutive sequence, then we can specify them as such, without having to go through the tedious business of enumerating them one by one. In this program we use:

```
checkset := [1..maxcourses];
```

thereby filling it with the values 1 to 20. The sequence does not have to be numerical; it merely has to follow some order, frequently the ASCII order. When one wishes to check if a character is, say, a lowercase letter, to see if it should be transformed to uppercase, one might well do this by checking to see if it is in the set ***lowercase***, initialised with:

```
lowercase := ['a'..'z'];
```

5. Initialisation is, as always, important. We are not actually incrementing or summing as we did with numerical variables in earlier examples; we are, however, doing something which is analogous. We shall build up sets by the use of the UNION operator. Using the symbol +, it even looks like summation, although it is not. We are, though, adding items to a set as we build up a picture of the subjects which a student is studying. Therefore, we have to be certain that before we add the first subject, the set of choices is actually empty, i.e. that it contains nothing left over from a previous user. It is simple to do this initialisation: one simply writes, in our program:

```
oneset := [];
```

where [] means ''the empty set''. It is simple, but you have to remember to do it.

Initialisation matters — not only with numbers

6. Having initialised our ***checkset*** to contain all the possible values for course codes, we can use it for data-checking. This enables us not only to detect errors in whatever is input, but also to avoid run-time errors arising, for example, from an attempt to add the code 21 to a set which is defined to hold values only in the range 1 to 20. The check is as simple and obvious as one might wish. Having read one input item into ***onecourse***, we merely check with:

```
if not ( onecourse in checkset ) then ............................
```

report an error, do NOT add it to the list of courses taken by this student.

One hopes that the logic is clear. If the current value of ***onecourse*** is, say, 27, then it clearly is not one of the values to which ***checkset*** was initialised, since they were made up of 1..20. In that case, the clause:

```
not ( onecourse in checkset )
```

will evaluate to TRUE. The THEN branch of the conditional statement will be followed, the error will be reported, and nothing will be added to the list of this student's courses. If, on the other hand, the value of ***onecourse*** had been 9, then that clause would have evaluated to FALSE, the ELSE branch would have been followed, and another subject would have been added to this student's list of courses. The verbal expression of the action can at times be convoluted. In this case one would have to say that it is not true (i.e. it is FALSE) that 9 is not in the range 1..20. With more complex expressions, doing it verbally can be very confusing, with a large range of NOTs following close upon each other's heels. In this case, it is relatively simple to follow — although surprisingly open to error. In larger cases, one really has to resort to boolean algebra to work out what will happen.

IN is a powerful data-checking operator

7. To accumulate the choices for one student we merely use the Union operator (+). Note that Union is an operator which works on 2 sets, i.e. it is of the form:

```
newset := oneoldset + anotheroldset;
```

It is unlike IN, which does not require 2 sets. Rather it uses a set element and a set, i.e.

```
if setelement IN theset then
```

Thus in our example if the value of ***onecourse*** which had just been read was 9, we could not add the value 9 to the set ***oneset***. That is, we could not write:

```
oneset := oneset + onecourse;
```

because then we would be trying to Union a set with a set element. So, in order to ensure that we Union a set with another set, we have to turn ***onecourse*** from an integer (in fact a valid integer in appropriate sub-range because we have checked to ensure that it is between 1 and 20) into a set containing one and only one integer. We do this quite simply by surrounding it with set brackets, i.e. by making it ***[onecourse]*** and by writing:

```
oneset := oneset + [onecourse];
```

In this way we can gradually accumulate the values which are to be stored in ***oneset*** to represent one student's choice of courses.

Union requires 2 sets. IN does not

8. Having constructed the choices for one student in ***oneset***, all that is left to do is to store it in the array of sets. We do this with:

```
list [index] := oneset;
```

The question of efficiency arises again. We could have added the course codes one at a time to ***list [index]*** directly without using the temporary variable ***oneset***. However, as explained earlier this would have incurred the overhead of additional operations to find out, for each Union, the location of ***list [index]***. The way it is done in this program, the machine has to find the location of that array cell once and once only.

The same considerations recur frequently

9. Having read the data-file, constructed a set of codes for each student, and stored them away in the array for future use, the last thing to do on the input phase is to make a note of how many students are in the list. We do this in the usual way by transferring the contents of ***index*** to ***total*** to preserve it until the end of the program. We then move on to the output phase.

This is done basically by two simple FOR loops. The first one goes through all the students. For each value of ***index*** i.e. for each student, the machine will extract his or her set of choices from the array and store it in ***oneset***. As usual this is done for reasons of both clarity and efficiency.

Having got ***oneset*** for a particular student, the machine then goes through all the possible valid values (1..20) to see if they are contained within that set. If a particular value is IN the set, it is printed out. Note that, since we are going sequentially from 1 to 20, any values which are printed will automatically be in ascending order. Thus using a set for our purpose kills two birds with one stone: it not only gets rid of double counting and omits erroneous entries, it also does our sorting for us.

Implementation is usually simple if the idea is clear

PROBLEM STATEMENT 13 THE LIBRARY AGAIN — USING A CHECKING SET

TOPICS COVERED Modifying an outline program
Adding data-checking via sets

In chapter two we introduced a simple library computerisation problem where we developed a menu procedure to allow us to select a number of actions. If the user typed an invalid selection, that program crashed. We now wish to develop a robust program using the concept of sets.

PROGRAM

```
program library(input,output);
{-----------------------------------------------}
procedure borrow;
begin
                writeln('borrowing book')
end;
{-----------------------------------------------}
procedure return;
begin
                writeln('returning a book')
end;
{-----------------------------------------------}
procedure addbook;
begin
                writeln('adding a book to the library')
end;
{-----------------------------------------------}
procedure deletebook;
begin
                writeln('deleting book from library')
end;
{-----------------------------------------------}
```

```
procedure join;
begin
                writeln'joining library')
end;
{-----------------------------------------------}
procedure leave;
begin
                writeln('leaving library')
end;
{-----------------------------------------------}
procedure printloaned;
begin
                writeln('print books loaned to borrower')
end;
{-----------------------------------------------}
procedure findborrower;
begin
                writeln('find who has borrowed a book')
end;
{-----------------------------------------------}
function terminate: boolean;
begin
                terminate := true;
                writeln('thank you for using the library — bye')
end;
{-----------------------------------------------}
function menu: boolean;
var             ch :   char;     valid : set of char;
{-----------------------------------------------}
procedure display;
begin           writeln('Welcome to the library — what facility do
                you wish to use?');
                writeln; writeln('Borrow a book —            type b');
                writeln('Return a book —                     type r');
                writeln('Add a book to the library —         type a');
                writeln('Delete a book from the library —    type d');
                writeln('Join the library —                  type j');
                writeln('Leave the library —                 type l');
                writeln('Print out books on loan —           type p');
                writeln('Find who has a borrowed a book —type f');
                 writeln('Terminate using the library — type t')
end;
{-----------------------------------------------}
```

```
begin                 valid: = ['b','r','a','d','j','l','p','f','t','B',
                          'R','A','D','J','L','P','F','T'];
              repeat display;
                 readln(ch);
              until ch in valid;
              menu:=false;
              case ch of
                          'b','B' : borrow;
                          'r','R' : return;
                          'a','A' : addbook;
                          'd','D' : deletebook;
                          'j','J'  : join;
                          'l','L'  : leave;
                          'p','P' : printloaned;
                          'f','F'  : findborrower;
                          't','T'  : menu := terminate
              end
end; {menu}
{------------------------------------------------}
begin         {MAIN PROGRAM}
              while not menu do
end.
```

{Yes, that really is the main program}

DISCUSSION

The only change we have made in this program compared to the one given in chapter two is the addition of the set ***valid*** which contains the set of valid responses. The repeat loop in ***menu*** ensures that only valid responses are passed into the case statement.

A good outline program is easy to extend

PROBLEM STATEMENT 14 STRING CLEANING AND SETS

TOPICS COVERED

- Data preparation
- Cleaning out unwanted characters
- Building sets by union
- Selection of groups
- Using OR

Write a program that reads a line of characters from the standard input and prints out all characters that are upper or lower case letters of the alphabet. Digits, special symbols (e.g. '!' or '*') and control characters should not be printed. The line length is sixty characters and the line structure must be preserved.

PROGRAM

```
program stringsexample1 (input, output);
{ remove non-alphabetic characters
from a line of characters while preserving the line structure according to
problem statement 14 }
const
        linelength = 60;
var
        lowercase, uppercase, alphabet : set of char;
        count        : integer;
        nextch       : char;
begin   { main program }
        { initialisation }
        lowercase := ['a'..'z'];
        uppercase := ['A'..'Z'];
        alphabet := lowercase + uppercase;
        {input a line of text and output it with non-alphabetic characters
        removed}

        writeln('Enter up to ',linelength:2,' characters on the next line,');
        writeln('non-alphabetic characters will be removed.');
        count := 0;
        while not eof do
        begin
                while (not eoln) and (count < linelength) do
                begin
                        count := count + 1;
                        read(nextch);
                        if nextch in alphabet then write(nextch)
                end;
                { preserve the line structure of the input }
                readln;
                writeln
        end
end.
```

RESULTS

Sample run one

Enter up to 60 characters on the next line,
non-alphabetic characters will be removed.

Sample run two

Enter up to 60 characters on the next line,
non-alphabetic characters will be removed.
1

Sample run three
Enter up to 60 characters on the next line,
non-alphabetic characters will be removed.
a
a

Sample run four
Enter up to 60 characters on the next line, non-alphabetic characters will be removed.
ab12ab!@ab^G^LABa^HbAB
ababababABabAB

Sample run five
Enter up to 60 characters on the next line, non-alphabetic characters will be removed.
aaaaaaaaaaaaaaaaaaaaaaaaaaaaaaaaaaaaaaaaaaaaaaaaaaaaaaaaaaaa
aaaaaaaaaaaaaaaaaaaaaaaaaaaaaaaaaaaaaaaaaaaaaaaaaaaaaaaaaaaa

Sample run six
Enter up to 60 characters on the next line,
non-alphabetic characters will be removed.
aaaaaaaaaaaaaaaaaaaaaaaaaaaaaaaaaaaaaaaaaaaaaaaaaaaaaaaaaaaaaaaa
aaaaaaaaaaaaaaaaaaaaaaaaaaaaaaaaaaaaaaaaaaaaaaaaaaaaaaaaaaaa

Sample run seven
Enter up to 60 characters on the next line,
non-alphabetic characters will be removed.
aaaaaaaaaaaaaaaaaaaaaaaaaaaaaaaaaaaaaaaaaaaaaaaaaaaaaaaaaa12BBa
aaaaaaaaaaaaaaaaaaaaaaaaaaaaaaaaaaaaaaaaaaaaaaaaaaaaaaaaaa

DISCUSSION

1. No matter how carefully data are prepared for processing, mistakes will inevitably be made. A good program should always test that its input data are valid and be able to react sensibly when given bad data. The more important the application, the more important it is that stringent checks should be applied. Data-checking allows one to filter out data that are obviously wrong before processing takes place. It also stops input that would violate the program's design limitations. This example illustrates the use of sets to filter strings of characters. Valid characters pass through the filter; invalid ones are stopped.

Sets are useful for some forms of data-checking
What matters is that there IS some data-checking

2. Words are formed from strings of characters. The characters that may appear in a word vary from one language to the next. English and French

have similar alphabets, but the Russian alphabet is different from both of them. In addition to letters of the alphabet there are digits and special characters. The special characters include brackets, punctuation marks and mathematical symbols. Computers have other special characters called control characters. The most common is the newline character, which is what the terminal adds to the input when you press the RETURN key. Control characters can be written in different ways. For example control-g (formed by holding down the control key and typing the letter ″G″) may be abbreviated to ctrl-g, ^G, or g. The ^G notation will be used here. Since the alphabet, digits and special characters are sets of characters, it is natural to represent them as sets in Pascal. We have written a program that uses sets to remove numeric and special characters from a line of text, leaving only letters of the alphabet.

Characters are merely images of an underlying code

3. The program must read a line of text from the standard input, one character at a time. If the character is a letter of the alphabet, it is printed otherwise it is discarded. Lines that are too long for the program are truncated. We start by declaring the alphabet to be a set containing all the upper case letters from 'A' to 'Z' and all the lower case letters from 'a' to 'z'. For clarity, separate sets are used for upper and lower case letters. It would be equally correct to write

```
alphabet := ['a'..'z','A'..'Z']; instead of

lowercase := ['a'..'z'];
uppercase := ['A'..'Z'];
alphabet := lowercase + uppercase;
```

In this context the '+' operator means set union, not arithmetic addition. ***alphabet*** is the union of ***lowercase*** and ***uppercase***. It contains all the characters in ***lowercase*** and all the characters in ***uppercase***. Two other set operators are provided, intersection and set difference. A * B denotes the intersection between two sets A and B. (All the elements that are in A and in B.) A − B is the set of all elements in A that are not also elements of B.

There are several ways to create a set

4. After ***alphabet*** has been initialised, the program prints a prompt telling the user that they are expected to type in a line of text. In an application, the user would normally be told exactly what was required, for example a name or an address. Then these lines of Pascal code would form part of a larger data input and validation routine. The prompt also warns users of a limitation in the program's design. The line must not be longer than

sixty characters. Limits like this simplify later processing. It would be harder to write a program that worked when the maximum line length was not fixed in advance. A global constant has been used to store the maximum line length. This makes the meaning of the first writeln statement clearer and the program easier to modify. Compare:

''Enter up to', linelength:2,' characters...''

with

''Enter up to', 60:2,' characters...''.

5. The ***while not eof*** loop stops the program trying to read anything when there is no input. Characters are read and filtered using the inner WHILE loop. This loop is executed once for each character read. It stops when it reaches the end of the line or the maximum number of characters have been input. To test whether the character is a letter of the alphabet, we use the simple IF test

if nextch in alphabet

It returns the value true if the next character is a member of the alphabet and false otherwise. Only characters that satisfy this set membership test are written to the standard output. READLN and WRITELN statements are put after the end of the WHILE loop. They ensure that the line structure of the output mirrors that of the input.

Re-use structures which you know already work

6. Our test runs show that the program appears to work. Non-alphabetic characters are removed, long lines are truncated and the line structure is preserved. However the seventh test run highlights an important detail. When there are more than sixty characters on the input line, only the first sixty are read. Even if some are discarded, the program does not look further along the line to see if there are valid characters that could take their place. This is an example of the program protecting itself from data that violate its design limitations. It is also an example of an incomplete problem specification. All the specification says is that ''The line length is sixty characters and the line structure must be preserved''. No guidance is given on what to do if there are more than sixty characters. Alternatively the program could be designed to echo up to the first sixty valid characters, even if more than sixty have to be read from the input line. Then the WHILE loop would be written as follows.

```
{-----------------------------------------------------------------------}
count := 1;
while (not eoln) and (count <= linelength) do
begin
        read(nextch);
        if nextch in alphabet then
        begin
              write(nextch);
              count := count + 1
        end
end;
{-----------------------------------------------------------------------}
```

Notice that the statement which increments ***count*** has been moved inside the IF test. It now counts the number of valid characters that have been read, not the total number of characters. To make the WHILE loop work correctly, 'count' must be initialised to one instead of nought. The condition (***count*** < ***linelength***) must be replaced by (***count*** <= ***linelength***), or the loop will only read up to ***linelength−1*** valid characters.

When the structure is clear, modifications are usually simpler to make

7. This program will work if it is run using a Pascal system that supports sets of at least 52 characters. (***alphabet*** contains 26 upper case and 26 lower case letters.) The maximum size of sets varies from one implementation to another. If the full alphabet set is too big, try splitting it into smaller sets. In place of

```
if nextch in alphabet
```

try writing

```
if (nextch in lowercase) or (nextch in uppercase)
```

Both are better than

```
if (nextch = 'a') or (nextch = 'b') or (nextch = 'c') or (nextch = 'd')...
```

At the very least it saves a lot of typing

8. There is one more potential problem when dealing with sets of characters. Each character is represented in the computer's memory by an integer number, called its character code. There are several different sets of character code in common use. ASCII (American Standard Code for Information Interchange) and EBCDIC (Extended Binary-Coded-Decimal Interchange Code) are among the most popular. In ASCII, upper and lower case letters are allocated two blocks of codes. The letters 'A' to 'Z' have the (octal) codes 101 to 132 and 'a' to 'z' have the codes 141 to 172. We have written ['A'..'Z'] as an abbreviation for ['A','B','C',....,'X','Y','Z'].

When given that abbreviation, some compilers test for set membership by evaluating the condition

if ***chcode(nextch)*** >= chcode(A)) and (chcode(nextch) <= chcode(Z))

where chcode(char) is replaced by the character code of the character concerned. This works if all the letters have contiguous values. In a few sets of character codes, notably EBCDIC, this is not true. Then it is best to write out the set in full.

If your machine does not use ASCII, beware our advice on sets!

PROBLEM STATEMENT 15 COMPILERS AND LEXICAL ANALYSERS

TOPICS COVERED
- Recognising language constructs
- Ignoring comments — Skipping while reading
- Recognising identifiers and reserved words
- The use of sets in a lexical analyser

One task facing a compiler writer is that of recognising standard identifiers, and reserved words. This is usually part of the function of the lexical scanner. In this exercise we wish to read a Pascal program and count the number of occurrences of reserved words. For this purpose we shall assume reserved words have been written in upper case. We shall also count the number of identifiers found. These are defined as words written in lower case. Words are defined to be sequences of letters.

PROGRAM

```
PROGRAM scanner (input,output);
{compile this program using the -s flag if using Berkeley Pascal}
CONST stcomment = '{';
      endcomment = '}';
      stringsymb = '''';
TYPE  letters = SET OF char;
VAR   ch    : char;
      ucase, lcase   : letters;
      reserved, idents   : integer;
BEGIN {initialise sets and counts}
      reserved := 0; idents := 0;
      ucase := ['A'..'Z']; lcase := ['a'..'z'];
      REPEAT read(ch);
           IF ch = stcomment THEN
           {comment found skip until end of it}
           BEGIN
                REPEAT
                          read(ch)
                UNTIL ch = endcomment;
                read(ch)
           END;
```

```
          IF ch = stringsymb THEN {string found skip until end of it}
          BEGIN
               REPEAT
                    read(ch)
               UNTIL ch = stringsymb;
               read(ch)
          END;
          IF ch IN ucase THEN
          BEGIN
               reserved := reserved + 1;
               REPEAT
                    read(ch)
               UNTIL NOT (ch IN ucase)
          END;
          IF ch IN lcase THEN
          BEGIN
               idents := idents + 1;
               REPEAT
                    read(ch)
               UNTIL NOT (ch IN lcase)
          END
     UNTIL eof;
     writeln('no of reserved words',reserved);
     writeln('no of identifiers',     idents)
     END.
```

RESULTS

When writing any program such as this, which takes as its input a program, an obvious test is to run the program with itself as input. In this case we would get the result:

```
no of reserved words  36
no of identifiers     46
```

DISCUSSION

The use of sets to identify what class of character we have just read makes this problem fairly easy. The only slightly tricky bit is ignoring comments and strings. The solution offered will not cope with nested comments. In order to do this some form of count would have to be maintained of how many opening comment symbols had been read, in order to ensure that the appropriate number of closing symbols were found. Without the loop to skip strings the letters A and Z would be counted as reserved words. Note that we did not use a compound conditional (if .. then .. else if .. then) in the loop because after recognising one feature (comment string, identifier, or reserved word) it is perfectly possible to find another immediately. A feature of all such programs is that the last character read which allowed us to detect the end of a feature may be the start of another feature. Therefore in recognising, say, an identifier we assume that we have already found the first letter.

Most complete programs can still be improved.
Finishing a program does not stop you thinking about it

6

Arrays and user-defined types

PROBLEM STATEMENT 16	**HOUSEHOLD EXPENSES — AND VECTORS**
TOPICS COVERED	The idea of objects and operations Arrays as structured objects The value of user-defined types Vectors — filling, adding, displaying Local operations Var and value parameters The use of MOD for formatting

You have a text-file containing information about the household expenses of a number of households. This text-file is called ***vecfile***, for reasons which will become obvious shortly. Each household occupies 3 lines in the file; there is one line each for Gas, Electricity, and Mortgage payments. Thus, household number 1 takes up lines 1–3, household number 2 takes up lines 4–6, and so on. Each line contains 12 real numbers. They are to be interpreted as representing the expenditure on the relevant item for each month of the year, i.e. January's gas bill, February's gas bill, right down to December's. Then, on the next line we have 12 real numbers representing 12 monthly electricity bills.

Your task is to produce relatively tidy output representing the monthly expenditure of each family on each item, plus their total annual expenditure. It should be in the form:

Household No. 1

Gas expenses
data data data data data data data data data data data data
Total gas expenses

Electricity expenses
ditto

Mortgage expenses
ditto

Overall expenses
ditto

PROGRAM

```
{-----------------------------------------------------------------------}
{PROGRAM USING VECTORS, PROCEDURES AND A FUNCTION
}
program vecfill(input,output,vecfile);
const    max=12;
type     vector=array[1..max] of real;
var gas,  electric,mortgage,overall      : vector;
    index                                : integer;
    vecfile                              : text;
{PROCEDURE TO READ DATA FROM THE TEXT-FILE AND FILL
A VECTOR WITH THEM}
procedure fillvector( var subfile : text; var sublist : vector);
var      index : integer;
begin    for index := 1 to max do
                 read (subfile, sublist[index]);
         readln(subfile)
end; {fillvector}
{---------------------------------------------------------------}
{PROCEDURE TO DISPLAY A VECTOR}
{IT INCLUDES A FUNCTION TO SUM THE VALUES IN THE
VECTOR}
procedure displayvector (sublist : vector);
var      index : integer;
{-—-—-—-—-—-—-—-—-—-—-—-—-—-—-—-—-—-—-—-}
{NESTED FUNCTION FOR SUMMING VALUES IN THE VECTOR}
function sum (anylist : vector) : real;
var      index : integer;
         temp : real;
begin    temp := 0.0;
         for index := 1 to max do
                 temp := temp + anylist [index];
         sum := temp
end; {sum}
{-—-—-—-—-—-—-—-—-—-—-—-—-—-—-—-—-—-—-—-}
begin    {Main body of procedure <displayvector>}
         for index := 1 to max do
         begin  write (sublist[index]:9:2);
                if (index mod (max div 2)=0) then
                           writeln
         end
```

```
          writeln('Total expenses were ',sum(sublist):8:2,' pounds');
          writeln('------------------------------------------------------------');
end; {displayvector}
{-----------------------------------------------------------------}
procedure addvectors(a,b,c:vector; var suboverall:vector);
var       index : integer;
begin     for index := 1 to max do
                 suboverall[index] := a[index] + b[index] + c[index]
end; {addvectors}
{-----------------------------------------------------------------}
begin     {MAIN}
          index := 0;
          reset(vecfile);
          while not eof(vecfile) do
          begin     index := index +1;
                    fillvector(vecfile,gas);
                    fillvector(vecfile,electric);
                    fillvector(vecfile,mortgage);
                    page(output);
                    writeln('Household No.',index:3,' Gas expenses':20);
                    displayvector(gas);
                    writeln(' Electric expenses':36);
                    displayvector(electric);
                    writeln(' Mortgage expenses':36);
                    displayvector(mortgage);
                    addvectors(gas,electric,mortgage,overall);
                    writeln(' Overall expenses':36);
                    displayvector(overall);
          end
end.
```

DISCUSSION

1. Each list of expenses, although it consists of 12 numbers, can be thought of as a single object. We do tend to talk about (and certainly think about) our expenses as single objects. For example, we may use the phrase "this year's electricity bills", but there is an important sense in which it is that these numbers make up a single object. In this program we try to represent them as a single object. A list of 12 months' expenses clearly contains 12 numbers, but it is still only 1 list. So we have defined a type to represent that list. We have called the type ***vector*** following the usual mathematical nomenclature for a one-dimensional array. It is a one-dimensional, 12-item array of reals (since we are dealing with money and the decimal places matter!).

Arrays often help to turn lists into comprehensible objects

2. In this program we shall use 3 vectors, one each for gas, electricity and mortgage expenses. We can use these over and over again. Given the specification of the task, once we have read in the data for household number 1, added them up, and printed them up, we do not need to retain them in the computer's memory. There are problems (the majority) in which we do need to retain data for a significant period of time. This is not one of them. We can just re-use the vectors (gas, electric, and mortgage) for households number 2,3,.. and so on. Thus our data structures are very simple. We need only 3 vectors no matter how many households we have to process.

Types and variables can be re-used many times

3. Having defined the type ***vector*** we shall need to perform operations on objects (variables) of that type. It is very common for types and procedures to be linked logically in this way. Indeed, one of the advantages of a strongly typed language like Pascal is that it encourages the programmer to think what they wish to do and permits them to define linked objects and operations. With the standard simple types this is the case — you can do things to integers that you cannot do to characters, for example. It is the same with user-defined types.

Note that the fact that parameters to a procedure must have a type name means that the procedure be used only with objects of the specified type(s) and thus the logical link is not only strong, it is enforced by the language.

Types and procedures are logically linked

4. We have 3 procedures which are relevant here. Firstly we have to fill each vector with values, i.e. we have to read 12 real numbers from the data-file and put them in their correct places in ***gas***, ***electric***, and ***mortgage***. This has to be done before we can do anything else with each vector. Note that it is the same operation on the same sort of object in each case. It obviously makes sense to define this operation as a procedure and then to use this procedure as often as we wish. Naturally we have called this procedure ***fillvector*** with the intention of making the program to some extent self-documenting.

Filling a vector is a single operation on a single object
(No matter how many operations it itself consists of !)

5. A further procedure displays the contents of a vector and the sum of its constituent elements. This has to be done many times. Unsurprisingly we have called the relevant procedure ***displayvector***. When we use it we merely write:

```
displayvector (gas);
or
displayvector (electric);
```

It is possible that we might have set up a more complex structure, say an array of vectors (a list of lists). Suppose that we had called these big arrays ***gaslist***, ***eleclist***, and ***mortlist***. Then we could have displayed a lot of vectors using the same procedure, with something like:

```
for index := 1 to n do
begin
    displayvector( gaslist[index]);
    displayvector(eleclist[index]);
    displayvector(mortlist[index])
end;
```

Procedure are nearly always more useful than you think originally

6. One of the things that we need to do is to add up the annual expenditure on each item. We have to end up with a single value, a single cash sum. We could do this by having a procedure with a VAR parameter to represent this total sum. However, Pascal does have a special means of permitting us to calculate single values — the FUNCTION. Although this is used a great deal in mathematical programming, there is no reason why it should not be used in other contexts if this is the natural thing to do. In this case it is. It is a natural extension of our principle of trying to represent things by an appropriate structure or operation. If our purpose is to calculate a single integer, real, character or boolean value, a function is the natural way to do it. So we have defined a function to calculate the single value representing the total of the elements of a vector of reals. We can therefore write code such as:

```
writeln (sum(gas):6:2);
or
if sum(mortgage) > 3000 then writebank(letter);
```

Of course, there are built-in, pre-defined functions in Pascal, such as SQR, SQRT, ABS, TRUNC, ODD and so on. Beginning programmers often neglect these, and even more so neglect to write their own functions. Of course, one does not write a function merely for the pleasure of it. However, if it is the way that one thinks about an operation, it is the right thing to do. One example which is frequently needed is a function to calculate powers and roots. To the surprise of every beginner, this is not a standard pre-defined part of Pascal.

Use functions whenever it is natural to do so

7. Of course, calculating the value of a function is not without cost. Whenever you use a statement like

```
writeln(sum(gas));
or
total := total + sum(gas);
```

the machine has to undertake a calculation. It has to perform however many operations are included in the definition of ***sum***. For a small function this may not be a great overhead, especially if the function is called only a small number of times. If, however, the function is a very complex one with a large number of statements within it, or if it is called many times, this overhead may become intolerable, and may counterbalance the clarity obtained by using the function in the first place. In this case, it is worth while assigning the value of the function to a temporary variable and then using that temporary variable instead of the function call. If, for example, you need to use the value of ***sum(gas)*** 10 times, you might calculate it once, store its value in a temporary value (called, say, ***tempgascost***), and refer to THAT on the next 9 occasions. For example:

```
tempgascost := sum(gas);
total := total + tempgascost;
gastotal := gastotal + tempgascost;
writeln('This month''s gas cost', tempgascost:6:2);
```

In this way we do not have to recalculate ***sum(gas)*** many times. We merely have to look up its value — a much faster undertaking.

Temporary variables can save time with frequently used functions

8. This function is used only when we are displaying vectors. Where should we put it? This is a matter of some debate. As we need it only when we are displaying vectors, there is a strong case for declaring the function INSIDE the procedure ***displayvector***, so that it becomes a function LOCAL to that procedure. This means that it can be used only inside that procedure and cannot be called by other procedures or, for that matter, by the main program. One might argue that you can never be sure that you will never need it outside the procedure ***displayvector*** and that therefore you should declare it as a GLOBAL function in the main declaration section at the beginning of the program. It would then be available to any procedure (or function) and to the main program.

In general, we have adopted the view that if you need something only locally, you should declare it only locally. This applies as much to procedures and functions as to variables. It safeguards you from making some silly mistakes, although we appreciate that such mistakes are less common with functions than they are with variables (where you can alter a value accidently, disastrously, and usually very mysteriously). If you discover later that you need the function globally, it is usually a simple matter to move it using an ordinary line editor.

Like objects, operations which are needed only locally should ideally be declared only locally

9. The final procedure ***addvectors*** merely adds up all the components of each of the three main vectors for gas, etc. and stores them in their correct places in a new vector, called ***overall***, so that we have a representation of the household's expenditure on all 3 items combined, for each month of the year. Ideally one would like to write this as a function. However, functions can, in the current standard as it is widely accepted and implemented, return only simple types (reals, integers, chars, booleans and pointers). They cannot produce a single object which is a structured type. They cannot, in other words, return sets, records or arrays. Thus we cannot write a function whose result type is a vector. The following would be illegal in a normal compiler:

```
function addvectors(a,b,c:vector):vector;
```

although things are moving that way. They have not got there yet so in order to be able to perform a calculation on 2 or more vectors and return a new vector containing the result, we have to do it by means of a VAR parameter, i.e.

```
procedure addvectors(a,b,c:vector; var suboverall:vector);
```

To return structured types, you have to use VAR parameters

10. There is one small formatting tip hidden away in the depths of function ***sum***. Often we wish to print things out using a FOR loop. However, our output may be rather lengthy and will eventually run off the side of the page (or screen). Thus, we may wish to ensure that only 4, 6, 9 or some other number of items are printed on each line, thus getting our output in column form — with 4, 6, or 9 columns. The principle is very simple. As usual to print things across the page we use ***write*** (NOT ***writeln***). When we wish to move to a new line, we merely put in a ***writeln***. The only question is "Where do we put it?" Suppose that we wish to go to a new line after every four items, thus getting four-column output. We merely have have to ensure that we have a ***writeln*** after every fourth item. How do we do this? We use ***index***, the loop control variable. We ensure that the new line comes after items 4, 8, 12, 16, etc. by checking whether ***index*** is exactly divisible by 4. If it is, we put in a ***writeln***; if it isn't, we don't. The way to find out if an integer is divisible by 4 is to test using the MOD operator. If you divide ***a*** by ***b*** and the

remainder is 0, then ***a*** is an exact multiple of ***b***. So the test in this case would be:

```
if (index mod 4=0) then writeln;
```

To get different numbers of columns all we have to do is to vary the value of 4 in the above example. In the program above we have made it depend upon ***max*** in that the quantity by which we mod is (max div 2).

MOD is a useful operator for tidy formatting

PROBLEM STATEMENT 17 BATTLE OF HASTINGS — AND FUNCTIONS

TOPICS COVERED
Mathematical functions
A power function
The principle of hiding operations
Nested functions Implementation limits — very large numbers
A trick with field-widths

There is an apocryphal story about a British Army officer who was promoted from the rank of lieutenant to that of captain in the year 1966. The administrator who sent him the letter announcing the promotion officially was not a very good proof-reader. Instead of telling him that he was promoted with effect from 1st January 1966, it unfortunately claimed that he was promoted with effect from 1st January 1066. Now, like most good officers, this one had either a sense of initiative or a sense of humour. He wrote back to the Ministry of Defence immediately, thanking them for this long overdue promotion. He also pointed out that it was an official, legally-binding document and that he would hold them to it. Therefore, he claimed, he was entitled to back pay starting from the date on which he was officially promoted i.e. the date in 1066.

This letter caused some sense of concern among the mandarins at the Ministry of Defence. Clearly, if they owed money, they owed it with the interest which the government had been gathering on it for all that period of time. The sum concerned would not be trivial, even at a relatively modest rate of interest. Fortunately, one of their number had a sense of initiative (or humour) similar to that of the officer. The new captain duly received a letter informing him that his claim was accepted as entirely justified, and apologising for the delay in payment. However, it pointed out, they had been looking into the records and had discovered that in the year of his promotion there had taken place a battle at a place called Hastings. As far as they could ascertain he was (officially and legally) the only officer of the period whom they could still trace. He was therefore the person responsible for the equipment which had been lost at that battle. The Ministry had valued the equipment lost and, again with a due allowance for a modest rate of interest, had calculated how much he owed them for the lost equipment. Miraculously it turned out to be exactly the amount which they owed him in back pay. Therefore they proposed to deduct this amount from his back pay and he would be regarded as having discharged all his responsibilities. Thus, the legal niceties were observed, honour was satisfied and everyone had a quiet laugh.

When we heard this story, the first question which came to mind was "How much would be involved in a debt accumulating over such a long period?" Even at a low rate of interest (say 5%) it could still be substantial, since the process is not one of simple interest, but of compound interest, i.e. one gets interest on the interest. The problem was "just how substantial would the sum be?" The calculation is one of compound interest. At 5% per annum, after 1 year £1 will be worth £1.05. After 2 years it will be worth 1.05 × 1.05. After the third year it is 1.05 × 1.05 × 1.05 ...... and so on. In other words the main task is to calculate 1.05 to the power of how many years our investment has to run.

Pascal does not have a built-in power function. Therefore we have to write one. Similarly it does not have a built-in function for calculating compound interest so we have to write that as well. The program below was intended to do such calculations for interest rates from 1.0 to 10.5%. It nearly did so.

PROGRAM

```
program hastings ( output );
const   battledate = 1066;
        today=1986;
        startamount=100;
var     rate, finishamount : real;
{-----------------------------------------------------------------}
function compound ( start: real; years : integer; rate : real ): real;
{----------------------------------------------}
function power ( rate : real; years : integer ): real;
begin   power := exp ( ln (rate) * years );
end; {power}
{----------------------------------------------}
begin
        compound:=( power((rate/100) + 1, years) ) * start
end; {compound}
{----------------------------------------------}
```

```
begin    {MAIN}
         rate:=1.0;
         repeat   finishamount := compound (startamount, (today -
                  battledate),rate);

                  writeln('At ',rate:1:1,'% you owe £',finishamount:2:2);
                  rate:=rate + 0.5
         until rate > 10.5
end.
```

RESULTS

At 1.0% you owe £945505.11
At 1.5% you owe £88870754.91
At 2.0% you owe £8168795444.00
At 2.5% you owe £734439726883.46
At 3.0% you owe £64602113842956.53
At 3.5% you owe £5560601973534692.90
At 4.0% you owe £468459612551623690.00
At 4.5% you owe £38635559985238859000.00
At 5.0% you owe £3120003953570334600000.00
At 5.5% you owe £246753239500099620000000.00
At 6.0% you owe £19115956940738476000000000.00
At 6.5% you owe £1450905586101574700000000000.00
At 7.0% you owe £107913423464829680000000000000.00
At 7.5% you owe £7866600791942389800000000000000.00
At 8.0% you owe £562153667033900350000000000000000.00
At 8.5% you owe £39387564718845109000000000000000000.00
At 9.0% you owe £2706313508860397100000000000000000000.00

DISCUSSION

1. The first thing which should notice about this program is that it fails. How does it fail, and why? It is supposed to perform the calculation with interest rates ranging from 1.0% to 10.5%. If you peruse the results you will see that the last entry is for 9.0%. What, then, happened to 9.5, 10 and 10.5% ? The machine did, in fact, try to perform the computation, but the result which it obtained was too large to fit into the space allocated to a real number. If you count carefully you will see that the capital value of the equipment, accumulating at 9% per annum, is roughly 2.7 times 10 to the power 36. That is a big number, but it is one that my machine can represent. The result of the next calculation, however, produces a result that goes beyond 10 to the power 38, which is the largest number which our machine can represent. So, 9.5% is too much — the answer is too big to be stored as a real number. In fact, the problem is the storage of the exponent.

Just because it works, that doesn't mean that it won't fail!

2. In order to run this program to generate a series of numbers, one does not actually need any input. All the values which are needed for the computation are included either as global constants (***battledate, today, startamount***), or as variables whose values vary automatically with no intervention from the user (***rate, finishamount***). Because of this we do not need even to mention the standard file ***input*** in the program heading. One tends to do that almost automatically, but in a few cases it is not strictly necessary. In such cases, and this is one of them, one can omit even that mention. In the usual way of making the program fit the problem we say ''we don't need any input — therefore we won't allow for any''. The structure of the problem is the main factor which should determine the nature of the program.

If you don't need something — don't use it

3. As you can see here, functions can be nested one inside the other. In this case it is clear that the main calculation can be performed using a function, since all it does is to return a single number each time — the value of the equipment after all that interest has been added. So we have a function called ***compound*** — obviously for calculating compound interest. This in turn needs a power function, so we provide one. As this power function is needed and used only inside ***compound*** that is where we declare it.

Nest operations so that you see only as much as you need

4. The power function is straightforward, requiring only a knowledge of how to calculate powers using logarithms. Many beginners write power functions using a FOR loop to multiply the rate by itself 2,3,4.. etc. times over. In our present example, that would work quite well, since we are calculating using whole numbers of years. In fact, year is declared to be an integer. If, on the other hand we had wished to be able to raise numbers to fractional powers like 0.25, or 1.5, the continuous multiplication method would not work. The method used in the function here would, however, work. The only modification needed is to ensure that ***years*** is declared to be a real, not an integer. Of course, since the fourth root of ***x*** is the same as ***x*** to the power of 0.25 we have written a function which will not only raise to any (representable) power, but will also work out roots. This is a very flexible tool. Note that the function body consists of only one statement.

It doesn't have to be complicated to be useful

5. Note that the incrementing of ***rate*** is done using a ***repeat*** loop. It could also have been done using a ***while*** loop. Indeed, there is a strong argument for using a ***while*** loop in most circumstances. The third form of loop construct — the FOR loop — could not, however, have been used here. This is because ***rate*** is a real number. If we wrote:

```
for rate := 1.0 to 10.0 do ........
```

after the machine had performed one iteration with rate = 1.0, what value would it assign for the second iteration — 1.1, 1.01, 1.001, 1.0001 or what? The answer is that we do not know. In the integers there is a natural scaling — there is no integer between 1 and 2. Similarly with characters: there is no character between 'J' and 'K'. With real numbers it is different: between 1.0 and 2.0 there is an infinity of possible values which they can take. So we have to specify the steps explicitly.

You cannot use reals as FOR loop control variables

6. Note that in the printing section of the program we have used some rather unusual field-widths. We ask for the rate of interest to be printed out with a field-width of 1:1 not, say, 8:1 or any other sensible value. Why is this? It certainly seems strange to ask for something to have a total field-width of one character, and at the same time to have only one character after the decimal point. Where is the room for the decimal point, one is tempted to ask?

Of course, the reason is in effect a trick to produce a particular format of output. We must have the decimal places part of the specification correct. We want only one decimal place, so we ask for only one decimal place. For the total width, the first figure, we would normally use a reasonably large value to accommodate the values which are likely to be calculated. This is ideal when we are printing out tables of numbers, or string headings which have to be neatly aligned. If everything is, say, 8 characters wide, it will be neatly aligned. Its shortcoming is that it may leave many or few (or no) blank spaces at the beginning. If, as in the case of the equipment value, what we are printing is a set of money values, there will be blanks between the currency symbol and the actual number. If we were printing this on a cheque, it would leave room for forgers to get to work — and to get to work at the more disastrous end of the number, to add at the more significant end!

By using a field-width which is obviously too short, we have effectively forced the machine to return to its default setting which is to print as many characters as it needs to, and thus to get rid of any potential leading blanks. Mind you, if we were tabulating data, this would not lead to tidy output, since numbers would not necessarily be lined up neatly. Where they were printed would depend upon how long they were. In fact, if the machine had not failed when it did, and had managed to carry on and calculate the answer for rate = 10.0, we would immediately have had the numbers moved one place to the right, and the output would have started to become untidy. As it happens, we have achieved the result which we desired.

Tricks are useful in some places — as long as you are careful to ensure that they are portable.

PROBLEM STATEMENT 18 UPPER-CASE CONVERSION — STRING FUNCTIONS

TOPICS COVERED

- Functions do not have to be numerical
- Result types must be simple
- Case conversion
- ORD CHR and ASCII
- Constants for efficiency

One wishes, for purposes of clarity, coding, producing posters, or whatever, to transform all lower case letters in a file to upper case letters. The basic structure which we would like to see is:

```
reset(lowerfile);
rewrite(upperfile);
while not eof (lowerfile) do
begin
        readstring(lowerfile, oneline);
        transform(oneline);
        writestring(upperfile, oneline,true)
end;
```

We already have procedures for reading and writing strings, so we can simply copy the ***readstring*** and ***writestring*** from other programs. What though of the procedure ***transform***? We wish this to transform lower case letters to upper case. However, we have to be careful not to alter other characters. Existing upper case letters must not be changed, nor must digits, blank spaces, or other non-alphabetical characters. We have seen an attempt to do this in chapter 5.

There are two problems. The first is to select the characters to be transformed whilst ignoring those to be left unchanged. We already know that this can be done using sets. What, though, of the actual transformation? The user-defined function ***uppercase***, which is used in the procedure ***transform***, is the crucial step. It is given below.

PROGRAM FRAGMENTS

```
{----------------------------------------------------------------}
{Function which does case transformation for ASCII systems}
function uppercase (aletter:char) : char;
begin    if letter in ['a'..'z'] then
                uppercase := chr (ord(aletter) − 32)
         else   uppercase := aletter
end; {uppercase}
{----------------------------------------------------------------}
```

```
{More general version of the same function}
function uppercase (aletter : char) : char;
begin   if aletter in ['a'..'z'] then
                    uppercase := chr( ord('A')-ord('a') + ord(aletter))
        else    uppercase := aletter
end; {uppercase}
{--------------------------------------------------------------------}

procedure transform (var somestring : string);
var     index : integer;
begin   for index := 1 to stringlength do
                    somestring [index] := uppercase (somestring [index])
end; {transform}
```

DISCUSSION

1. The actual procedure ***transform*** is obvious. Using the loop control variable ***index*** we merely step along each character of the string in turn, replacing it with its upper case version.

2. Note that we have assumed a constant called ***stringlength*** and have written the procedure to work generally. When writing this procedure we do not need to know the value of ***stringlength***. In various applications it might be as little as 3 (see the voting program in this book), as much as 80 (which is usually a screenful) or even 132 (which is a common width for printer paper). This is an example of how using constants and writing our program in a modular fashion, re-using old code, can not only save effort, but can also minimise the risk of errors.

Constants and modularity become more important the more you use them

3. The main task, though, is performed by the function ***uppercase***. This takes a single parameter (a single character). Note that although ***oneline*** and its matched parameter ***somestring*** are packed arrays of char, ***somestring[index]*** is not — it is a single character. Do not confuse single characters and arrays of them.

Not only does the function take in a single character as its only parameter, it also returns a single character since its result type is CHAR.

Functions do not have to return numbers — they can return any simple type

4. The function itself consists of a single statement — an IF .. THEN .. ELSE. The IF part, the boolean test, is of a kind with which we are already familiar. It tests to see whether the character which is currently being processed — ***aletter*** or ***somestring[index]*** — is in the set of lowercase letters ['a'..'z'].

5. If it is in that set then it is transformed and ***uppercase*** takes on the

transformed value. What, though, if ***somestring[index]*** is already a capital letter or a digit, for example? The answer is simple; the function ***uppercase*** merely takes on the value of the character untransformed, just as it was passed in, using the assignment statement:

```
uppercase := aletter
```

In this way we transform those characters which need to be changed and leave unchanged those which should be left in such decent tranquillity. It is not infrequent for beginners to overlook the obvious case in which one does no transformation.

Ensure that you consider any possible ELSEs before leaving conditionals

6. How is the actual transformation done? To understand this, we need to know how the machine represents characters. Basically it has to turn them into numbers according to some pre-defined code. The most widely used code is the ASCII code. In this code, for example, the lower case letters run from 97 ('a') to 122 ('z'), while the upper case ones run from 65 ('A') to 90 ('Z'). This means that the code for an upper case letter is always 32 lower than that for its lower case equivalent.

Pascal has two built-in functions which allow us to go from characters to their numerical codes and back again. To get the code of a particular character we use the ORD function. Suppose that ***aletter*** has the value 'A'. Then the statement:

```
avariable := ord (aletter);
```

will result in ***avariable*** taking on the value 65. If ***aletter*** had happened to be 'z', then ***avariable*** would take on the value 122.

To go the other way we use the CHR function. Thus if ***avariable*** had the value 65, the statement:

```
aletter := chr (avariable);
```

would give ***aletter*** the value 'A'. This would apply for all values within the range of the code system.

We have shown in the first version of the function a simple statement which will work on systems using the ASCII code (or any code with an interval of 32). Suppose that ***aletter*** has the value 'b'. What will happen to ***uppercase***? Firstly the machine determines that 'b' is clearly IN the set ['a'..'z']. It must therefore take the THEN branch of the conditional statement, not the ELSE one. It will go through the following steps:

```
aletter         is   'b'
ord (aletter)   is    98
98 -32          is    66
chr(66)         is   'B'
uppercase       :=   'B'
```

Functions can, of course, use other functions

7. Although this will work on machines using the ASCII code, which is a very large proportion of the total, it will not necessarily work on all machines. One can make the function rather more general, and take away its dependence on the value 32. As long as the upper case/lower case interval is constant, we can calculate the gap by the expression:

```
gap := ord('A') — ord ('a');
```

Then whenever we have the ord of a lower case letter we merely have to add ***gap*** to it to get the ord of its upper case equivalent. A simple CHR will turn this back to the upper case character.

In the second version of the function we do this rather inefficiently for the purpose of concise exposition. Each time the function is called the gap is recalculated. This might be done hundreds, thousands, or millions of times during the running of the program. Clearly, it would be preferable to have a global variable (or even a constant) with the appropriate value, like ***gap*** mentioned above. This could be set, or calculated, once at the beginning of the program and merely referred to in the function. With more space in this book we would have done it that way!

Functions can often be made more flexible and general with a little thought

7

Tackling a problem — making the bricks into a wall

PROBLEM STATEMENT 19	**PALINDROMES AND STRING MANIPULATION**
TOPICS COVERED	Manipulating strings Reading to a delimiter Padding strings Simple encryption Putting it all together

Assuming that the maximum length of a string is 25 characters, write functions or procedures to do the following:

1) read a string of characters terminated by a space
2) read a string of characters terminated by end-of- line
3) read a string of characters terminated by either space or end-of-line
4) write a string of non-space characters
5) find the length of a string of non-space characters
6) reverse a string
7) encode a string by rotating the characters by a given factor
8) decode a string which was encoded by the above procedure
   (If we assumed that we only used the letters a–z then if we rotated by a factor of 5 then every a would be replaced by f, b by g, c by h, and so on. At the end of the alphabet z would be replaced by e; in other words we wrap round the end of the sequence. The same principle can be extended to the set of ASCII characters).
9) check if a string is a palindrome

The above procedures/functions should be checked by writing a program which will read in a sentence from a text-file, find the first palindrome, and encode the sentence by rotating it by the length of the first palindrome. Sentences which contain no palindromes should be rotated by a factor of 10. A second program should decode sentences encoded by the first. Sentences will consist of a sequence of words (maximum length 25) separated by single spaces, and without punctuation. For ease of programming we will terminate sentences by end-of-file not by a full-stop, and the end-of-file marker may be assumed to occur after an end-of-line.

PROGRAM FRAGMENTS

The two string reading READING procedures

```
{-----------------------------------------------------------}
procedure readtospace(var source : text; var result : string);
{procedure to read up to first space}
var     ch : char;
        i,j : 1..lengthplus1;
begin
        i := 1;    {initialise count of characters}
        read(source,ch);
        while (ch <> ' ') and (i <= maxlength) do
        begin
                result[i] := ch;
                i := i + 1;
                read(source,ch)
        end;
        {ignore rest of word if over maxlength}
        if i > maxlength then        {find next space}
                while ch <> ' ' do read(source,ch);
                for j := i to maxlength do        {pack out rest with spaces}
                        result[j] := ' '
end; {readtospace}
{-----------------------------------------------------------}
procedure readtoeoln(var source : text; var result : string);
{procedure to read up to end-of-line}
var     ch : char;
        i,j : 1..lengthplus1;
begin   i := 1; {initialise count of characters}
        read(source,ch);
        while (not eoln(source)) and (i <= maxlength) do
        begin
                result[i] := ch;
                i := i + 1;
                read(source,ch)
        end;
        if eoln(source) then
        begin
                result[i] := ch;
                i := i + 1
        end;
        {ignore rest of word if over maxlength}
```

```
          readln(source);            {move on to next line}
          for j := i to maxlength do result[j] := ' '    {pack out rest with
          spaces}
end; {readtoeoln}
{-------------------------------------------------------------}
```

THE ENCODING PROGRAM

```
program encrypt(straight,coded);
{program to encrypt sentences (containing no punctuation) by rotating
 letters by the length of the first palindrome. The uncoded sentence will be
 on a file called straight, and the coded sentence will be output to a file called
 coded
}
const     maxlength = 25;
          lengthplus1 = 26;
          defaultrot = 10;
          linelength = 80;
type      index = 1..maxlength;
          string = packed array[stringindex]of char;
var       rotator              : stringindex;
          found                : boolean;
          word, codedword : string;
          linecount            : integer;
          straight, coded  : text;
{-------------------------------------------------------------}
procedure combinedread(var source : text; var result : string);
{procedure to read up to first space or end-of-line}
var       ch : char;
          i,j : 1..lengthplus1;
          begin i := 1;             {initialise count of characters}
          read(source,ch);
          while (not eoln(source)) and (ch <> ' ') and (i <= maxlength) do
          begin  result[i] := ch;
                 i := i + 1;
                 read(source,ch)
          end;
          if eoln(source) then
          begin  result[i] := ch;
                 i := i + 1
          end;
          {find next space or eoln and so ignore rest of word if over
          maxlength}
          while (not eoln(source)) and (ch <> ' ') do
                 read(source,ch);
          if eoln(source) then
                 readln(source);
```

```
            for j := i to maxlength do
                    result[j] := ' '
end; {combinedread}
{-----------------------------------------------------------}
function length(var given : string):stringindex;
{function returns length of string—var parameter to economise on storage}
var         i : 0..maxlength;
begin       i := 0;
            repeat i := i + 1;
            until (given[i] = ' ') or (i = maxlength);
            if i = maxlength then
                    length := i
            else    length := i − 1
end; {length}
{-----------------------------------------------------------}
procedure writestring(var dest : text; var given : string);
{procedure to write a string—var parameter used to economise on storage}
var         i : stringindex;
begin       for i := 1 to length(given) do
                    write(dest,given[i])
end; {writestring}
{-----------------------------------------------------------}
procedure reverse(var fwd, backward : string);
{procedure to reverse the string given in fwd and place it in backward}
var         len, i : stringindex;
begin       len := length(fwd);
            for i := 1 to len do
                    backward[i] := fwd[len + 1 − i];
            {fill rest of backward with spaces}
            for i := len + 1 to maxlength do
                    backward[i] := ' '
end; {reverse}
{-----------------------------------------------------------}
procedure encode(var plain, coded : string; rotfactor : integer);
{procedure to encode string plain into string coded by rotation by rotfactor}
var         i : stringindex;
begin       for i := 1 to maxlength do coded[i] := ' ';
            for i := 1 to length(plain) do
                    coded[i] := chr(ord(plain[i])+rotfactor)
end; {encode}
{-----------------------------------------------------------}
function palindrome(var given : string):boolean;
{returns value true or false depending upon whether given string is palin-
drome or not}
var         temp : string;
begin       reverse(given,temp);
            palindrome :=(given = temp)
```

```
end; {palindrome}
{--------------------------------------------------------------}
begin    {main program}
         reset(straight);
         repeat   combinedread(straight,word);
                  found := palindrome(word)
         until found or eof(straight);
         if not found then
         rotator := defaultrot else
         rotator := length(word);
         reset(straight);
         rewrite(coded);
         linecount := 0;
         repeat   combinedread(straight,word);
                  linecount := linecount + length(word);
                  if linecount > linelength then
                  begin writeln(coded);
                        linecount := length(word)
                  end;
                  encode(word,codedword,rotator);
                  writestring(coded,codedword);
                  write(coded,' ')
         until eof(straight);
         writeln(coded)
end.
```

THE DECODING PROGRAM

Rather than give a complete program again we will simply show the procedure ***decode*** which is substituted for the procedure ***encode*** in the above program. The main program has, of course, also got to be altered so that the file ***coded*** is read from and the file ***straight*** is written to.

```
{--------------------------------------------------------------------}
procedure decode(var coded, plain : string; rotfactor : integer);
{procedure to decode string coded in to string plain by reverse rotation by
rotfactor}
var      i : stringindex;
begin    for i := 1 to length(coded) do
                plain[i] := chr(ord(coded[i])-rotfactor)
end; {decode}
```

RESULTS

Here is the original uncoded file <straight>

the quick brown fox jumped over the lazy dog
no palindromes yet madam

Using a utility to take an octal dump of the file where we interpret each byte as a character we get the following output where a byte containing 040 is a space, and one containing 012 a newline character.

```
0000000 164 150 145 040 161 165 151 143 153 040 142 162 157 167 156 040
         t   h   e       q   u   i   c   k       b   r   o   w   n
0000020 146 157 170 040 152 165 155 160 145 144 040 157 166 145 162 040
         f   o   x       j   u   m   p   e   d       o   v   e   r
0000040 164 150 145 040 154 141 172 171 040 144 157 147 012 156 157 040
         t   h   e       l   a   z   y       d   o   g  \n   n   o
0000060 160 141 154 151 156 144 162 157 155 145 163 040 171 145 164 040
         p   a   l   i   n   d   r   o   m   e   s       y   e   t
0000100 155 141 144 141 155 012
         m   a   d   a   m  \n
0000106
```

Now after running the encode program the file ***coded*** looks like this

ymj vznhp gwt|s kt} ozruji t{jw ymj qf~ itl st ufqnsiwtrjx ~jy rfifr

We have lost the new line in the original, but we expected that. It also looks to be one character short. Using our octal dump facility again explains this. The character 'z' which is represented by octal 172 has been encrypted as 177. This is a non-printable character.

```
0000000 171 155 152 040 166 172 156 150 160 040 147 167 164 174 163 040
         y   m   j       v   z   n   h   p       g   w   t   |   s
0000020 153 164 175 040 157 172 162 165 152 151 040 164 173 152 167 040
         k   t   }       o   z   r   u   j   i       t   {   j   w
0000040 171 155 152 040 161 146 177 176 040 151 164 154 040 163 164 040
         y   m   j       q   f 177   ~       i   t   l       s   t
0000060 165 146 161 156 163 151 167 164 162 152 170 040 176 152 171 040
         u   f   q   n   s   i   w   t   r   j   x       ~   j   y
0000100 162 146 151 146 162 040 012
         r   f   i   f   r      \n
0000107
```

Now we run the decoding program and we get a new version of the file ***straight***.

the quick brown fox jumped over the lazy dog no palindromes yet madam

The new line has of course not reappeared, but otherwise we have successfully decoded the message. An octal dump follows for completeness.

```
0000000 164 150 145 040 161 165 151 143 153 040 142 162 157 167 156 040
          t   h   e       q   u   i   c   k       b   r   o   w   n
0000020 146 157 170 040 152 165 155 160 145 144 040 157 166 145 162 040
          f   o   x       j   u   m   p   e   d       o   v   e   r
0000040 164 150 145 040 154 141 172 171 040 144 157 147 040 156 157 040
          t   h   e       l   a   z   y       d   o   g       n   o
0000060 160 141 154 151 156 144 162 157 155 145 163 040 171 145 164 040
          p   a   l   i   n   d   r   o   m   e   s       y   e   t
0000100 155 141 144 141 155 040 012
          m   a   d   a   m      \n
0000107
```

DISCUSSION

1. Some implementations of Pascal include facilities for reading and writing packed arrays of char directly. This is not a feature of standard Pascal, and it is therefore useful in writing portable programs to be able to quickly produce i/o routines for strings. The problem asked for three versions of the input routine, only one of which (***combinedread***) is actually used in the final program.

2. The procedure ***readtospace*** contains three loops. The first reads characters and places them in the array ***result*** until either the maximum number of characters has been read or a space is found. Only one of the next two loops will be executed. The first skips to the next space if the word being read was too long. The second pads out the array ***result*** with spaces. This makes life easier when we try to use the array, and it is always good practice to be sure of what values are stored in any data structure.

Always make sure that all parts of a data structure are fully defined

3. The basic structure of the procedure ***readtoeoln*** is very similar. The first loop merely has a different termination condition (end-of-line rather than space). Since end-of-line becomes true after reading a character, but before the character is inserted into the array ***result*** an additional test is required here. The process of skipping to the next word is trivial; we just need to do a ***readln***. Once again the array ***result*** is packed with spaces.

Once you have developed a working program structure, use it again where appropriate

4. The procedure ***combinedread*** is a fairly straightforward combination of these two procedures. The existence of the three versions illustrates the need to be clear what exactly is to be read when asking for a string to be read in.

Always make sure that you have a precise problem specification

5. The function ***length*** is used in the procedures ***writestring***, ***reverse***, ***encode***, and ***decode***. It might be argued that this is inefficient in that it causes the string to be scanned twice. The code for ***length*** (or its equivalent) could be included in the other procedures. Nevertheless the length of a string is a useful parameter to be able to determine.

Inefficiency can frequently be justified

6. Note that we have used var parameters rather than value parameters for passing arrays around. This saves space for one important reason. When we use a var parameter, all that is actually passed is the ADDRESS of the variable. In the case of an array this address is merely the location in memory at which the array starts. It is a single pointer value, taking up perhaps 4 bytes. If, on the other hand, we use a value parameter, then a copy of the entire array is passed to the procedure. If the array is large, this could involve both a lot of time for the copying and a lot of space to store the copy of the array, which might well take up thousands of bytes. In this example,we have chosen to save space, even though it introduces two problems. Firstly, we may inadvertently change something which we do not really wish to change. Secondly, we are unable to use the procedure to handle string CONSTANTS. We can pass only named variables to it.

Efficiency and safety may well be in conflict

7. The procedures ***encode*** and ***decode*** make use of the standard functions ***ord*** and ***chr*** which convert characters into and from their ASCII codes. Only one procedure is really needed as decoding could be done by passing a negative rotation factor. We have shown the code for both just for clarity.

Sometimes verboseness aids readability

8. The function to test for a palindrome makes use of the fact that in Pascal it is possible to compare packed arrays of char of identical size. This function is thus almost trivial.

Use language facilities when they are appropriate

9. Finally a few words on the main program. This is reasonably straightforward. The only complication was the need to prevent the output being just one long line. This is done by counting how many characters have been output, and doing a ***writeln*** when necessary. Another possibility would have been to note when the input had an end-of-line (possibly by setting a

flag in the string reading procedure ***combinedread***), and outputting new lines to match those in the input.

A program is never finished .. there's always more

PROBLEM STATEMENT 20 CHECKING FOR INVALID DATES

TOPICS COVERED
- More on string handling
- Breaking a problem down
- Using subranges
- Using enumerated types
- Sets to accumulate errors
- String constant arrays for error messages

Dates can be written in many different ways. The purpose of this exercise is to show how a number of different date formats can be read by one program, and converted into a standard format. We will also aim to produce as robust a program as possible.

Write a program that will read dates written in any of the following formats:

Month day year e.g.

January 23 1985
January 22 85
Jan 19 85
Feb 3 1984

day Month year e.g.

19 Nov 1985
23 December 1985
29 Feb 84
1 October 1982

(i.e. the month may be written out in full or abbreviated to the standard three letter forms — you may assume that the initial letter is always a capital letter. The year may be given as either a four digit or two digit number).

The program should check that the dates are valid. Appropriate error messages are:-

Invalid month (e.g. when a month name has been misspelled)
Invalid day (e.g. when a day is not allowed in a particular month)
Invalid year (e.g. when a year out of this century is given)

These error messages may be printed out in the order most appropriate for the given input. ALL appropriate error messages should be printed.

For valid dates the program should print out the date in the standard format:

dd/mm/yy

where

dd is a 1 or 2 digit number for the day,
mm is a 1 or 2 digit number for the month,
yy is a 2 digit number in the range 00 to 99 representing years this century.

The data will consist of a number of dates on standard input with one per line, possibly with leading or trailing blanks, and terminated by end-of-file. The program should not crash even if nonsense data are presented to it. The output should be in two columns: the left hand column containing the date in the input format, the right hand column the date in the standard format or a list of error messages.

PROGRAM

```
program dateconvertor(input,output);
type    dy         = 1..31;
        mon        = (jan,feb,mar,apr,may,jun,jul,aug,sep,octo,nov,dec);
        yr         = 0..99;
        errtypes   = (dayincorrect,dayinvalid,monthincorrect,
                      yearincorrect,earlyend);
        errorset   = set of errtypes;
var     currch : char;
        day    : dy;
        month : mon;
        year   : yr;
        errors : errorset;
        digits : set of char;
        chcount: integer;
{-----------------------------------------------------}
procedure skipspaces(var currch : char; var chcount : integer);
{skip all spaces until first non-space character found}
begin   while (currch = ' ') and (not eoln) do
        begin read(currch);
              chcount := chcount + 1;
              write(currch)
        end
end; {skipspaces}
```

```
{-------------------------------------------------------}
procedure readday(var currch : char; var day : dy; var errors : errorset;
                  var chcount : integer);
{read in day of month}
var     localday : integer;
begin   localday := ord(currch)-ord('0');
        read(currch);
        chcount := chcount + 1;
        write(currch);
        while (currch <> ' ') and (not eoln) do
        begin localday := localday * 10 + ord(currch) — ord('0');
              read(currch);
              chcount := chcount + 1;
              write(currch)
        end;
        if eoln then
              errors := errors + [earlyend];
        if (localday >= 1) and (localday <= 31) then
              day := localday
        else  begin day := 1;
                    errors := errors + [dayincorrect]
              end
end; {readday}
{-------------------------------------------------------}
procedure readmonth(var currch: char; var month : mon;
                    var errors : errorset; var chcount : integer);
{read in the month}
const   maxlength = 9;
type    indexrange = 1..maxlength;
        string = packed array[indexrange]of char;
var     monstring : string;
{-------------------------------------------------------}
procedure readstring(var currch : char; var monstring : string;
                     var chcount : integer);
{read a string terminated by space}
var     length : indexrange;
begin   for length := 1 to maxlength do
              monstring[length] := ' ';
        length := 1;
        monstring[length] := currch;
        read(currch);
        chcount := chcount + 1;
        write(currch);
```

```
            while (currch <> ' ') and (length < maxlength) and (not eoln) do
            begin  length := length + 1;
                   monstring[length] := currch;
                   read(currch);
                   chcount := chcount + 1;
                   write(currch)
            end;
            if (length = maxlength) and (currch <> ' ') then
                   monstring[length] := currch;
            while currch <> ' ' do
            begin  read(currch);
                   chcount := chcount + 1;
                   write(currch)
            end
      end; {readstring}
      {------------------------------------------------------------}
      begin  readstring(currch, monstring, chcount);
            if eoln then
                   errors := errors + [earlyend];
            if (monstring='Jan      ') or (monstring = 'January  ') then
                   month := jan
            else if (monstring = 'Feb ') or (monstring = 'February ') then
                   month := feb
            else if (monstring = 'Mar') or (monstring = 'March    ') then
                   month := mar
            else if (monstring = 'Apr') or (monstring = 'April    ') then
                   month := apr
            else if (monstring = 'May') or (monstring = 'November') then
                   month := may
            else if (monstring = 'Jun ') or (monstring = 'June     ') then
                   month := jun
            else if (monstring = 'Jul  ') or (monstring = 'July     ') then
                   month := jul
            else if (monstring = 'Aug') or (monstring = 'August  ') then
                   month := aug
            else if (monstring = 'Sep ') or (monstring = 'September') then
                   month := sep
            else if (monstring = 'Oct ') or (monstring = 'October  ') then
                   month := octo
            else if (monstring = 'Nov') or (monstring = 'November') then
                   month := nov
            else if (monstring = 'Dec') or (monstring = 'December') then
                   month := dec
            else   begin  month := jan;
                          errors := errors + [monthincorrect]
                   end
      end; {readmonth}
```

```
{-----------------------------------------------------------}
procedure readyear(var currch : char; var year : yr; var errors : errorset;
                          var chcount : integer);
{read the year}
var       localyr : integer;
begin     localyr := ord(currch)-ord('0');
          read(currch);
          chcount := chcount + 1;
          write(currch);
          while (currch <> ' ') and (not eoln) do
          begin  localyr := 10 * localyr + ord(currch) - ord('0');
                 read(currch);
                 chcount := chcount + 1;
                 write(currch)
          end;
          if currch <> ' ' then
                 localyr := 10 * localyr + ord(currch) - ord('0');
          if (localyr >= 0) and (localyr <= 99) then
                 year:= localyr
          else   if (localyr >= 1900) and (localyr <= 1999) then
                        year := localyr - 1900
                 else   begin year := 0;
                              errors := errors + [yearincorrect]
                        end
end; {readyear}
{-----------------------------------------------------------}
procedure printout(day : dy; month : mon; year : yr; var errors : errorset;
                        chcount : integer);
{print out date or error messages}
type      string = packed array[1..16]of char;
var       errormess : array[errtypes]of string;
          err : errtypes;
{-----------------------------------------------------------}
procedure checkdate(day : dy; month : mon; year : yr; var errors : errorset);
{check if date valid}
var       maxdays : 28..31;
begin     case month of
                 jan, mar, may, jul, aug, octo, dec :      maxdays := 31;
                 apr, jun, sep, nov :                      maxdays := 30;
                 feb :  if (4 * (year div 4) = year) and (year <> 0) then
                              maxdays := 29
                        else maxdays := 28
          end;
          if day >  maxdays then
                 errors := errors + [dayinvalid]
end; {checkdate}
{-----------------------------------------------------------}
```

```
begin    errormess[dayincorrect]   := 'day incorrect ';
         errormess[dayinvalid]     := 'day invalid ';
         errormess[monthincorrect] := 'month incorrect ';
         errormess[yearincorrect]  := 'year incorrect ';
         errormess[earlyend]       := 'date incomplete ';
         write(' ':35-chcount);
         if errors = [] then checkdate(day,month,year,errors);
         if errors = [] then
         begin write(day:2,'/');
               case month of
                     jan  : write('1/');
                     feb  : write('2/');
                     mar  : write('3/');
                     apr  : write('4/');
                     may  : write('5/');
                     jun  : write('6/');
                     jul  : write('7/');
                     aug  : write('8/');
                     sep  : write('9/');
                     octo : write('10/');
                     nov  : write('11/');
                     dec  : write('12/')
               end;
               if year < 10 then writeln('0',year:1)
               else writeln(year:2)
         end
         else   begin   for err :=dayincorrect to earlyend do
                                  if err in errors then
                                  write(errormess[err]);
                                  writeln
         end
end; {printout}
{-------------------------------------------------------------}
begin    {main program}
         repeat  chcount := 1;
                 errors := [];
                 digits := ['0'..'9'];
                 read(currch);
                 write(currch);
{initially skip any leading spaces, currch will then contain first non-space
character}
                 skipspaces(currch, chcount);
                 {check to see if day comes first}
                 if currch in digits then
                 begin readday(currch,day,errors,chcount);
                       skipspaces(currch,chcount);
                       readmonth(currch,month,errors,chcount)
                 end
```

```
                  else {assume month comes next}
                       begin readmonth (currch,month,errors,
                                        chcount);
                             skipspaces(currch,chcount);
                             readday(currch,day,errors,chcount)
                       end;
                  skipspaces(currch,chcount);
                  readyear(currch,year,errors,chcount);
                  printout(day,month,year,errors,chcount);
                  readln;
                  if not eof then
                  if eoln then
                  begin readln;
                        writeln
                  end
        until eof
end.
```

RESULTS

```
January 23 1985          23/1/85
January 22 85            22/1/85
Jan 19 85                19/1/85
Feb 3 1984               3/2/84
19 Nov 1985              19/11/85
23 DfRfg 1985            month incorrect
19 Feb 75                19/2/75
29 Feb 85                day invalid
1 October 1982           1/10/82
23 January 1985          23/1/85
3 Feb 76                 3/2/76
29 Feb 83                day invalid
Sept 31 89               month incorrect
32 Sptrfe 67             day incorrect month incorrect
October 19 1956          19/10/56
28 February 44           28/2/44
2 Mar 54                 2/3/54 28
Apf 1986                 month incorrect
1 Jan 567                year incorrect
xxxxxxxxxxxxxxxxxxxxx    day incorrect month incorrect date incomplete
Jan 1 1980               1/1/80 30
Fegh 1976                month incorrect
31 Decembor 2098         month incorrect year incorrect
31 Dec 2098              year incorrect
6 Jun 23                 6/6/23
```

DISCUSSION

1. We can immediately divide the problem of reading a date into three subproblems, reading the day, the month and the year. It is also useful to have a procedure which skips over spaces between, and before, dates (hence the procedure ***skipspaces***).

Always try to split a large problem into smaller, more manageable pieces

2. The parameter ***chcount*** is used to count how many characters have been output. We need this to enable us to produce the output in two columns when we have no idea how long the item in the first column is going to be.

The absence of carriage control in Pascal can be overcome

3. Note that every time we read a character we also output it. This is the easiest way of outputting the date in its input form.

Always output the data read in. Not only does this enable you to check that the program is actually reading the data, but also you do not end up with a program which produces a useless answer (like 42!)

4. The procedure ***readday*** reads the input character by character and performs its own conversion to a number. This is necessary to make the program robust. If we used Pascal's facilities for reading integers, a non-numeric input character would cause the program to crash.

The only safe thing to read is a character. Assuming that it will always be anything else makes a program less robust

5. In order to record what errors we have found we are going to use a set which will contain all the errors detected. At the end we will then simply look through the set, error by error, and print out those messages which are required.

Techniques, such as set-checking, can be re-used

6. The procedure ***readmonth*** makes use of a procedure defined within it — ***readstring*** — to read the name of the month. The longest name of a month is September, with nine letters. Unfortunately in comparing strings there is little alternative to the rather cumbersome compound IF used in this procedure.

Turning for the moment to the main program we see that the first non-space character is tested to see if it is a digit or not. If it is then we assume the date is of the form "day month year". Otherwise the form "month day year" is assumed.

Detail is often tedious; it is still necessary

7. After reading the date, the procedure ***printout*** is invoked to print the date in standard format or the list of error messages. It is in this procedure that we make use of the variable ***chcount***. Before printing out the date we must check if it is valid. This needs to be done only if the input process has detected no errors so far (an empty error set). Checking the date consists of checking whether the month has 28, 29, 30 or 31 days, and whether the day given is valid. A simple case statement is used to do this. Note the use of the operator DIV which produces an integer result to check if the year is divisible by 4. Also note that the year 1900 was not a leap year (the year 2000 will be since it is divisible by 400). We use a case statement again to write out the value of the enumerated type representing the month. The value ***octo*** is used for October because ***oct***, in our compiler, is a reserved word used with octal numbers. This is an unfortunate choice by the writers of the Berkeley Pascal compiler.

**Programming starts with a broad problem definition.
It often finishes with a great deal of detail**

PROBLEM STATEMENT 21	**TAX BILLS**
TOPICS COVERED	Revision and combination of existing material Defensive programming Making it easy to change Hiding local operations Tidy output Conditionals v. loops for data-checking

Write a program that calculates and prints a person's yearly income tax bill given their gross annual income and their total allowances in pounds.

The program should print a message saying which tax year the calculations are for and it should check that the input data are valid. The gross income must be greater than or equal to zero and the allowances claimed must be greater than or equal to the lower personal allowance for that tax year. Print a warning when an invalid input is found. For an invalid gross income print the message ''Gross income must not be negative. Please check and re-enter your income.'' If the user does not claim at least the lower personal allowance, print the message ''A lower personal allowance of XXXX pounds is available. You may also be eligible for other allowances. Please check and re-enter your allowances.'' XXXX should be replaced by the figure for that tax year.

To work out the income tax due, subtract the allowances from the gross income to get the taxable income. If this is less than or equal to zero, no income tax is payable. Otherwise the first part suffers tax at the basic rate.

Any surplus is taxed at the higher rates. In the 1985/6 tax year, the following rates applied.

Lower personal allowance = 2205 pounds
Basic rate = 30% on the first 16200 pounds of taxable income
Higher rates = 40% ,, ,, next 3000 ,, ,, ,, ,,
45% ,, ,, ,, 5200 ,, ,, ,, ,,
50% ,, ,, ,, 7900 ,, ,, ,, ,,
55% ,, ,, ,, 7900 ,, ,, ,, ,,
60% ,, ,, remainder

Your program should use these rates, but it should be written so that they can be changed easily. If there is tax to pay, the program should print the message "Income tax payable in pounds : ", followed by the amount. Otherwise it should print the message "No income tax to pay."

PROGRAM

```
program taxexample2 (input, output);
{Calculate and print the annual amount of income tax payable according to
problem statement 21. }
const   lowerallowance = 2205; { the lower personal allowance for this tax
                                 year }
        taxyear = 1985;
type    taxrange = (basic,band1,band2,band3,band4,band5);
var     yearlyincome, taxallowances : integer;
        yearstax : real;
        valid    : boolean;
{------------------------------------------------------------------------}
function taxdue(grossincome, allowances : integer) : real;
{Calculate the yearly tax payable on gross income after deducting allow-
 ances, but without rounding or truncating any fractions of pence.}
const   lowestrate = basic;        {these two constants would need to be
                                     changed }
        highestrate = band5;        {if the number of tax bands were
                                   altered }
        penultimaterate = band4;  { = pred(highestrate) }
var     taxableincome, taxpayable : real;
        thisrate  : taxrange;
        done      : boolean;
        taxrate   : array [lowestrate..highestrate] of integer;
        sumatrate array [lowestrate..penultimaterate] of real;
begin   { TAXDUE }
        {Initialise the percentage rate for each tax band and the range of
        each band, except the last, in pounds. }
```

```
        taxrate[basic] := 30;
        taxrate[band1] := 40;
        taxrate[band2] := 45;
        taxrate[band3] := 50;
        taxrate[band4] := 55;
        taxrate[band5] := 60;
        sumatrate[basic] := 16200.00;
        sumatrate[band1] := 3000.00;
        sumatrate[band2] := 5200.00;
        sumatrate[band3] := 7900.00;
        sumatrate[band4] := 7900.00;
        taxpayable := 0.0;
        thisrate := lowestrate;
        taxableincome := grossincome - allowances;
        done := taxableincome <= 0.0;
        {Work out the tax payable on taxable income falling in each tax
        band except the highest. }
        while not done and (thisrate <> highestrate) do
        begin   if taxableincome <= sumatrate[thisrate] then
                begin   { There will be tax to pay in higher
                        band(s). So deduct tax for the full
                        range covered by this band.
                        }
                        taxpayable := taxpayable +
                                (taxableincome / 100.0) *
                                taxrate thisrate];
                        taxableincome := taxableincome - suma-
                        trate[thisrate];
                        done := true

                end
                else    begin{ This is the highest rate at which income is
                        taxed. So deduct tax on the portion of
                        income that falls into this band.
                      }
                        taxpayable := taxpayable +
                             (sumatrate[thisrate] / 100.0) *
                             taxrate[thisrate];

                        taxableincome := taxableincome -
                                        sumatrate[thisrate];
                        thisrate := succ(thisrate)
                end
        end;
        if taxableincome > 0.0 then
                { tax any surplus at the highest rate }
        taxpayable := taxpayable + (taxableincome / 100.0) *
                                taxrate[highestrate];

        taxdue := taxpayable
    end; { TAXDUE }
```

```
{----------------------------------------------------------------------------------}
begin { MAIN }
      { input & validate the gross income & allowances for this tax year }
      writeln;
      writeln('Calculations for the ',taxyear:4,'/',(taxyear+1):4,' tax year.');
        writeln;
        valid := false;
        repeat  write('Enter gross income in pounds : ':31);
                readln(yearlyincome);
                if yearlyincome > = 0 then
                        valid := true
                else    begin
                          writeln;
                          writeln('Gross income must not be negative.');
                          writeln('Please check and re-enter your income.');
                          writeln
                        end
        until valid;
        valid := false;
        repeat  write('Enter allowances in pounds : ':31);
                readln(taxallowances);
                if taxallowances > = lowerallowance then
                        valid := true
                else begin
                        writeln;
                        writeln('A lower personal allowance of ',
                                        lowerallowance:4,' pounds is available');
                writeln('to single people. You may also be eligible for other');
                writeln('allowances. Please check and re-enter your allowances.');
                        writeln
                     end
        until valid;
        { calculate the income tax payable }
        yearstax := taxdue(yearlyincome, taxallowances);
        { output the results }
        writeln;
        if yearstax > 0.0 then
        writeln('Income tax payable in pounds : ', yearstax:1:2)
        else    writeln('No income tax is payable.')
end.
```

RESULTS

Sample run one

Calculations for the 1985/1986 tax year.
Enter gross income in pounds : -100
Gross income must not be negative. Please check and re-enter your income.
Enter gross income in pounds : -1850
Gross income must not be negative. Please check and re-enter your income.
Enter gross income in pounds : 1850
Enter allowances in pounds : 2205
No income tax is payable.

Sample run two

Calculations for the 1985/1986 tax year.
Enter gross income in pounds : 30000
Enter allowances in pounds: 3455
Income tax payable in pounds : 9472.50

Sample run three

Calculations for the 1985/1986 tax year.
Enter gross income in pounds : 7520
Enter allowances in pounds : 2205
Income tax payable in pounds : 1594.50

DISCUSSION

1. In the first tax example, we saw how to calculate the weekly amount of income tax that an employee should pay. As written, the program has severe shortcomings. It will print a tax bill, even if it is given the wrong information. Worse still, if the employee number is wrong the bill will go to the wrong employee. This illustrates the old computing adage ''garbage in, garbage out''. You can't force people to supply correct information. However you can write programs that check all their inputs for mistakes. If it is possible to recover from erroneous input, the program should do so. Otherwise, it is better to print nothing than to print garbage.

Remember -- G I G O

2. The United Kingdom's system of personal taxation is among the most complicated in the world. It requires that personal allowances and other deductions for each tax year must be subtracted from any taxable income. When there are more allowances and deductions than taxable income, there is no liability to income tax. But if there is a surplus, income tax must be paid. Our program is designed to work out the amount of income tax that is due on that surplus. The rules for calculating allowances, deductions and taxable income are changed each year, after the Chancellor of the Exche-

quer has delivered the main spring budget. In this exercise, we shall use the allowances and rates of taxation that applied during the 1985/6 tax year. They are outlined in the problem statement and examples are given below. We shall further simplify the problem by assuming that the total allowances and deductions have already been calculated and that the gross annual income is known. This still leaves a task which isn't trivial, as witnessed by the difficulty that many people experience when they have to do it for their annual tax return

Real-life problems vary in their degree of complexity yet you must understand the problem if you are going to solve it

3. The program starts by printing a message giving the tax year. Each tax year runs from April 6th in one calendar year to April 5th in the next calendar year, so tax years cut across calendar years. The program stores the tax year as a global constant called ***taxyear***. In this example it is 1985. To print the tax year, we use the following writeln statement.

```
writeln('Calculations for the ',taxyear:4,'/',(taxyear+1):4,' tax year.');
```

This prints the year as 1985/1986. The expression ***(taxyear+1):4*** is a convenient way of printing the second part of the date without storing 1986 as a second constant, whose presence might cause confusion.

Tidy labelling helps the user

4. Next the program asks for the gross annual income and the total value of any allowances. Both must be given in whole pounds. If the gross income is negative, a warning message is printed and the user must re-enter the amount. Notice that the program keeps asking for a new amount until it is given a positive value. Finally it prints the amount of income tax payable, or the message "No income tax is payable" if none was due. The field-width specification :1:2 prints the amount of tax. This gives two places for the pence and at least one place before the decimal point for the pounds. If one place was not enough, more would be allocated automatically. Programmers sometimes work out how many spaces are needed to print the largest possible amount and put that value in place of the '1' above. This practice has been inherited from other programming languages where you have to give the maximum, rather than the minimum, number of places. The resulting output is not as tidy because extra spaces appear when small values are printed.

If a trick works once, use it again — as long as it does not destroy the program structure or cause mystification

5. The amount of income tax payable could have been printed using either

```
if yearstax = 0.0 then
          writeln('No income tax is payable.')
else      writeln('Income tax payable in pounds : ',yearstax:1:2)
```

or

```
if yearstax <> 0.0 then
          writeln('Income tax payable in pounds : ',yearstax:1:2)
else      writeln('No income tax is payable.')
```

Both appear to work. They will not print garbage because ***taxdue*** always returns a non-negative value. What would happen if the ***taxdue*** function were modified by an inexperienced programmer who made a mistake? Then ***taxdue*** might sometimes return a negative value and the program would print negative tax bills. To guard against this, we write

```
if yearstax > 0.0 then
          writeln('Income tax payable in pounds : ',yearstax:1:2)
else      writeln('No income tax is payable.')
```

This works even if ***yearstax*** is negative. It is an example of defensive programming. The ***taxdue*** function should never return a negative value. But even if it does not, the program will still print a sensible message. The only thing that it does not check for is tax bills that are unduly large. You might like to add a suitable test for this condition.

Defensive programming nearly always pays off in the long run

6. One problem, which is not obvious, arises because the gross income is stored as an integer. Computers with small words (like eight bit micro computers) cannot store large integers. The gross annual income of even a moderately well paid employee would cause the program to crash with an integer overflow if it were running on a small computer. There is a standard identifier (implementation-dependent) called ***maxint*** the value of which you can print using the following short program.

```
program printmaxint (output);
begin
          writeln('maxint = ',maxint)
end.
```

If the value that your computer prints is too small and a bigger computer isn't available, try declaring the variables ***yearlyincome*** and ***taxallowances*** as real numbers. You will also need to alter the ***taxdue*** function so that it expects two real arguments instead of two integer ones.

Occasionally implementation makes a difference — but not often

7. Sometimes novices use an IF–THEN statement to read and validate data. To understand why this is wrong, consider the following fragment of code. It would go where the first REPEAT–UNTIL loop appears in the main program.

```
writeln('Enter allowances in pounds : ':31);
readln(yearlyincome);
if yearlyincome < 0      then
begin
        writeln('Gross income must not be negative.');
        writeln('Please check and re-enter your income.');
        readln(yearlyincome)
end;
```

This asks for another amount if the first one is invalid. But it will fail if the second amount is also invalid. REPEAT–UNTIL is a better choice than either a FOR loop or a WHILE–DO loop in this piece of code. A FOR loop is inappropriate because we do not know in advance how many times an invalid amount will be entered. A WHILE loop could be used. But because the conditions in the WHILE–DO statement will be tested before any of the statements in the loop body are executed, an extra ***readln(yearlyincome)*** statement would be needed before the loop started. When you know that something must be done once, but may have to be done nought or more extra times, the REPEAT–UNTIL loop is best. When the task might not have to be done at all, the WHILE–DO is preferable. (An example is reading text from a file, because no attempt should be made to read anything if the file is empty or you have reached the end. A REPEAT–UNTIL loop would not work because it would always try to read something, even if the file was empty.)

Conditionals are not loops — do not confuse them

8. The total allowances are read and validated in a similar way to the gross income. But this time the test is whether the allowances claimed exceed the lower personal allowance. This was 2205 pounds in 1985/6. Bachelors, spinsters, widows, widowers and parties to a marriage who have separated may claim the lower personal allowance. There are other allowances that an individual may also be eligible for, but it is beyond the scope of this exercise to delve further into the tax system. We check that at least the minimum allowance is being claimed. The program could be extended to check that

the allowances being claimed are not excessive. Tax avoidance (trying to minimise your tax bill by lawful means) is legitimate; tax evasion (not paying all monies due to the Inland Revenue) is not.

9. The function ***taxdue*** calculates the amount of income tax that must be paid to the Inland Revenue. Although it is only used once, we still declare it as a function because it makes the main program easier to read. Clarity is more important than brevity. ***taxdue*** is declared with two formal parameters, ***grossincome*** and ***allowances***. They are both value parameters. The income tax due is returned as a real number. When ***taxdue*** is called by the statement

```
yearstax := taxdue(yearlyincome, taxallowances);
```

in the main program, it is given two actual parameters: ***yearlyincome*** and ***taxallowances***. Since we are using value parameters, the value of ***yearlyincome*** is copied into ***grossincome***, which acts as a local variable inside the function. Similarly, the value of ***taxallowances*** is copied into ***allowances***. The function deliberately uses copies of the values stored in ***yearlyincome*** and ***taxallowances***. It does not change the value of either variable in the main program. This makes it easier to verify that the program is correct. Variable parameters should be used only when the copying operation would be expensive, for example when a large array had to be passed to a frequently called function. Any assignment to a variable parameter or a global variable is called a side effect. You should avoid writing functions that use side effects because they can be hard to debug. When you see such assignments in other people's programs treat them with suspicion; they could signal that the function does something that was not intended.

Beware the var — use it only when you know that you need it

10. Before looking at how the ***taxdue*** function works, we shall explain how to calculate the amount of income tax owed in three imaginary cases. All individuals whose income exceeds the lower personal allowance may be liable to income tax. The lower personal allowance is set at a level that means only the low paid are exempt from income tax. Undergraduate students at University usually fall into this category. According to the 1985/6 regulations, their maintenance grant is exempt from taxation. If their only other income was, say, ten pounds interest from a National Savings Bank account and earnings of 540 pounds from vacation employment in a factory, the tax calculation would be

Gross Income	=	550 pounds
Allowances	=	2205 pounds
Taxable Income	=	Gross Income − Allowances
	=	550 − 2205
	=	−1655

The taxable income is less than zero, so no income tax is payable. Contrast this with an office worker earning 8500 pounds and claiming the lower personal allowance. Their taxable income is 6295 pounds (8500− 2205). Recall from the problem specification that basic rate tax at 30% is payable on the first 16200 pounds of taxable income. The tax bill is

Tax Payable = (Taxable Income / 100) * Basic Tax Rate
= 62.95 * 30
= 1888.50 pounds

Finally, consider a company director with a taxable income of 44000 pounds. The income tax bill is

Tax Payable = Tax at the basic rate:
On the first 16200 pounds at 30% = 4860 pounds
plus tax at the higher rates:
On the next 3000 pounds at 40% = 1200
" " " 5200 " " 45% = 2340
" " " 7900 " " 50% = 3950
" " " 7900 " " 55% = 4345
On the balance of 3800 pounds at 60% = 2280

18975 pounds

The ***taxdue*** function calculates the amount of tax due in the same way that we have done in our examples. ***taxpayable*** is initialised to zero and ***thisrate*** is set to the lowest rate, which is basic rate. Taxable income is worked out by subtracting the allowances from the gross income. If it is less than or equal to zero, the income was less than the allowances and no income tax is payable. Then ***done*** becomes true and the function returns 0.0 as the tax payable. The statement

```
done := taxableincome <= 0.0
```

is preferable to

```
if taxableincome <= 0.0 then
        done := true
else    done := false;
```

It should be used instead of an IF test whenever the only action of the the test is to alter the value of a boolean variable.

While taxable income is greater than zero, the function considers each tax band in turn. If there is no more tax to be deducted at a higher rate, tax is deducted at the current rate and ***done*** is set to true. Otherwise tax is deducted for the full amount of taxable income falling in the current band and ***thisrate*** is set to the next highest band. Enumerated types are used to name each tax band, ranging from ***basic*** for basic rate to ***band5*** for the top rate. In both cases, the amount on which tax has been deducted is subtracted from ***taxableincome***. After the WHILE loop has finished ***taxableincome*** will be less than or equal to zero unless there is surplus income to be taxed at the top rate. The last IF test handles this condition and the function returns the income tax payable.

To make the program as flexible as possible, the tax rate and the width of each tax band are stored in arrays called ***taxrate*** and ***sumatrate***. The values are easily modified if the Chancellor alters them in a budget. For example, the basic rate of tax was cut from 30% to 29% for the 1986/7 tax year. This change is reflected by one alteration in the program. Changes in the number of tax bands are easy to support because the array bounds are all declared as constants within the function. One thing that the program design can be criticised for is the wasteful initialisation of both arrays every time the ***taxdue*** function is called. It is only necessary on the first call. If the function was going to be used often, it would be worth writing a separate procedure to initialise the array and calling that procedure once at the start of the main program. This program is more robust than its predecessor. It can be modified to cope with changes in tax legislation from one year to the next. (As long as the present personal taxation system is not replaced by a completely different system.) However a different copy of the program is needed for each tax year. You should try to think of ways to modify the program so that it could cope with several different tax years.

Design for flexibility

11. Note how the program hides away lots of details. The function ***taxdue*** is self-contained. Information is passed into it using two parameters and one real number is returned by the function as its result. There are three constants and six variables declared WITHIN the function. They are invisible outside it. One might discuss whether the constants need to be local, since they cannot be changed anyway (after all, they are constants!), but the variables really should be local to the function.

It should be possible for someone else to take this function away and re-write it in the light of tax changes in the next Budget and to be confident that whatever they do, they will not corrupt anything else in the program. This is the purpose of using local variables when they are needed only locally and to restrict communication with outer blocks to parameters and function results.

If you can hide it, do so

PROBLEM STATEMENT 22 AREAS OF SHAPES

TOPICS COVERED Modularity
Using procedures and functions
A clear structure makes coding simpler

Write a program to calculate and print the areas of circles, rectangles and triangles. It should display a menu of all the different shapes that can be chosen and invite the user to choose one. Only choices that are in the menu should be accepted. Any others must be rejected and the user asked to choose differently. The program should ask for and validate all the information that it needs to work out the area of a shape. The length and width are required for rectangles; the base length and perpendicular height are required for triangles and the radius is required for circles. Ensure that all measurements are greater than or equal to zero. Print the area to as many decimal places as the user would like, up to a maximum of eight. When one calculation has been completed, ask if the user would like another one. Stop if their answer is no, but carry on if it is anything else.

PROGRAM

```
program shapes (input, output);
{ Calculate the areas of shapes according to problem statement 22. }
const   maxdecimals = 8;    { the greatest no. of decimal places that will }
                            { be printed for a result }
        pi   = 3.1415926;
type    validshape = (circle,rectangle,triangle);
var     finished, validchoice : boolean;
        area           : real;
        answer         : char;

{------------------------------------------------------------------------}
procedure getvalue (var value : real);
{ Prompt the user to enter a value. Only non-negative ones are accepted. }
var     valid : boolean;
begin   { GETVALUE }
        valid := false;
        repeat  writeln;
                write('enter value : ');
                readln(value);
                if value >= 0 then valid := true
                else begin
                        writeln;
                        writeln('Value must not be negative.');
                        writeln('Please check and re-enter.')
                     end
        until valid
end; { GETVALUE }
```

```
{--------------------------------------------------------------------}
procedure printname ( shape : validshape );
{ Print a shape's name if it is a valid shape }
var     thisshape : validshape;
begin   { PRINTNAMES }
        for thisshape := circle to triangle do
        if shape = thisshape then
        case shape of
                circle    : write('circle ');
                rectangle: write('rectangle ');
                triangle  : write('triangle ')
        end
end; { PRINTNAMES }
{--------------------------------------------------------------------}
procedure printheader( shapename : validshape );
begin   { PRINTHEADER }
        write('You have asked for the area of a ');
        printname( shapename );
        writeln('to be calculated.')
end;
{ PRINTHEADER }
{--------------------------------------------------------------------}
function circlearea : real;
{ Return the area of a circle }
var     radius : real;
begin   { CIRCLEAREA }
        printheader( circle );
        writeln('What is the radius ?');
        getvalue( radius );
        circlearea := pi * sqr( radius )
end; { CIRCLEAREA }
{--------------------------------------------------------------------}
function rectanglearea : real;
{ Return the area of a rectangle }
var     length, width : real;
begin   { RECTANGLEAREA }
        printheader( rectangle );
        writeln('What is the length ?');
        getvalue( length );
        writeln('What is the width ?');
        getvalue( width );
        rectanglearea := length * width
end; { RECTANGLEAREA }
{--------------------------------------------------------------------}
```

```
function trianglearea : real;
{ Return the area of a triangle }
var       base, height : real;
begin     { TRIANGLEAREA }
          writeln('What is the base length ?');
          getvalue( base );
          writeln('What is the perpendicular height ?');
          getvalue( height );
          trianglearea := (base * 0.5) * height
end; { TRIANGLEAREA }
{------------------------------------------------------------------}
procedure entermenu ( var area : real; var validchoice : boolean );
{ Menu driven procedure for selecting a shape and calculating its area. Only
choices that are in the menu will be accepted. }
var       menu  : set of char;
          choice : char;
begin     { ENTERMENU }
          validchoice := false;
          menu := ['c','C','r','R','t','T','n','N'];
          { print the menu }
          writeln('Which shape would you like to find the area of ?');
          writeln('You may choose from :');
          writeln;
          writeln('Circles       — type c');
          writeln('Rectangles  — type r');
          writeln('Triangles    — type t');
          writeln('None of these — type n');
          writeln;
          repeat { solicit a choice }
                    write('enter choice : ');
                    readln(choice);
                    writeln;
                    if choice in menu then
                    begin     validchoice := true;
                              case choice of
                                        'c','C' : area := circlearea;
                                        'r','R' : area := rectanglearea;
                                        't','T' : area := trianglearea;
                                        'n','N' : begin
                    write('The program can''t')
                    write ('work out areas for')
                    writeln (other shapes.');
                                                  writeln;
                                                  validchoice := false
                                                  end
                                                  end
                    end else writeln('Choice not in menu; Please re-enter')
          until choice in menu
end; { ENTERMENU }
{------------------------------------------------------------------}
```

```
procedure printarea ( area : real; validchoice : boolean );
{ Print an area if the program was able to calculate it (validchoice was true).
The user is asked what precision to use.
Replies outside the range 1..maxdecimals are ignored and defaults of 1 or
maxdecimals places used instead. }
var     decimals : integer;
begin   { PRINTAREA }
        if validchoice { it was possible to calculate the area } then
        begin
        write('How many decimal places ')
        writeln('would you like printed for the areas ?');
        write('Between 1 and ',maxdecimals:1,);
        writeln(' can be printed.');
                writeln;
                write('enter value : ');
                readln( decimals );
                if decimals > maxdecimals then
                decimals := maxdecimals
                else if decimals <= 0 then decimals := 1;
                writeln('area = ',area:1:decimals,' square units');
                writeln
        end
end; { PRINTAREA }
{-----------------------------------------------------------------------}
begin   { MAIN }
        area := 0.0;
        finished := false;
        validchoice := false;
        { calculate and print the areas of shapes chosen by the user }
        repeat
                entermenu( area, validchoice );
                printarea( area, validchoice );
                write('Do you want another calculation (y/n) ? ');
                readln(answer);
                writeln;
                if (answer = 'n') or (answer = 'N') then finished := true
        until finished
end.
```

RESULTS

Which shape would you like to find the area of? You may choose from:

```
Circles          — type c
Rectangles       — type r
Triangles        — type t
None of these    — type n
enter choice : q

Choice not in menu; Please re-enter enter choice : c

You have asked for the area of a circle to be calculated.
What is the radius?
enter value : -9.8
Value must not be negative. Please check and re-enter.
enter value : 1
How many decimal places would you like printed for the area?
Between 1 and 8 can be printed.
enter value : 2
area = 3.14 square units
Do you want another calculation (y/n)? y

Which shape would you like to find the area of?
You may choose from:
Circles          — type c
Rectangles       — type r
Triangles        — type t
None of these    — type n
enter choice : r
You have asked for the area of a rectangle to be calculated.
What is the length?
enter value : 2
What is the width?
enter value : 2
How many decimal places would you like printed for the area?
Between 1 and 8 can be printed.
enter value : 0
area = 4.0 square units
Do you want another calculation (y/n)? Y
Which shape would you like to find the area of? You may choose from:
Circles          — type c
Rectangles       — type r
Triangles        — type t
None of these    — type n
enter choice : t
You have asked for the area of a triangle to be calculated.
```

What is the base length?
enter value : 2
What is the perpendicular height?
enter value : 1
How many decimal places would you like printed for the area?
Between 1 and 8 can be printed.
enter value : 9
area = 1.00000000 square units
Do you want another calculation (y/n)? no

DISCUSSION

1. The task of working out the areas of different shapes is not a difficult one. It is something that almost everybody learns at school. Remembering the way to do it for a particular shape can be harder. If you were asked, would you remember that the area of a triangle is half the base times the perpendicular height or that the area of a circle is pi times the radius squared? Perhaps you would, but the principle applies to more complicated shapes like a rhombus or an ellipse. This exercise embodies those simple geometric rules in a Pascal program. The problem has been kept straightforward so that you can concentrate on how functions and procedures are used to build a complete program. Some of them, like the procedure to control a menu, are used elsewhere in this book. This underscores two important points. The first is that whenever possible, you should build up complicated routines from simple ones. This makes the program easier to read and understand. It also makes it easier to maintain and modify. The second point is that you try to reuse code, even if it was originally written for another purpose. This enables you to achieve greater productivity, building on what has already been done, instead of endlessly re-inventing the same things with minor variations.

Don't re-invent the wheel

2. To understand how the program works, start by looking at the main program. Notice how short the code is compared to the rest of the program. Its brevity means that you can take in the structure without having to delve into any functions or procedures. This is the hallmark of a clearly written program. You can see that all it has to do is call two procedures, ***entermenu*** and ***printarea***. Then it asks the user if another calculation is wanted. If the answer is no, which is abbreviated to 'n' or 'N', the program stops. Otherwise another choice is made and processed. Once you understand what the main program does, try sketching the hierarchy of procedures and functions. This gives you a deeper appreciation of the program's structure. Working top–down, you should get a sketch like this one.

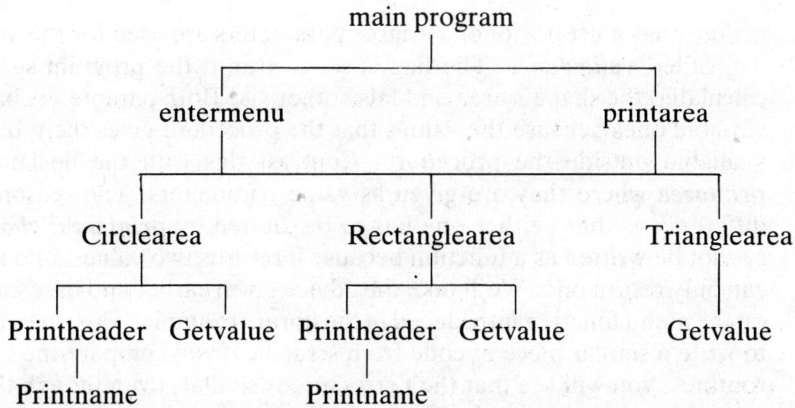

Each procedure or function call is shown. Procedure names begin with a small letter, functions start with a capital letter. For a complicated program, you might have to use several small diagrams instead of one big one. As a rule of thumb, use separate diagrams if a single one would not fit on a page. We shall now look at each procedure and function in more detail.

If the structure is clear, the coding is simpler

3. The main program calls two procedures. ***printarea*** prints an answer to the required number of decimal places. It takes two arguments, the area and a flag called ***validchoice***. Both are set by ***entermenu***. If the flag is true, the program was able to work out an answer, which is then printed by this procedure. False means that no answer was returned, perhaps because the user asked for a shape that was not in the menu. Then no value should be printed. Areas are printed using an integer variable to hold the second part of the field-width specification for area. Users can choose to print areas to any accuracy between one and eight decimal places. Their job is to give the measurements to enough decimal places to justify this accuracy. That is one thing which the program does not check. Requests to print more than the maximum, or less than the minimum, number of decimal place are overruled. If more than the maximum number of places are requested, only the maximum number are printed. If less than one place is asked for we print one by default. Some Pascal implementations will let you give a field-width specification of nought and will not print any decimal places. Others do not allow this, so it is best to play safe and ask for one if you want a portable program. (In Jensen & Wirth's *Pascal User Manual and Report*, second edition, the only stipulation is that the fraction length field-width specification must be a natural number. Implementors differ over whether to treat nought as a natural number!)

Limit your tricks to those which are portable

4. ***chooseshape*** is an important routine. You can tell this from the position that it occupies in the hierarchy. It is responsible for displaying a menu, ensuring that the user's choice is on the menu and starting any further

actions that must be done. Variable parameters are used for the area and a flag called ***validchoice***. The flag is set to true if the program successfully calculated the shape's area and false otherwise Both parameters have to be variable ones because the values that the procedure gives them have to be available outside the procedure. Contrast this with the declaration for ***printarea*** where they are given as value parameters. The reason for this difference is that neither one has to be altered by ***printarea***. ***chooseshape*** cannot be written as a function because it returns two values, and functions can only return one. We'll take the advice given earlier and base ***entermenu*** on the menu function introduced in the library example. This saves us having to write a similar piece of code from scratch. If you compare the two menu routines, you will see that their structure is similar, even though they print menus for different applications. So it is not hard to take a copy of one routine and modify it to get the other. Part of the programmer's art is knowing when it is best to re-use a piece of code and when it is best to start afresh.

Menu-driven programs guide users through the facilities that are provided. They give a complete list of the options available at each stage. This program has one menu. Complicated programs often have several, nested to different depths below the top-level menu. Despite their extra complexity, the principle is still the same; show the user what is available at each stage so that the program is as easy to use as possible. Menus are a good interface for beginners and inexperienced users. Experienced users generally prefer typing commands to working down through a menu. Since they already know what is available, it is quicker to type something like −area circle 3− (meaning find the area of a circle of radius three units) than to go through a sequence of menu-driven prompts.

Think of the user

5. The second half of ***entermenu*** calls one of three different functions to calculate the area of a shape chosen from the menu. Each function works out the area of a different shape using a different method. But the details of how they work are not allowed to intrude into the procedure which controls the menu. This illustrates a second use of procedures and functions; they hide things that do not need to be visible until later. In the menu we only need to know that if a valid shape is chosen, a function will be called that calculates the area and returns the result as a real number. We are not interested in the mechanics of calculating the area of a circle, a square or a triangle. Breaking up a program in this way allows each routine to be kept short. Think how much harder it would be to understand what the program did if you were given a two hundred line listing that was not broken up into procedures and functions. Consider breaking up any routine that is longer than about a page. This limits the complexity of each one and makes your intentions clearer. Often there will be several different ways that a program could be split into routines. Another part of the programmer's art is working out how

to do it so that the structure of the program mirrors the way that the problem is divided into simpler sub-problems.

Hide things unless they really need to be visible

6. The three functions ***circlearea***, ***rectanglearea*** and ***trianglearea*** have several things in common. Each one returns the area as a real number and calls the procedures ***printheader*** and ***getvalue***. None of them have any arguments because no information is required from other parts of the program. The only differences arise because different rules and different sets of dimensions are needed to work out the area of each shape. The functions all print a similar header and read dimensions in a similar way. So it is sensible to write each of these sub-tasks as separate procedures. This illustrates a final advantage of procedures and functions. They allow you to do the same or similar tasks as many times as you like, but you have to write the code only once.

The ***getvalue*** procedure asks the user to enter a value and check that it is not negative. If an invalid number is entered, a warning message is printed and a new number must be typed. The code to do this is based on the statements used to validate entries in the second tax example. Once again, old code has been re-used with minor modifications. It could also have been written as a procedure, the decision being a matter of taste. Some implementations allow you to print enumerated types using the ***write*** and ***writeln*** standard procedures. But this facility is not always available, so a ***printname*** procedure is included. This is called by the ***printheader*** procedure which is used by all three functions. By sharing the same procedure it is easier to change the printed message, because the alterations only have to be done once, not three times. It also makes the program appear more uniform to the user. Similar messages are printed for each shape chosen from the menu. As we said earlier, the problem solved in this exercise was not difficult. But you will find that several of the routines can be applied to a wide range of problems. You should now understand more about the use of procedures and functions. Other lessons, like how to design programs well, can't be learnt just by reading books. The best way to master them is by writing programs of your own.

Uniformity breeds familiarity, which in turn breeds comfort

8

Arrays and arrays of records

PROBLEM STATEMENT 23	**MATRICES — TWO-DIMENSIONAL ARRAYS**
TOPICS COVERED	Two-dimensional arrays for elementary maths The use of nested FOR loops Initialisation Optimisation Subranges for safety Modular design for clarity Conformant arrays

Write a program that gets the user to enter two matrices. If they can be multiplied together, the program should calculate the product. Then it should print the two matrices and their product. If this is not possible, it should print the message ''The two matrices cannot be multiplied together''. Print the matrices so that all the elements in a row are on the same line and all the columns are lined up. Leave two blank spaces between each element in a row. The user must be asked to choose the dimensions of each matrix. Your program should reject any dimension smaller than one or larger than fifty. Each element is a real number.

Two matrices can be multiplied together if the number of columns in the first matrix equals the number of rows in the second matrix. Then the product will have as many rows as the first matrix and as many columns as the second matrix.

PROGRAM

```
program matrices (input, output);
{This program reads in two matrices. If they are compatible, they are
 multiplied together and the product is printed, according to problem
 statement 23.
}
const  matsize  = 50; { the maximum size of rows or columns in matrices }
type   matindex= 1..matsize;
       matrix   = array [matindex,matindex] of real;
```

```
var     first, second, result  : matrix;
        frows, fcols, srows,
        scols, rrows, rcols    : matindex;
        doneit                 : boolean;
{----------------------------------------------------------------------}
procedure getvalue (var value : matindex );
{Prompt the user to enter one dimension for a matrix. Only values in the
 range 1 to matsize inclusive are accepted.
}
var     valid : boolean;
        temp : integer;
begin   { GETVALUE }
        valid := false;
        repeat write('enter value : ');
               readln(temp);
               writeln;
               if temp < 1 then
               begin  writeln('Value must not be negative.');
                      writeln('Please check and re-enter.')
               end
               else   if temp > matsize then
                      begin  writeln('Value must not be greater than ',
                                      matsize:1,'.');
                             writeln('Please check and re-enter.')
                      end
                      else begin
                             value := temp;
                             valid := true
                      end
        until valid
end; { GETVALUE }
{----------------------------------------------------------------------}
procedure matread ( var a : matrix;
var lastrow, lastcol : matindex);
{Find out what size matrix is to be read. If it is smaller than matsize rows by
 matsize columns, read it in, one element at a time.
}
var     row, col : matindex;
begin   { MATREAD }
        writeln('How many rows does this matrix have? ');
        getvalue( lastrow );
        writeln('How many columns does this matrix have? ');
        getvalue( lastcol );
        writeln('You have asked for a ',lastrow:1,' by ',lastcol:1,' matrix.');
        writeln('Type the elements of your matrix, one at a time : ');
        writeln;
```

```
          for row := 1 to lastrow do
          begin  writeln('Row ', row:1);
                 for col := 1 to lastcol do
                 begin
                         write('col ', col:1, ' : ');
                         readln( a[row, col] )
                 end;
                 writeln
          end
end; { MATREAD }
{----------------------------------------------------------------------------}
procedure matprint ( a : matrix; lastrow, lastcol : matindex);
{ Print a matrix with the elements of each row appearing on a new line. }
var                     row, col        : matindex;
begin  { MATPRINT }
          for row := 1 to lastrow do
          begin for col := 1 to lastcol do
                         write( a[row, col]:8, ' ' );
                 writeln
          end
end; { MATPRINT }
{----------------------------------------------------------------------------}
procedure matmultiply ( a, b : matrix;
                                  amaxrow, amaxcol, bmaxrow,
                                  bmaxcol : matindex;
                                  var result      : matrix;
                                  var rmaxrow, rmaxcol : matindex;
                                  var doneit      : boolean );
{ Multiply two matrices, a and b, together if the number of columns in the
  first matrix equals the number of rows in the second matrix.
}
var     i, j, k : matindex;
        temp : real;
begin  { MATMULTIPLY }
        if amaxcol = bmaxrow then
                 begin  rmaxrow := amaxrow;
                        maxcol := bmaxcol;
                        for i := 1 to amaxrow do
                                  for j := 1 to bmaxcol do
                                  begin  temp := 0.0; { initialise this element of
                                                              the product to zero
                                                        }
                                         for k := 1 to amaxcol do
                                                  temp := temp + a[i,k] * b[k,j];
                                         result[i,j] := temp
                                  end;
                        doneit := true
                 end
        else doneit := false
end; { MATMULTIPLY }
```

```
{------------------------------------------------------------------------}
begin  { MAIN }
       { Read in two matrices containing real numbers. If they are compat-
         ible, multiply them together and print the product. Otherwise print
         an error message.
       }
       doneit := false;
       matread( first, frows, fcols );
       matread( second, srows, scols );
       matmultiply( first, second, frows, fcols, srows, scols,
                    result, rrows, rcols, doneit );
       if doneit then
       begin  matprint( first, frows, fcols );
              writeln;
              writeln(' MULTIPLIED BY');
              writeln;
              matprint( second, srows, scols );
              writeln;
              writeln(' EQUALS');
              writeln;
              matprint( result, rrows, rcols );
       end
       else writeln('The two matrices cannot be multiplied together.')
end.
```

RESULTS

Sample run one

```
How many rows does this matrix have?
enter value : 2
How many columns does this matrix have?
enter value : 2
You have asked for a 2 by 2 matrix.
Type the elements of your matrix, one at a time :
Row 1
col 1 : 1
col 2 : 2
Row 2
col 1 : 3
col 2 : 4
How many rows does this matrix have?
enter value : 2
How many columns does this matrix have?
enter value : 1
You have asked for a 2 by 1 matrix.
Type the elements of your matrix, one at a time :
Row 1
col 1 : 5
Row 2
col 1 : 6
```

```
1.0e+00  2.0e+00  3.0e+00  4.0e+00
MULTIPLIED BY
5.0e+00  6.0e+00
EQUALS
1.7e+01  3.9e+01
```

SAMPLE RUN TWO

```
How many rows does this matrix have?
enter value : -1
Value must not be negative.
Please check and re-enter.
enter value : 51
Value must not be greater than 50.
Please check and re-enter.
enter value : 1
How many columns does this matrix have?
enter value : 1
You have asked for a 1 by 1 matrix.
Type the elements of your matrix, one at a time :
Row 1
col 1 : 1
How many rows does this matrix have?
enter value : 2
How many columns does this matrix have?
enter value : 1
You have asked for a 2 by 1 matrix.
Type the elements of your matrix, one at a time :
Row 1
col 1 : 1
Row 2
col 1 : 2
The two matrices cannot be multiplied together.
```

DISCUSSION

1. The array is probably the most widely known data structure, because in many languages it is the only structured data type explicitly available. The simplest form of an array is a one-dimensional array (or vector). This is a finite, ordered, homogeneous structure. In other words, it consists of a fixed number of elements arranged in a set order, with all the elements being of the same type. In Pascal it is not possible to put a mixture of different types of element in the same array. So the vector

A[1] = 42; A[2] = 'Fred'; A[3].workphone = 4772;

would not be allowed because the elements are of different types: an integer, a string and a record. This restriction makes Pascal arrays less flexible than arrays in other languages like Smalltalk-80. But Pascal gains in speed what it loses in flexibility, because computers can manipulate homogeneous arrays more efficiently than non-homogeneous ones.

All the elements of an array must be of the same type

2. An array variable whose components are also arrays is called a matrix. To declare a variable, A, as a matrix with two rows and four columns of real numbers, we would write:

```
const  lastrow = 2;
       lastcol = 4;
       type matrixtype = array [1..lastrow, 1..lastcol] of real;
var    A : matrixtype;
```

Then the i-th row of the j-th column would be accessed by A[i,j], as long as i was in the range 1..2 and j was in the range 1..4. Matrices are useful when it is necessary to keep many items in memory at once and to access them all quickly and uniformly. By uniform access, we mean that elements selected at random can be accessed in about the same time. Contrast this with elements stored in a sequential file. There, access time depends on where the desired element is compared to the last element accessed.

Arrays lend themselves to uniform processing

3. Matrices are useful for programming and problem solving. One of their most common applications is solving systems of linear equations in mathematical, engineering and graphics problems. The equations model some aspect of the real world, for example the wing of an aircraft. Being able to solve them might make the difference between knowing that the aircraft will fly and hoping that it won't crash. Unfortunately, the topic of solving systems of equations is beyond the scope of this book. Instead we will tackle a more modest problem, that of multiplying two arrays together.

Familiarity with matrices is essential if you are to do numerical work

4. A matrix, in the mathematical sense, is a rectangular array of numbers. The numbers are each entries in the matrix. Its size is determined by the number of rows and the number of columns that occur in the matrix. For example, the matrix:

```
1 2 3
4 5 6
```

is a two row by three column matrix (written 2×3). Two matrices can only be multiplied together if the number of columns in the first one equals the number of rows in the second one. Then the product will have as many rows as the first matrix and as many columns as the second matrix. Suppose that A is a 3×4 matrix and B is a 4×7 matrix.

$$\underset{3\times 4}{A} \quad \underset{4\times 7}{B} = \underset{3\times 7}{AB}$$

Then the product AB is a 3×7 matrix. But it is not possible to form the product BA.

$$\underset{4\times 7}{B} \quad \underset{3\times 4}{A} = \underset{\text{not defined!}}{BA}$$

The number of columns in the first matrix does not equal the number of rows in the second matrix. So the two matrices cannot be multiplied together in this order. Matrices are not commutative over multiplication. For any two ordinary numbers, a and b, ab = ba. But AB <> BA when we are dealing with matrices. Look at how two matrices are multiplied together to form the product.

$$\begin{matrix}1 & 2\\ 3 & 4\end{matrix} \times \begin{matrix}5 & 6\\ 7 & 8\end{matrix} = \begin{matrix}(1*5+2*7) & (1*6+2*8)\\ (3*5+4*7) & (3*6+4*8)\end{matrix} = \begin{matrix}19 & 22\\ 43 & 50\end{matrix}$$

The entry in the first column of the first row of the product (written [1,1]) is worked out by multiplying together corresponding entries from the first row of the first matrix and the first column of the second matrix and adding up the resulting products. This gives 1 * 5 + 2 * 7, which is nineteen. Element [1,2] is found by multiplying together corresponding entries from the first row of the first matrix and the second column of the second matrix. To get the element in the j-th column of the i-th row of the product, multiply together the corresponding entries from the i-th row of the first matrix and the j-th column of the second matrix. If the matrices are named A, B and C respectively then the multiplication can be done using three nested FOR loops.

$$\underset{n\times m}{A} \quad \underset{m\times p}{B} = \underset{n\times p}{AB}$$

```
for i := 1 to n do
        for j := 1 to p do
                for k:= 1 to m do
                        C[i,j] = C[i,j] + A[i,k] * B[k,j]
```

Nested FOR loops do a great deal of work very simply

5. Try working through these loops to multiply together the 2×2 matrices

given earlier. Only two more things need to be added to make this a complete Pascal routine. The first is a test to ensure that we execute the loops only when the two matrices can be multiplied together. The test is whether the number of columns in A equals the number of rows in B. The second thing is not as obvious. We must remember to initialise all the elements of C to zero. This must be done because the first time that the statement at the centre of the loops is executed, it adds the product of two elements from A and B to whatever it finds in the appropriate element of C. Pascal does not guarantee that the element in C will automatically be initialised to anything before first being used. This is the programmer's responsibility. There are two ways to initialise C: all at once or one element at a time. To do it all at once, we must put a pair of nested FOR loops before the ones given above.

```
for row := 1 to n do
      for col := 1 to p do
            C[row,col] := 0.0;
```

The alternative is to initialise each element before it is first accessed. We can do this by altering the three nested loops given previously.

```
for i := 1 to n do
      for j := 1 to p do
      begin
            C[i,j] := 0.0;
            for k:= 1 to m do
                  C[i,j] = C[i,j] + A[i,k] * B[k,j]
      end;
```

When you use matrices, initialisation remains important

6. This method is used in the ***matmultiply*** procedure of the program with one enhancement. A temporary variable is added to speed up the inner loop.

```
for i := 1 to n do
      for j := 1 to p do
      begin
            temp := 0.0;
            for k:= 1 to m do
                  temp := temp + A[i,k] * B[k,j];
            C[i,j] := temp
      end;
```

temp replaces C[i,j] inside the loop because the computer can access variables faster than it can access array elements. Each access may only save a few milliseconds, but many accesses will be required to multiply two large arrays together, so the savings will add up. Some Pascal compilers would do the optimisation automatically, but you ought to include it just to be sure. The price paid for this gain in efficiency is a reduction in the clarity of the program. It is worth optimising routines when they will be frequently used or when a fast response is essential. Otherwise the amount of work required to improve them can be more than offset by other costs like the programmer's time.

Optimisation is worth while — if the optimised code is frequently used

7. There are three more procedures in the program; ***getvalue***, ***matread*** and ***matprint***. ***getvalue*** is an extension of the ***getvalue*** procedure used elsewhere in this book. It reads and validates the dimensions of each array. In this program it checks for two types of invalid data instead of one. Dimensions smaller than one or larger than the maximum value are rejected. The dimension must be read into a local integer variable before testing. It cannot be read directly into ***value*** because ***value*** is declared as a variable of type ***matindex***, an integer subrange from ***1..matsize***. Any attempt to read a dimension outside these limits into that variable would make the program crash. Instead, a temporary integer variable is used and the dimension is copied into ***value*** only if it lies within the required limits. This is not the only way that the procedure could be written. Here is an alternative.

```
valid := false;
repeat
          write('enter value:');
          readln(temp);
          valid:=(temp>0 ) and (temp<=maxsize)
          if not valid then
          begin
                    writeln('Values must be in the range 1 to ',
                                   maxsize:1);
                    writeln('Please check and re-enter.')
          end
until valid;
```

The code is more succinct, but the error message that it prints is less informative. It says what the range of valid inputs is, not whether the input was too big or too small. Either alternative is correct, the choice is a matter of personal taste.

You can check data, even when it involves changing types

matread calls ***getvalue*** twice to read the dimensions of the array. Then it uses two nested loops to read the matrix elements. They are read one at a time working from left to right across the first row, then the second row and so on until the whole array has been entered. The prompt reminds the user which element to enter next. This is especially helpful when entering large arrays, because it is easy to lose track of where you are. ***matprint*** prints out a matrix in the same order that ***matread*** read it. The single digit field-width specification forces the value to be printed in decimal floating point form. This may be harder to read, but has the advantage of keeping the columns lined up. If the number of decimal places were also specified, the columns would not be straight if the matrix contained a mixture of large and small values.

8. Pascal was designed for teaching programming. Since its introduction in the early 1970s, it has become the dominant teaching language in computer science courses. However it contains defects that make it hard to write programs well. One defect, which is present in the international Pascal language standard (compliance level 0), is that the size of arrays cannot vary while a program is running. The size is declared as part of the array's type. This makes it hard to write efficient general purpose routines that will process arrays of different sizes at different times. The matrix multiplication program overcomes this difficulty by fixing the maximum size of each array and using parameters to record how much space was really used. This wastes space when the arrays are smaller than the maximum size. The problem is not confined to matrix multiplication; other tasks, including string manipulation and sorting, are affected. Some versions of Pascal correct this defect by offering non-standard extensions to the language. But they should be treated with caution because reliance on non-standard features makes it hard to move programs from one system to another. Compliance level 1 of the international Pascal language standard introduces conformant array parameters as a standard way of overcoming the defect. Their use is briefly described below, but none of our programs rely on them because they are not yet available on most Pascal systems.

Conformant arrays are coming — but they are not yet common

9. Conformant array parameters allow a function or procedure to operate efficiently on arrays of different sizes. Consider a function that calculates the mean of some real numbers stored in an array. The same function should be able to work with different sized arrays. This is straightforward to implement using a conformant array parameter.

```
{-----------------------------------------------------------------}
function mean (var a : array [low..high : integer] of real) : real;
var    index : integer;
       sum : real;
begin  {MEAN}
       sum := 0.0;
       for index := low to high do
                   sum := sum + a[index];
       mean:= sum / (high - low + 1)
end; {MEAN}
{-----------------------------------------------------------------}
```

The identifiers ***low*** and ***high*** represent the upper and lower bounds of array ***a***. The same function can be applied to arrays that are declared with different sizes. For example, given the declarations

```
var    distance              : array [1..100] of integer;
       height                : array [1..25] of real;
       avdistance, avheight  : real;
```

mean could be called by the statements

```
avdistance := mean( distance ); avheight := mean( height );
```

If ***distance*** was correctly initialised, the mean value of its one hundred elements would be calculated and stored in ***avdistance***. ***low*** would be set to one and ***high*** would be set to one hundred. Similarly in the second call ***low*** would be set to one, ***high*** would be set to twenty five and the mean value of the twenty five elements in ***height*** would be calculated and stored in ***avheight***. Conformant array parameters can also be used to select part of an array. This is useful in recursive algorithms that work by splitting a problem into smaller sub-problems and solving each one recursively. The only proviso is that conformant array parameters may not be declared as value parameters, even if the calling routine does not modify the array.

10. We have used the classical method to multiply matrices together. It does the job in a time proportional to the cube of the size of the arrays. There are more advanced methods that are faster for large matrices. They work by reducing the number of multiplications that have to be done. However, our method is faster for most normal size problems. Its main weakness is that it will give the wrong answers if very large and very small elements are multiplied together. It is possible to overcome this limitation by scaling. Another weakness is that the user cannot alter the value of an element if it has been wrongly typed. You could add another procedure that prints an array and allows the user to correct any elements that are wrong.

Code is rarely fixed. Bear future development in mind

PROBLEM STATEMENT 24 STOCK CONTROL AND STRUCTURED FILES

TOPICS COVERED
- Records
- The advantages of mixed types in one object
- Arrays of records
- Sorting records — whole records can be swapped
- Structured files — elements are records

Write a program to do the following stock control tasks.

Read stock records from a structured file called ***stockfile*** into an array of stock records called ***stock***. The stock array should be large enough to hold fifty items. Stop when the file is exhausted or when the first fifty records have been read. If there were no stock records because the file was empty, ask the user to enter an item's details. Continue reading item details until there is no more space in the array, or there are no more items. Each stock record should contain the following details. The field names we have used for each detail are also shown.

An item reference, ***reference***
A brief description of the item, ***description***
(Two strings, each up to twenty characters long.)

The item's unit cost, ***unitcost***
(The cost is represented as a real number.)

The current stock level, ***stocklevel***
Re-order level, ***reorderlevel***
Re-order quantity, ***reorderqty***
(Three integer numbers.)
The item's re-order status, ***reorderstatus***
(This is a single character: 'R' if an order has already been placed, a space otherwise.)

Read all these details except the re-order status. If the number of units in stock is less than or equal to the re-order level, ask if an order for more units has already been placed. Set ***reorderstatus*** to 'R' if it has been placed and set it to a blank space otherwise.

When the items have been read into the array, sort them into ascending order of reference. The sort should be done in place.

Print the sorted list of items, using the following format for each item.

```
ITEM REFERENCE   : itemsreferencestring
DESCRIPTION      : itemsdescriptionstring
UNIT COST        : n.pp pounds
STOCK LEVEL      : nn
re-order message
```

The item reference and description should be no more than twenty characters long. There should be at least two blank spaces between the end of the reference and the description field header. Unit cost should be printed with two places after the decimal point for the pence and as many digits as required for the pounds. Stock level should be printed using however many digits are required. The re-order message should be "This item will be reordered" – if the number in stock is at or below the re-order level and an order has not already been placed. If an order has already been placed, print the message "n more units are on order", where n is the re-order quantity.

After the stock listing, print re-order notes for items that have reached or fallen below their re-order level and have not yet been re-ordered. Set their re-order status to 'R' when the note has been printed. Each re-order note should be formatted as follows.

```
ITEM REFERENCE   : itemsreferencestring
DESCRIPTION      : itemdescriptionstring
Please supply nn units of this item at n.pp pounds per unit.
```

The first line of text is to be printed as described above. On the second line, replace nn with the re-order level and n.pp with the unit price.
Finally, write all the updated records back to the stock file.

PROGRAM

```
program stockcontrol (input, output, stockfile);
{
Write a stock control program according to problem statement 24.
}
const stringlength = 20; { maximum length of each string }
      maxitem = 50; { maximum no. of items in stock }
type  string      = packed array [1..stringlength] of char;
      stockitem = record
                    reference, description   : string;
                    unitcost                 : real;
                    stocklevel, reorderlevel,
                    reorderqty               : integer;
                    reorderstatus            : char
      end;
      stkfiletype = file of stockitem;
      stockarray = array [1..maxitem] of stockitem;
var   stockfile     : stkfiletype;
      stock         : stockarray;
```

```
        index, lastitem     : integer;


{------------------------------------------------------------------------}
procedure readstring( var datafile : text; var name : string );
{ Read a string of up to stringlength characters from datafile. }
var i : integer;
begin { READSTRING }
        { initialise the string to contain blanks }
        for i := 1 to stringlength do
                name[ i ] := ' ';
        i := 0;
        while (not eoln(datafile)) and (i < stringlength) do
        begin
                i := i + 1;
                read(datafile, name[ i ])
        end;
        readln(datafile)
end; { READSTRING }
{------------------------------------------------------------------------}
procedure readitem( var newitem : stockitem );
{
Prompt the user for details about an item of stock. If the number of units
held in stock is at or below the re-order level ask if an order for replacements
has already been placed.
}
var     response : char;
begin { READITEM }
        with newitem do
        begin
                write('enter item reference :     ');
                readstring(input, reference);
                write('enter description :     ');
                readstring(input, description);
                write('unit cost (in pounds) :     ');
                readln(unitcost);
                write('how many are in stock :     ');
                readln(stocklevel);
                writeln;
                write('what is the reorder level     ? ');
                readln(reorderlevel);
                write('what is the reorder quantity     ? ');
                readln(reorderqty);
                reorderstatus := ' ';
                if stocklevel <= reorderlevel then
                begin
                        write('are they on order (y/n)     ? ');
```

```
                    readln(response);
                    if (response = 'y') or (response = 'Y')
                        then reorderstatus := 'R'
                end
        end
end; { READITEM }
{-----------------------------------------------------------------------}
procedure writestring( name : string; newline : boolean );
var     i : integer;
begin { WRITESTRING }
        for i := 1 to stringlength do
                write( name[ i ] );
        if newline
                then writeln
end; { WRITESTRING }
{-----------------------------------------------------------------------}
procedure writeitem( item : stockitem );
{ Print all an items' details except the re-order level & re-order quantity. }
begin { WRITEITEM }
        with item do
        begin
                write('ITEM REFERENCE   : ');
                writestring( reference, false );
                write(' DESCRIPTION    : ');
                writestring( description, true );
                writeln('UNIT COST      : ',unitcost:1:2,' pounds');
                writeln('STOCK LEVEL : ',stocklevel:1);
                if stocklevel <= reorderlevel
                    then if reorderstatus = 'R'
                        then writeln(reorderlevel:1,' more units are on order')
                        else writeln('This item will be reordered')
        end;
        writeln
end; { WRITEITEM }
{-----------------------------------------------------------------------}
procedure getstock( var stockfile : stkfiletype;
                    var stocktable : stockarray;
                    var lastitem : integer
                    );
{ Read details about all items held in stock from stockfile and print the total
number of items (if>0). If the file was empty, ask the user if they would like
to add any details. After the details for each new item have been entered,
ask the user if there are any more items. Continue until the user says no, or
there is no more space to store them in the stocktable.
}
var     index : integer;
        finished : boolean;
        response : char;
```

```
begin { GETSTOCK }
        { read details from stockfile into stocktable. }
        index := 0;
        reset( stockfile );
        while (not eof(stockfile)) and (index < maxitem) do
        begin
                index := index + 1;
                stocktable[ index ] := stockfile^;
                get( stockfile )
        end;
        lastitem := index;
        if lastitem > 0 then writeln('There are details for ',lastitem:1,' items on file.')
                else begin
                        writeln('There are no stock items on file.');
                        finished := false;
                        while (not finished) and (lastitem < maxitem) do
                        begin
                                write('Do you want to add details for an item?');
                                readln(response);
                                if (response = 'y') or (response = 'Y') then
                                begin
                                        lastitem := lastitem + 1;
                                        readitem(stocktable[lastitem])
                                end
                                else finished := true;
                                writeln
                        end
                    end;
                    if lastitem = maxitem  then
        writeln('There is no more room for new items')
end; { GETSTOCK }
{-----------------------------------------------------------------------}
procedure putstock( stocktable : stockarray;
                        lastitem : integer;
                        var stockfile : stkfiletype
                        );
{ Sequentially copy each item stored in stocktable into a record in the
structured file stockfile.
}
var     index : integer;
begin { PUTSTOCK }
        index := 0;
        rewrite( stockfile );
        while index < lastitem do
```

```
        begin
                index := index + 1;
                stockfile^ := stocktable[ index ];
                put( stockfile )
        end
end; { PUTSTOCK }
{-------------------------------------------------------------------}
procedure sortstock( var stocktable : stockarray;
                        lastitem : integer
                        );
{ Sort the elements of stocktable into reference order using Shell sort.
}
var     i, j, increment : integer;
        temp            : stockitem;
begin { SORTSTOCK }
        increment := lastitem div 2;
        while increment > 0 do
        begin
                for i := increment + 1 to lastitem do
                begin
                        j := i - increment;
                     while j > 0 do
                        if stocktable[j].reference > stocktable[j+increment].reference
                        then
                        begin
                                temp := stocktable[j];
                                stocktable[j] := stocktable[j+increment];
                                stocktable[j+increment] := temp;
                                j := j - increment
                        end else j := 0 { break }
                end;
                increment := increment div 2
        end
end; { SORTSTOCK }
{-------------------------------------------------------------------}
procedure reorder( var item : stockitem );
{
Print a re-order note for any stock item that is below its re-order level and
has not already been ordered. Then update the reorderstatus.
}
begin { REORDER }
        with item do
        begin
                write('ITEM REFERENCE : ');
                writestring( reference, false );
                write(' DESCRIPTION    : ');
```

```
            writestring( description, true );
            write('Please supply ',reorderqty:1,' units of this item');
            writeln(' at ',unitcost:1:2,' pounds per unit.');
            writeln;
            {
            update the reorderstatus to avoid any duplicate orders
            }
            reorderstatus := 'R'
        end
end; { REORDER }
{-------------------------------------------------------------------}
begin { MAIN }
        {
        Get information about each item of stock and sort the items in order
        of item reference.
        }
        getstock(stockfile, stock, lastitem);
        sortstock(stock, lastitem);
        {
        Print a sorted listing of all items in stock, followed by re-order notes
        for any item that is at or below the re-order level and has not already
        been re-ordered.
        }
        if lastitem > 0 then
        begin
            writeln;
            writeln('STOCK FILE LISTING...');
            writeln;
            for index := 1 to lastitem do
                writeitem(stock[index]);
            writeln;
            writeln('RE-ORDER NOTES FOR LOW STOCK LEVEL ITEMS..
            writeln;
            for index := 1 to lastitem do
            if stock[index].stocklevel <= stock[index].reorderlevel then
                if stock[index].reorderstatus <> 'R' then
                        reorder(stock[index]);
            {
            Write a copy of the sorted and updated details back to
            stockfile.
            }
            putstock(stock, lastitem, stockfile)
        end
end.
```

RESULTS

SAMPLE RUN ONE

```
There are no stock items on file.
Do you want to add details for an item? no
```

SAMPLE RUN TWO

```
There are no stock items on file.
Do you want to add details for an item? yes
enter item reference          : VER SS/DD 48 40
enter description             : 5.25 inch floppy discs
unit cost (in pounds)         : 12.80
how many are in stock         : 340

what is the reorder level     ? 200
what is the reorder quantity  ? 400

Do you want to add details for an item? y
enter item reference          : VER DS/DD 96 80
enter description             : 5.25 inch floppy discs
unit cost (in pounds)         : 20.50
how many are in stock         : 173

what is the reorder level     ? 200
what is the reorder quantity  ? 200
are they on order (y/n)       ? y

Do you want to add details for an item? y
enter item reference          : ACR AP 80
enter description             : printer ribbon
unit cost (in pounds)         : 3.65
how many are in stock         : 30

what is the reorder level     ? 50
what is the reorder quantity  ? 25
are they on order (y/n)       ? n

Do you want to add details for an item? n

STOCK FILE LISTING...
ITEM REFERENCE: ACR AP 80        DESCRIPTION  : printer ribbon
UNIT COST     : 3.65 pounds
STOCK LEVEL   : 30
This item will be reordered

ITEM REFERENCE: VER DS/DD 96 80  DESCRIPTION  : 5.25 inch floppy
UNIT COST     : 20.50 pounds
STOCK LEVEL   : 173
200 more units are on order
```

ITEM REFERENCE: VER SS/DD 48 40 DESCRIPTION :5.25 inch floppy disk
UNIT COST : 12.80 pounds
STOCK LEVEL : 340

RE-ORDER NOTES FOR LOW STOCK LEVEL ITEMS...

ITEM REFERENCE: ACR AP 80 DESCRIPTION : printer ribbon
Please supply 25 units of this item at 3.65 pounds per unit.

SAMPLE RUN THREE

There are no stock items on file.
Do you want to add details for an item? y
enter item reference : 360-1 M-F
enter description : 9 pin M-F cable
unit cost (in pounds) : 28
how many are in stock : 43

what is the reorder level ? 20 what is the reorder quantity

{ Details for the other 48 items have been omitted }

Do you want to add details for an item? y
enter item reference : 006-2 M-M
enter description : 15 pin M-M cable
unit cost (in pounds) : 32
how many are in stock : 21

what is the reorder level ? 20
what is the reorder quantity? 20
There is no more room for new items

STOCK FILE LISTING...

ITEM REFERENCE: 006-2 M-M DESCRIPTION : 15 pin M-M cable
UNIT COST : 32.00 pounds
STOCK LEVEL : 21

{ Details for the other 48 items have been omitted }

ITEM REFERENCE: 360-1 M-F DESCRIPTION : 9 pin M-F cable
UNIT COST : 28.00 pounds
STOCK LEVEL : 43
RE-ORDER NOTES FOR LOW STOCK LEVEL ITEMS...

{ There were no items that needed to be re-ordered }

DISCUSSION

1. Stock is a valuable resource that has to be managed properly. Holding too much stock is wasteful because it ties up capital that could be used to better effect elsewhere. But failure to replace stock items soon enough results in lost sales. Stock control systems are used to improve an organisation's stock management. They help an organisation to monitor its stock levels more effectively than is usually possible by manual methods. When an item is running short, an order note can be printed automatically and a new supply delivered just before the existing one runs out. To do this, we need to know the re-order level and the re-order quantity for each item in stock. These are chosen to take into account how long the new stock will take to arrive. They should also allow for seasonal variations and any discounts that may be obtained by placing one large order instead of several small ones. The first computerised stock control systems processed batches of orders. This was done overnight or at weekends, depending on how quickly the enterprise turned over its stock. Later systems worked interactively, printing out orders as stock was sold. In this exercise, we shall develop part of a simple batch system.

Understanding the problem is the first step in solving it

2. The problem specification states our requirements, describing the input and output formats in detail. Although this application differs from the others in this book, routines from the earlier exercises can be re-used to make it easier to write the program. ***readstring*** and ***writestring*** have both been used before. The sorting routine is based on the Shell sorting algorithm which was introduced as an improvement to insertion sort in the sorting example. Apart from converting it into a procedure, we have also changed it to use global data structures. This is necessary because so many different data structures are involved that it would be confusing and inefficient to pass them all as variable parameters. The line

```
if stocktable[j].reference > stocktable[j+increment].reference
```

replaces

```
if table[j] > table[j+increment]
```

to ensure that the items are sorted according to their references. By changing the field name, it would be possible to sort on any other field. Changing the condition from greater than to less than would reverse the order of the items. One disadvantage with this algorithm is that items with the same reference are not guaranteed to be left in the order that they were originally entered.This problem could be overcome by sorting any items with the same reference on a second field or choosing a stable sorting algorithm.

There are many books that discuss the choice and implementation of sorting algorithms in detail. If you are contemplating an application that manipulates large numbers of stock items, you should read about some of the alternatives to Shell sort.

With algorithms, there is always a choice to be made

3. By using arrays of records, we have made the program less complicated than would have been possible if we had been forced to use different arrays to store the constituent fields of each record. This is how the items are declared using an array of structured records.

```
const
        stringlength= 20; { maximum length of each string }
        maxitem     = 50; { maximum no. of items in stock }
type
        string = packed array [1..stringlength] of char;
        stockitem = record
                reference, description              : string;
                unitcost                            : real;
                stocklevel, reorderlevel, reorderqty : integer;
                reorderstatus                       : char
        end;
        stkfiletype = file of stockitem;
        stockarray = array [1..maxitem] of stockitem;
var
        stockfile   : stkfiletype;
        stock       : stockarray;
```

The corresponding declaration if each field is stored in a separate array is more complicated.

```
const
        stringlength= 20; { maximum length of each string }
        maxitem     = 50; { maximum no. of items in stock }
type
        string = packed array [1..stringlength] of char; var
        stockfile1                              : text;
        reference, description                  : array [1..maxitem] of
                                                  string;
        unitcost                                : array [1..maxitem] of real;
        stocklevel, reorderlevel, reorderqty    : array [1..maxitem] of
                                                  integer;
        reorderstatus                           : array [1..maxitem] of char;
```

Structured files treat each item as a single entity. The alternative is to deal with one field at a time, storing each one in a separate data structure. Look at how much more work is required to swap items as they are being sorted. The three lines

```
temp := stocktable[j];
stocktable[j] := stocktable[j+increment];
stocktable[j+increment] := temp;
```

must be replaced by statements like the following ones to swap corresponding pairs of elements if the different fields are stored in different arrays.

```
strtemp := reference[first];
reference[first] := reference[second];
reference[second] := strtemp;
strtemp := description[first];
description[first] := description[second];
description[second] := strtemp;
realtemp := unitcost[first];
unitcost[first] := unitcost[second];
unitcost[second] := realtemp;
inttemp := stocklevel[first];
stocklevel[first] := stocklevel[second];
stocklevel[second] := inttemp;
inttemp := reorderlevel[first];
reorderlevel[first] := reorderlevel[second];
reorderlevel[second] := inttemp; inttemp := reorderqty[first];
reorderqty[first] := reorderqty[second];
reorderqty[second] := inttemp;
chartemp := reorderstatus[first];
reorderstatus[first] := reorderstatus[second];
reorderstatus[second] := chartemp;
```

Here the temporary variables are named to reflect the type of object that is being swapped. Other parts of the program also become more complicated. The moral is clear: for each problem choose the most suitable data structures provided in your programming language. If a good data structure is not available, or you choose not to use it, the task of programming becomes harder. You are forced to waste time and effort wrestling with the mechanics of information representation instead of solving the problem. By using structured records, all this work is done for you by the system! The only real drawback with this program is that the maximum number of items that can be processed is fixed. You can process no more items than will fit into the space you have reserved. Even if you use all the computer's memory, there will eventually come a time when it is insufficient. There are ways around this problem that dispense with arrays. They use files to store the data on backing storage devices, only bringing a small part of the data into main memory at each stage. Secondary memory can be expanded more easily and cheaply than main memory. Look at the personal details exercise in chapter nine (problem statement 26) to see how this can be done.

There are many data structures — choose a relevant one

4. To appreciate the structure of this program, sketch the procedure

hierarchy. The diagram we have given shows how the program is built up from its component procedures.

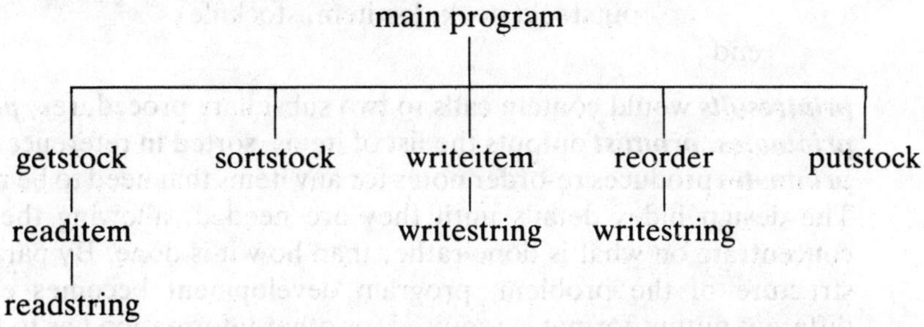

Learning how to draw these diagrams is not difficult. But it takes practice to reap their full benefit. At the design stage, they can be used to check that the program structure mirrors the way that the problem has been broken down into sub-problems. Each sub-problem ought to be solved by a separate sub-program. Later on, when the program needs to be extended, a structure diagram can be used to identify those parts of the program that need alteration.

Diagrams can clarify your visualisation of the problem

5. The same techniques can be applied when you have to modify someone else's program. If there is no documentation, or it is inadequate, start by working out the procedure hierarchy. This will help you to spot any structural weaknesses. Our program design has weaknesses that would make certain modifications harder than they ought to be.The problem can be divided into four sub-problems: input the data, process them, output the results and update the stock file. The first two sub-problems are adequately handled by ***getstock*** and ***sortstock*** respectively. ***putstock*** updates the stock file. All the output is printed by code that appears in the main program. Contrast this part of the main program with the corresponding part of the problem.

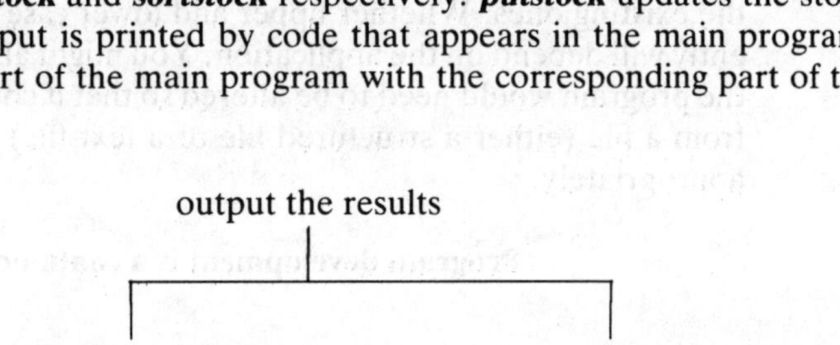

The main program would be clearer if separate procedures were called to print the sorted list and the re-order notes, rather than including the code in-line. A better way to structure the main program is outlined below.

```
if lastitem > 0 then
begin
    printresults(...) {suitable parameters must be added}
    putstock(stock, lastitem, stockfile)
end
```

printresults would contain calls to two subsidiary procedures, ***printlist*** and ***printnotes***. ***printlist*** outputs the list of items, sorted in reference order, and ***printnotes*** produces re-order notes for any items that need to be re-ordered. The design hides details until they are needed, allowing the reader to concentrate on what is done rather than how it is done. By paralleling the structure of the problem, program development becomes easier. If a different output format is required, or other information has to be printed, the changes that must be made are contained in a few clearly identified routines. Systematic modifications can be made faster than sporadic ones and the resulting program is more reliable.

Good programmers design programs whose structure mirrors that of the problem they are solving

6. This program tackles only one part of a batch stock control system: creating a stock file if one does not already exist and printing a sorted listing with re-order notes. It does the job adequately, but there are rough edges that would need smoothing out if the program were to be used seriously. Only the first fifty entries in the stock file are processed. Later entries are ignored and the program gives no warning of their existence. This means that valuable information could be lost. At the least, a production quality program should print a warning message. Ideally it should be able to process the extra entries. A full system would contain data validation procedures and would enable the user to modify the stock file selectively. As well as validating each entry individually, it would prevent any duplicate entries from being inserted. This is done by checking each new reference against all the existing ones. Whether upper and lower case letters are treated differently will depend on the application. You might also like to think about how the program would need to be altered so that it could read a batch of orders from a file (either a structured file or a text-file) and update the stock file appropriately.

Program development is a continuous process

PROBLEM STATEMENT 25 NORMALISATION AND SCALING

TOPICS COVERED: Matrix manipulation (multiplication, inversion, etc).
Handling multiple files
Procedure parameters

At the University of Fairplay students are allowed to select up to six courses from ten different units on offer. Each course is given by a different member of staff. In order to ensure that the final examination results for each student are comparable the collator of the marks applies a normalisation algorithm.

The average and standard deviation are calculated for each course offered. An overall average and standard deviation are calculated by totalling all the marks of all students on all courses. If a student obtained a mark of 62.5% on a course whose average mark was 50%, and the standard deviation was 12.5%, then he might be said to have a mark equal to the average plus one standard deviation. All the students' marks are expressed in this form. They are then normalised by using the average and standard deviation calculated over the total set of marks. For example if the overall average had been 48% and the standard deviation 11% then the above student would have a mark of 59% (48+11) on that course.

The collator requires a program to be written which will perform this normalisation process for him. In order to speed up the data input process when the results are known he creates two files to contain the names of the students and the numbers of the courses before the examinations. He has never had more than 25 students, and, as we said, there are 10 courses. When the marks are known he would like to input the following information:

a student number (in the range 1 to 25) and the number of courses taken (in the range 1 to 6) (on one line)
up to six pairs of numbers representing the course number, and mark obtained.
(on the following lines)

The desired output consists of a table showing:

For each student
the normalised mark in each course,
his average over all the courses he took (assuming each course is equally weighted),
the number of courses taken.

For each course
The average mark and standard deviation before normalisation.
The overall average and standard deviation.

All marks awarded are integers in the range 0–100. Results should be quoted to two decimal places. All course numbers consist of four characters. No student has a name longer than 30 characters.

PROGRAM

program normalise(input,output,names,numbers);
{program to normalise marks for up to 25 students who can choose up to 6 courses from a selection of 10. The names of students are stored in a file ***names***. The numbers of the course are stored in a file ***numbers***. The

```
marks are read from standard input, and the table of results printed on the
standard output}

const  maxstudents    = 25;  {maximum number of students}
       nocourses      = 10;  {number of courses}
       maxtaken       = 6;   {maximum number of courses taken}
       lengthname     = 30;  {maximum length of student name}
       lengthno       = 4;   {length of course number}
       nameandspace   = 35;  {space for names to left of table}
type   numbindex = 1..lengthno;
       studindex  = 1..maxstudents;
       crseindex  = 1..nocourses;
       crsnumber = packed array[numbindex] of char;
              {to hold number of a course}
var    marks        : array[studindex,crseindex] of -1..100;
       {the raw marks}
       studtakes    : array[studindex] of 1..maxtaken;
       {the number of courses taken by each student}
       crseave,            {the average for each course}
       crsedev      : array[crseindex] of real;
              {the standard deviation for each course}
       candidates   : array[crseindex] of studindex;
              {the number of candidates per course}
       overave,            {the overall average}
       overstddev   : real;        {the overall standard deviation}
       headings     : packed array[crseindex] of crsnumber;
       {array to hold course numbers}
   totalcand          : 0..maxstudents;
   names,       numbers       : text;
{-------------------------------------------------------}
procedure initialise;
{initialise the marks array — use -1 to indicate course not taken, the crseave
and crsedev arrays, the candidates array, and the overall average }

var    crse   : crseindex;
       stud   : studindex;

begin
       overave := 0;
       for crse := 1 to nocourses do
       begin
              candidates[crse] := 0;
              crseave[crse] := 0;
              crsedev[crse] := 0;
              for stud := 1 to maxstudents do
                     marks[stud,crse] := -1
       end
end; {initialise}
```

```
{-----------------------------------------------------------------}
procedure readmarks;
{read in marks from standard input}
var     crse,
        crseno : crseindex;
        stud : studindex;
        notaken : 1..maxtaken;
        mark : 0..100;
begin
        while not eof do
        begin
                {read number of current student, and how many courses he's
                taken}
                readln(stud, notaken);
                studtakes[stud] := notaken;
                {read in the marks}
                for crse := 1 to notaken do
                begin
                        readln(crseno, mark);
                        marks[stud,crseno] := mark;
                        {accumulate sum for each course and count candi-
                        dates. also accumulate overall total}
                        overave := overave + mark;
                        crseave[crseno] := crseave[crseno] + mark;
                        candidates[crseno] := candidates[crseno] + 1
                end
        end
end; {readmarks}
{-----------------------------------------------------------------}
procedure average;
{calculate averages for each course, and calculate overall average}
var     crse        : crseindex;

begin
        totalcand := 0;
        for crse := 1 to nocourses do
        begin
                crseave[crse] := crseave[crse] / candidates[crse];
                totalcand     := totalcand + candidates[crse]
        end;
        overave := overave / totalcand
end; {average}
{-----------------------------------------------------------------}
```

```
procedure deviations;
{calculate standard deviations}

var     crse    : crseindex;
        stud    : studindex;
        currstddev,
        currave,
        temp    : real;
begin
        for crse := 1 to nocourses do
        begin
                currstddev := 0;
                currave := crseave[crse];
                for stud := 1 to maxstudents do
                        if marks[stud,crse] >= 0 then
                        begin
                                temp := marks[stud,crse] - currave;
                                currstddev := currstddev + temp * temp;
                                temp := marks[stud,crse] - overave;
                                overstddev := overstddev + temp * temp
                        end;
                crsedev[crse] := sqrt( currstddev / candidates[crse] )
        end;
        overstddev := sqrt( overstddev / totalcand )
end; {deviations}
{-----------------------------------------------------------------}
procedure readnumbers;
{read in the course numbers}

var     crse    : crseindex;
        cnt     : numbindex;
begin
        reset(numbers);
        for crse := 1 to nocourses do
        begin
                for cnt := 1 to lengthno do
                    read(numbers, headings[crse][cnt]);
                readln(numbers)
        end
end; {readnumbers}
{-----------------------------------------------------------------}
procedure printheadings;

var     crse : crseindex;

begin
        write(' ':nameandspace);
```

```
        for crse := 1 to nocourses do
        write(headings[crse][1]:6);
        writeln(' Number Average');
        write(' ':nameandspace);
        for crse := 1 to nocourses do write(headings[crse][2]:6);
        writeln(' of');
        write(' ':nameandspace);
        for crse := 1 to nocourses do write(headings[crse][3]:6);
        writeln(' Courses');
        write(' ':nameandspace);
        for crse := 1 to nocourses do write(headings[crse][4]:6);
        writeln;
        writeln
end; {printheadings}
{-----------------------------------------------------------------}
procedure printresults; {print the results for each student}
var     stud      : studindex;
        crse      : crseindex;
        cnta      : 0..lengthname;
        cntb      : 1..nameandspace;
        studave   : real;
        sch       : char;

begin
        reset(names);
        stud := 1;
        while not eof(names) do
        begin
                cnta := 0;
                while not eoln(names) do
                begin
                        read(names,ch);
                        write(ch);
                        cnta := cnta + 1
                end;
                readln(names);
                for cntb := cnta + 1 to nameandspace do
                        write(' ');
                studave := 0;
                for crse := 1 to nocourses do
                begin
                        studave := studave + marks[stud,crse];
                        if marks[stud,crse] >= 0 then
                        write(overave - overstddev *
                        ((crseave[crse] - marks[stud,crse]) /
                        crsedev[crse] ):6:2 )
                        else write(0.0:6:2)
                end;
```

```
                    writeln(studtakes[stud]:4, studave / studtakes[stud]:10:2);
                    stud := stud + 1
          end
end; {printresults}
{-------------------------------------------------------------------}
procedure printsummary;
{print the pre-normalisation averages and standard deviations and the
overall average and standard deviations}

var       crse : crseindex;

begin
          writeln;
          write(' Raw Average',' ':lengthname − 11);
          for crse := 1 to nocourses do write(crseave[crse]:6:2);
          writeln;
          write(' Raw Standard Deviation',' ':lengthname − 22);
          for crse := 1 to nocourses do write(crsedev[crse]:6:2);
          writeln;
          writeln(' Overall Average : ',overave:6:2);
          writeln' Overall Standard Deviation : ',overstddev:6:2)
end; {printsummary}
{-------------------------------------------------------------------}
begin  {main program}
          initialise;
          readmarks;
          average;
          deviations;
          readnumbers;
          printheadings;
          printresults;
          printsummary
end.
```

RESULTS

Here is a short ***name*** file just to test the logic of the program.

C Babbage
A Lovelace
N Wirth
E Dijkstra
C Hoare

Here is a typical ***numbers*** file

c102
c112
c132
c142
c152
c202
c212
c222
c242
c262

Finally we have a typical set of input data that could be input from the terminal

1 3
1 23
4 34
6 27
3 6
1 24
2 24
3 24
5 35
8 56
9 89
2 4
10 40
9 35
8 45
7 36
4 6
2 34
3 45
4 34
5 76
6 56
7 34
5 6
10 67
8 45
6 34
4 53
2 56
1 67

Here is the ouput produced by the program given the above data

```
                c      c      c      c      c      c      c      c      c      c  N
Mean            1      1      1      1      1      2      2      2      2      2
                0      1      3      4      5      0      1      2      4      6
                2      2      2      2      2      2      2      2      2
C Babbage   31.23   0.00   0.00  31.64   0.00  27.13   0.00   0.00   0.00   0.00 3
25.67
A Lovelace   0.00   0.00   0.00   0.00   0.00   0.00  60.80  31.64  26.64  26.64 4
37.50
N Wirth     32.06  25.83  26.64   0.00  26.64   0.00   0.00  67.87  60.80   0.00 6
41.33
E Dijkstra   0.00  38.61  60.80  31.64  60.80  67.22  26.64   0.00   0.00   0.00 6
45.83
C Hoare     67.87  66.72   0.00  67.87   0.00  36.81   0.00  31.64   0.00  60.80 6
53.00
Raw Average 38.00  38.00  34.50  40.33  55.50  39.00  35.00  48.67  62.00  53.50
Raw SD      20.51  13.37  10.50   8.96  20.50  12.36   1.00   5.19  27.00  13.50
Overall Average : 43.72        Overall Standard Deviation : 17.08
```

DISCUSSION

1. Before looking at the program we ought to point out that with the limited number of students given in the example any normalisation process is unlikely to be particularly useful, and it could be argued that it is invalid to perform the exercise. Even the limit of 25 given in the specification might be considered rather low. However, the given data are adequate to test the logic of the program.

Beware of using a program to do a task that should not be done, but simple data sets can be useful in program testing

2. The required program involves three main stages — inputting the data, performing the normalisation, and outputting the results. In order to be able to write a program to execute any of these stages we must decide upon suitable data structures to store the information.

Develop a program by looking at both the algorithms required and the data structures
If the problem specifies the algorithm (as in this case) look at the data structures required first
If the data structures are specified look at the algorithms
If neither are given, keep both in mind

3. The basic information we have is the marks obtained by each student on the various courses. The obvious way of storing these data is in a two-dimensional array ***marks*** which is indexed by the number of students, and the number of courses. We intend to store only the raw marks here so each entry can be in the range 0 to 100. It is convenient to extend the range to include -1 which we use to indicate that a course is not taken.

Think twice before using the obvious subrange

4. In order to decide what other data structures we require let us consider what we are asked to calculate. For each course we need to calculate the average and standard deviation. Two one-dimensional arrays, ***crseave*** and ***crsedev***, are used to hold these values. To make these calculations we need to know the total marks awarded on the course and the number of students who have taken each course. The total can be accumulated in the ***crseave*** array, and we declare an array ***candidates*** to hold the number of students on each course. Finally we need to calculate the overall average and standard deviation. The variables ***overave***, ***overstddev***, and ***totalcand*** are used to do this. These variables may be considered to be overloaded in that we use them to build up intermediate values required to calculate the final values as well as using them to hold the final values. The benefit of overloading variables like this is the saving of storage space. The disadvantage is a slightly less readable program.

As always, there is a trade-off between efficiency and clarity

5. We have said that the first part of the program involves inputting the data. We are fortunate in that the problem specification clearly indicates the format of the input, and the procedure ***readmarks*** can be written almost directly from this specification. There are two features of this procedure that are worth noting. Firstly we use local variables ***stud***, ***crseno***, and ***mark*** to avoid repeated array accesses. Secondly we can accumulate totals of marks and number of candidates as we go ready for use in later calculations.

Looping is time consuming. Try to do as much as possible on each iteration to make it worth while

6. Having already obtained totals whilst reading in the marks, the process of calculating averages is fairly straightforward (see procedure **average**). Similarly calculating the standard deviations is fairly straightforward. Note again the use of local variables to avoid repetitive array accesses, and also the way we have to multiply a variable by itself because of the lack of a power operator in Pascal.

7. The actual normalisation can be carried out at the output stage, thus avoiding the extra storage that would be needed in order to hold these values. The actual formula is:

Calculate the difference between the mark awarded and the average for that course

(crseave[crse] − marks[stud,crse])

Divide this by the standard deviation

(crsedev[crse])

Multiply by the overall standard deviation

(overstddev)

Subtract from overall average

(overave).

Don't bother to store values you don't need again

8. Most of the rest of the program is fairly self evident. The apparent complexities of achieving a neat layout are merely tedious. The only other procedure we have not yet mentioned is the first, ***initialise***, which simply sets certain variables to appropriate initial values. Finally it must be emphasised that the solution offered is not a robust program. It relies on the use of Pascal subranges for its data-checking and will fail if a course is taken by fewer than two people (a standard deviation cannot be calculated in this case and perhaps should not be unless many more students take a course).

Robustness is a desirable property in a program, but sometimes it is prohibitively expensive to achieve

9. We should also perhaps comment on the user interface we have provided. This was clearly specified in the problem, but it is worth noting that sometimes a terse, apparently unfriendly, interface can be very friendly to an experienced user who knows what they are doing.

Tailor your program to your user

10. You will have noticed that despite our warnings about always using parameters with procedures and the advice to look with suspicion at parameterless procedures, none of the procedures in this program has any parameters. The reason for this is the way we tackled the problem. Each procedure performs one stage of the manipulation of the whole data structure available. Thus most procedures would have to have all the variables used as parameters. Normally using parameters makes a program more readable. In this case we claim that it would not. Suppose for the moment that we had fully parameterised all the procedures. Below are the procedure headings and main program as they would now appear.

```
{-----------------------------------------------------------}
procedure initialise(var overave : real; var candidates : candarray; var
crseave,crsedev : realarray;var marks : marksarray);
{initialise the marks array — use -1 to indicate course not taken, the crseave
and crsedev arrays, the candidates array, and the overall average }
```

This procedure requires all its parameters to be variable parameters as its purpose is to change (initialise) them.

```
{-----------------------------------------------------------------------}
procedure readmarks(var studtakes : takesarray;var marks:marksarray; var
candidates : candarray;var crseave : realarray; var overave : real );
{read in marks from standard input}
```

Once again variable parameters are required.

```
{-----------------------------------------------------------------------}
procedure average(var totalcand : studrange;var overave : real; var crseave :
realarray;var candidates : candarray);
{calculate averages for each course, and calculate overall average}
```

Only the parameters which contain the averages and accumulate the total number of candidates need to be variable parameters, but passing arrays as constant parameters is expensive in storage.

```
{-----------------------------------------------------------------------}
procedure deviations(var crseave, crsedev : realarray;var marks :
marksarray; var overstddev : real;var candidates : candarray;
overave : real;totalcand : studrange);
{calculate standard deviations}
```

A similar comment applies here.

```
{-----------------------------------------------------------------------}
procedure readnumbers(var numbers : text;var headings : headarray);
{read in the course numbers}

{-----------------------------------------------------------------------}
procedure printheadings(var headings : headarray);

{-----------------------------------------------------------------------}
procedure printresults(var names : text;var marks : marksarray; var crseave,
crsedev : realarray; var studtakes : takesarray;overave, overstddev : real);
{print the results for each student}

{-----------------------------------------------------------------------}
procedure printsummary(var crseave, crsedev : realarray; overave,
overstddev : real);
{print the pre-normalisation averages and standard deviations and the
overall average and standard deviations}
```

These print procedures do not require variable parameters but once again we use them to save storage.

```
{-----------------------------------------------------------------------}
```

```
begin {main program}
      initialise(overave, candidates, crseave, crsedev, marks);
      readmarks(studtakes, marks, candidates, crseave, overave);
      average(totalcand, overave, crseave, candidates);
      deviations(crseave, crsedev, marks, overstddev, candidates,
                 overave, totalcand);
      readnumbers(numbers, headings);
      printheadings(headings);
      printresults(names, marks, crseave, crsedev, studtakes, overave,
                   overstddev);
      printsummary(crseave, crsedev, overave, overstddev)
end.
{--------------------------------------------------------------------------------}
```

When procedures have a large number of parameters it is difficult to remember what order they were declared in. This can lead to strange errors if mistakes are made when the procedures are called. Imagine the confusion that could occur if the average and standard deviation arrays were passed in the wrong order. This would not cause a compile time error as they are both of the same type. Looking at the individual procedures would not give any clue to the cause of the error. Only when declaration and call were compared would it (hopefully) be obvious, and these may be several pages of listing apart.

If procedures have too many parameters, then when calling them it is difficult to know what parameters to pass

Procedures can be used in two ways — to work on part of the data used in a program, in which case parameters must be used, or — as in this case — to perform one step in a long manipulation of the whole of the data used, in which case parameters are less useful. One reason why parameters are useful is to show what variables a procedure may effect. This is particularly important when one procedure is called more than once (possibly working on different parameters). In this program each procedure is called only once, and merely serves to identify the individual steps in the program.

You can communicate among many people by passing around lots of slips of paper. You can also do it by letting them all write on the same blackboard !

9

Records and structured files

PROBLEM STATEMENT 26 PERSONAL DETAILS
TOPICS COVERED More on records
More on structured files

Write a program that constructs a file of personal details, reading each person's details from the keyboard and storing them as one record in a structured file called ***peoplefile***. The records should contain fields that store the following information.

Surname and initials	as a string of up to twenty characters.
National insurance number	as a string of up to twenty characters.
Home address	as three lines of up to twenty characters each.
Sex	as a character; 'm' or 'M' for male and 'f' or 'F' for female.
Gross annual income and tax allowances,	as two integers.
Income tax due	as a real number.

After each person's details have been read, the user should be prompted to enter details about any more people. When the last person's details have been read, reset the ***peoplefile***. Then read each record from the file in turn and use the gross annual income and the total tax allowances to calculate the amount of income tax due. Print each record in a three column format. Each column is to be twenty characters wide. The first column should have the name on the first line and the national insurance number on the second line. The second column should contain the address and the third column should contain the sex on one line, the gross earnings and tax allowances on the next line and the income tax due on the last line. Print the tax due, with two digits after the decimal point, and add headers to make clear the meaning of each number. After each record has been updated and printed, write it to a second structured file called ***taxfile***.

PROGRAM

```
program personaldetails (input, output, peoplefile, taxfile);
{
Read sets of personal details from the keyboard and store them in a
structured file called peoplefile. When the last one has been entered, read
them all back from peoplefile and calculate the amount of income tax that
each person owes. Print each person's details and store the amended records
in another structured file called taxfile
}
const  namelength   = 20;   { the maximum length of each string }
       addrlength   = 3;    { the number of lines in each address }
       taxyear      = 1985;
type   taxrange     = (basic,band1,band2,band3,band4,band5);
       taxratearray = array [basic..band5] of integer;
       taxbandarray = array [basic..band4] of real;
       string       = packed array [1..namelength] of char;
       addrtype     = array [1..addrlength] of string;
       individual   = record
                        name, natinsnumber: string;
                        address           : addrtype;
                        sex               : char;
                        income, allowances : integer;
                        taxdue            : real
       end;
var
       peoplefile, taxfile   : file of individual;
       person, newperson     : individual;
       taxrate               : taxratearray;
       sumatrate             : taxbandarray;
       response              : char;
       finished              : boolean;

{-------------------------------------------------------------------}
procedure readstring( var name : string );
{Read a string of up to namelength characters, after initialising it to contain
spaces.}
var    i : integer;
begin { READSTRING }
       for i := 1 to namelength do
              name[ i ] := ' ';
       i := 0;
       while (not eoln) and (i < namelength ) do
       begin
              i := i + 1;
              read( name[ i ] )
       end;
       readln
end; { READSTRING }
```

```
{-------------------------------------------------------------------------------}
procedure readaddress( var address : addrtype );
var     line : integer;
begin { READADDRESS }
        writeln('home address on ',addrlength:1,' lines');
        for line := 1 to addrlength do
        begin
                write('line ',line:1,' : ');
                readstring( address[ line ] );
        end
end; { READADDRESS }
{-------------------------------------------------------------------------------}
procedure readperson( var newone : individual );
{Read a person's details. taxdue is initialised to zero; it is calculated later.}
begin { READPERSON }
        with newone do
        begin
                writeln;
                write('surname and initials        : ');
                readstring( name );
                write('national insurance number : ');
                readstring( natinsnumber );
                write('sex (m/f)                   : ');
                readln( sex );
                writeln;
                readaddress( address );
                writeln;
                writeln('enter financial details for ',taxyear:4,'/',
                        (taxpayer year+1):4);
                write('gross income in pounds      : ');
                readln( income );
                write('tax allowances in pounds : ');
                readln( allowances );
                writeln;
                taxdue := 0.0
        end
end; { READPERSON }
{-------------------------------------------------------------------------------}
procedure writestring( name : string; newline : boolean );
var     i : integer;
begin { WRITESTRING }
        for i := 1 to namelength do
                write( name[ i ] );
        if newline
                then writeln
end; { WRITESTRING }
```

```
{---------------------------------------------------------------------------}
procedure writeperson( person : individual );
{
Print a person's details in three columns, each namelength characters wide.
The first column contains the name and national insurance number. The
second column contains the address and the third column contains the sex,
gross earnings, tax allowances and income tax due.
}
begin { WRITEPERSON }
        with person do
        begin
                writestring( name, false );
                writestring( address[1], false );
                if (sex = 'm') or (sex = 'M')
                        then writeln('sex : MALE')
                        else if (sex = 'f') or (sex = 'F')
                                then writeln('sex : FEMALE')
                                else writeln('sex : not known');
                writestring( natinsnumber, false );
                writestring( address[2], false );
                writeln('income : ', income:1, ' allowances : ', allowances:1 );
                write(' ':namelength);
                writestring( address[3], false );
                writeln('tax due : ', taxdue:1:2 );
                writeln
        end
end; { WRITEPERSON }
{---------------------------------------------------------------------------}
procedure initialise( var taxrate : taxratearray;
                        var sumatrate : taxbandarray );
{
Initialise the percentage rate for each tax band and the range of each band,
except the last, in pounds.
}
begin { INITIALISE }
        taxrate[basic]    := 30; taxrate[band1] := 40;
        taxrate[band2]    := 45; taxrate[band3] := 50;
        taxrate[band4]    := 55; taxrate[band5] := 60;
        sumatrate[basic] := 16200.00;
        sumatrate[band1] := 3000.00;
        sumatrate[band2] := 5200.00;
        sumatrate[band3] := 7900.00;
        sumatrate[band4] := 7900.00;
end; { INITIALISE }
{---------------------------------------------------------------------------}
```

```
procedure addtaxdetails ( var person : individual );
{
Calculate the yearly tax payably on gross income after deducting allow-
ances, but without rounding or truncating any fractions of pence.
}
const lowestrate = basic;    { these two constants would need to be changed }
      highestrate = band5;   { if the number of tax bands were altered }
var   taxableincome,
      taxpayable : real;
      thisrate   : taxrange;
      done       : boolean;
begin { ADDTAXDETAILS }
      taxpayable := 0.0;
      thisrate := lowestrate;
      taxableincome := (person.income - person.allowances);
      done := (taxableincome <= 0.0);
      {
      Work out the tax payable on taxable income falling in each tax band
except the highest.
      }

      while not done and (thisrate <> highestrate) do
      begin
            if taxableincome <= sumatrate[thisrate] then
            begin
                  {
                  There will be tax to pay in higher band(s). So deduct
                  tax for the full range covered by this band.
                  }
                  taxpayable := taxpayable +
                        (taxableincome / 100.0) * taxrate[thisrate];
                  taxableincome := taxableincome -
                  sumatrate[thisrate];
                  done := true
            end
            else begin
                  {
                  This is the highest rate at which income is taxed. So
                  deduct tax on the portion of income that falls into this
                  band.
                  }
                  taxpayable := taxpayable +
                        (sumatrate[thisrate] / 100.0) * taxrate[thisrate];
                  taxableincome:= taxableincome -
                  sumatrate[thisrate];
```

```
                    thisrate := succ(thisrate)
                end
            end;
            if taxableincome >0.0 then { tax any surplus at the highest rate }
                taxpayable := taxpayable +
                    (taxableincome / 100.0) * taxrate[highestrate];
            person.taxdue := taxpayable
        end; { ADDTAXDETAILS }
        {-------------------------------------------------------------------------}
        begin { MAIN }
            initialise( taxrate, sumatrate );
            {
            Read sets of personal details from the keyboard into a structured file
            called peoplefile.
            }
            writeln('Enter the first person''s personal details :');
            finished := false;
            rewrite( peoplefile );
            repeat
                readperson( newperson );
                peoplefile^ := newperson;
                put( peoplefile );
                write('Do you want to add details for any more people (y/n)? ');
                readln( response );
                if (response = 'n') or (response = 'N') then finished := true
            until finished;
            {
            Read records of personal details from peoplefile. Calculate the
            amount of income tax owed by each person, print that person's
            record and write the record to a structured file called taxfile
            }
            writeln;
            write('Each person''s income tax bill for ',taxyear:4,'/',
            (taxyear+1):4);
            writeln(' will be calculated');
            writeln('and all the personal details will be printed...');
            writeln;
            reset( peoplefile );
            rewrite( taxfile );
            while not eof(peoplefile) do
            begin
                person := peoplefile^;
                addtaxdetails( person );
                writeperson( person );
                taxfile^ := person;
                put( taxfile );
```

```
            get( peoplefile )
      end
end.
```

RESULTS

```
Enter the first person's personal details:

surname and initials         : Adams DB
national insurance number : WL 204 073 B
sex (m/f)                          : m

home address on 3 lines
line 1 : 43 Mercier Terrace
line 2 : Upper Newton
line 3 : UN1 3BA

enter financial details for 1985/1986

gross income in pounds       : 7520
tax allowances in pounds    : 2205

Do you want to add details for any more people (y/n)? y

surname and initials          : Mitchell DA
national insurance number : DS 546 608 C
sex (m/f)                           : ff

home address on 3 lines
line 1 : 12 School Lane
line 2 : Boreham
line 3 : BH3 4DZ

enter financial details for 1985/1986
gross income in pounds       : 1320
tax allowances in pounds    : 2205

Do you want to add details for any more people (y/n)? n

Each person's income tax bill for 1985/1986 will be calculated
and all the personal details will be printed...
Adams DB          43 Mercier Terrace   sex        : MALE
WL 204 073 B   Upper Newton            income   : 7520 allowances : 2205
                       UN1 3BA                   tax due  : 1594.50

Mitchell DA        12 School Lane        sex        : FEMALE
DS 546 608 C    Boreham                   income   :1320 allowances : 2205
                       BH3 4DZ                   tax due:  0.00
```

DISCUSSION

1. With the knowledge which we have so far, you will have noticed how hard it can be to store collections of items in arrays. Each element in an array has to be of the same type. So if we wanted to store the description of an item as a string and its price in pence as an integer, two separate arrays were needed. Splitting up the different components of each item and storing them in separate data structures meant that extra housekeeping was required and the program was harder to read. These problems could be overcome by using arrays of records to gather together all the components of each element and manipulate them as a single entity. This approach was adopted in the second stock control example (see chapter eight). However there is still one drawback. In ISO Pascal (compliance level 0), the size of an array is fixed when the program is written. It cannot be changed while the program is running. This is a severe disadvantage in many applications, where it is impossible to predict accurately how many data there will be in advance. If the estimate is too small, the program may crash. If it is too large, memory space will be reserved, but may never be used to store elements of the array. Both these disadvantages can be overcome by storing the elements as sequences of records in structured files. Alternatively, conformant arrays may be used if a Pascal system that satisfies the ISO standard to compliance level 1 is available. Conformant array parameters are briefly discussed in the matrix multiplication example in chapter 8 (problem statement 23).

**A record may contain elements of many different types.
In this respect, it is an unique data structure**

2. In the problem statement we are asked to use structured files to create and manipulate collections of personal details. The details for each person are to be stored as a record containing fields for their name, national insurance number, address, sex, gross income, tax allowances and amount of income tax due. The fields are of different types: strings, arrays of strings, integers and reals. Each person's details are read from the keyboard and stored as one record in a structured file called ***peoplefile***. Prompts are printed so that the user can see what they are expected to type. The amount of tax due is the only field which is not read. It is initialised to zero in the ***readperson*** procedure and calculated at a later stage. Each address is declared as an array of three strings. ***readaddress*** reads each one by calling ***readstring***. The sex is read as a single character. This is done using

```
readln(sex);
```

to read the first character typed. Any other characters on the input line are ignored. For convenience, a WITH statement is used. This automatically prefixes any field names in a person's record with the record name and a full-stop. If it were not used, we would have to type all the field names in full: ***person.name***, ***person.natinsnumber***, ***person.sex***, etc. After each person's details have been read, users are asked whether they would like to enter details about any more people. When the last person's details have been read, the ***peoplefile*** is reset. Then each record from the file in turn and the amount of income tax due is calculated using the the gross annual income and the total tax allowances.

Get the overall logic correct — and keep it simple

3. Next each complete record is printed using a three column format. Each column is twenty characters wide. In the program, the width is equal to the maximum length of each string, which is declared as a global constant. This makes it easy to alter the width if we decide to alter the program so that it will accept longer strings. The first column has the name on the first line and the national insurance number on the second line.The second column contains the address and the third column contains the sex on one line, the gross earnings and tax allowances on the next line and the income tax due on the last line. Where the meaning of a field may not be clear, labels are printed. After each record has been updated and printed, it is written to a second structured file called ***taxfile***.

Spend time on the output format — it may make the program usable

4. The program has been written re-using as many routines as possible from other exercises. The procedures to read and write strings are all used elsewhere and the procedure ***addtaxdetails*** is a slight enhancement of the ***taxdue*** function that you saw in problem 21, chapter 7. Instead of returning the tax due as a real number, it accepts a person's record as a variable parameter and updates the ***taxdue*** field of the record directly. To emphasise that one field in a record, rather than an ordinary variable, is being used we write ***person.taxdue*** at the end of the procedure. This convention of prefixing the field name with the record name and a full-stop is used when we work out the taxable income at the start of the procedure. There we write:

```
taxableincome := (person.income − person.allowances);
```

Notice also that a separate procedure has been written to initialise the tax tables used by the program. This is called once, at the start of the main program, not every time that ***addtaxdetails*** is executed.

Re-use working code. It is simpler and safer

5. Two advantages of using structured files in this way are that records can be read and written easily and the programmer is not limited by having to

declare the number of personal records in advance. Every structured file has a buffer variable associated with it that acts as a window on the file. It allows the program to manipulate a complete record, instead of having to refer to each field individually. In the main program we start by rewriting the ***peoplefile***. This allows us to write records to the file. The statements

```
peoplefile^ := newperson;
put(peoplefile);
```

assign a copy of the personal record just read by the ***readperson*** procedure to the buffer variable ***peoplefile***^ and write it to the end of the ***peoplefile***. Compare this with what would be required to do the same thing using text-files.

Using structured files saves effort — you can access whole records

6. At the end of the main program we read records from ***peoplefile***, update them using the ***addtaxdetails*** procedure, and write the updated records to another structured file called ***taxfile***. The statements

```
reset(peoplefile);

    and

rewrite(taxfile);
```

reposition the ***peoplefile*** buffer variable to the start of the ***peoplefile*** and prepare the ***taxfile*** for writing. Then the statement

```
person := peoplefile^;
```

reads the contents of the buffer variable into ***person***. That person's details are processed and the the updated record is written to the ***taxfile*** by

```
taxfile^ := person;
```

Put and get statements update the two buffer variables before the next record is processed. Records are read, updated and written until the ***peoplefile*** is exhausted. This program demonstrates how to create, read, write and modify structured files. You might like to extend it so that each person's details are validated as they are entered. You can easily do this by adapting the data validation routines introduced elsewhere in this book. If they were YOUR personal details, wouldn't you want to be confident that everything was correct?

PROBLEM STATEMENT 27 EXTERNAL SORTING

TOPICS COVERED: Implementing book algorithms
Merging files
Sorting externally held data

In order to make this problem reasonable within the context of this book, we must make some rather artificial restrictions. This is an exercise in manipulating files. For convenience we shall assume that we wish to sort a file of positive integers. This file is of unknown length. We assume that only ten integer values may be stored at once in main memory, i.e. we can only sort an array of length ten, and that we can create up to four internal files. The exercise is to perform a two-way tape merge. We shall use internal Pascal files to represent tapes. This is quite reasonable since Pascal files are strictly sequential. The initial data-file is to be split into sorted units of ten, and then merged according to the following pattern.

> The input is transferred in sorted blocks of 10 onto tapes 1 and 2 alternately.
> These blocks of sorted data are then merged onto tapes 3 and 4 alternately.
> The output from the next merge phase is put onto tapes 1 and 2 again.

This process is repeated until only one output block is produced, which is the complete sorted list.

PROGRAM

```
program exsort(input,output);
{program to simulate an external merge sort using Pascal files we assume
only 10 items may be sorted internally, and declare four files to represent the
tapes. -1 is used to mark the end of sorted blocks }

const  interblock  = -1;
       maxstore    = 10;
type   intfile     = file of integer{for convenience we are going to sort
                                     integer values}
var    file1, file2,
       file3, file4  : intfile;      {the internal files}
       done          : boolean;      {flag to mark end of sorting}
       length        : integer;      {records length of sorted block}
{------------------------------------------------------------------}
procedure merge(var from1,from2,tofile : intfile);
{merge a single sorted block from from1 and from2 to tofile; negative value
is used to mark end of block}
var    endfrom   : boolean;          {flag to mark that an input tape is
                                      exhausted}
```

```
begin
        endfrom := (from1^ < 0 ) or (from2^ < 0);
        {merge two blocks until one becomes empty by placing smaller of
        head items on to output file} while not endfrom do
        begin
                if from1^ < from2^
                        then begin
                                tofile^ := from1^;
                                get(from1);
                                endfrom := from1^ < 0
                        end
                        else begin
                                tofile^ := from2^;
                                get(from2);
                                endfrom := from2^ < 0
                        end;
                put(tofile)
        end;
        {now copy across rest of either input block which is not empty. Only
        one of the following loops will ever be executed in an instantiation of
        this procedure}
        while from1^ > = 0 do
        begin
                tofile^ := from1^;
                get(from1);
                put(tofile)
        end;
        while from2^ > = 0 do
        begin
                tofile^ := from2^;
                get(from2);
                put(tofile)
        end;
        tofile^ := interblock;
        put(tofile);
        get(from1);
        get(from2)
end; {------------------------------------------------------------------------}
procedure sort(var howmany : integer; var tofile : intfile);
{take integers from standard input and sort them (using bubble sort) onto
file tofile. Return how many numbers have been sorted in parameter
howmany }
var     list        : array[1..maxstore] of integer;     {the array for sorting}
        i,j,swap  : integer;                             {counters and swap variable}
begin
        {read in the data}
        howmany := 1;
        while (not eof) and (howmany <= maxstore) do
```

```
        begin
            readln(list[howmany]);
            howmany := howmany + 1
        end;
        howmany := howmany - 1;{forget final increment}
        {now the simple bubble sort}
        for i := howmany downto 2 do
            for j := 1 to i - 1 do
                if list[j] > list[j + 1]
                    then begin
                        swap := list[j];
                        list[j] := list[j + 1];
                        list[j + 1] := swap
                    end;
        for i := 1 to howmany do
        begin
            tofile^ := list[i];
            put(tofile)
        end;
        if howmany > 0 then
        begin
            tofile^ := interblock;
            put(tofile)
        end
    end; {------------------------------------------------------------------------}
    procedure mergepairs(var from1,from2,to1,to2 : intfile);
    begin
        repeat
            merge(from1,from2,to1);
            if not (eof(from1) or eof(from2))
                then merge(from1,from2,to2);
        until (eof(from1)) or (eof(from2));
        while not eof(from1) do
        begin
            to2^ := from1^;
            put(to2);
            get(from1)
        end;
        while not eof(from2) do
        begin
            to2^ := from2^;
            put(to2);
            get(from2)
        end
    end;
    {------------------------------------------------------------------------}
    {merge from one pair of files to another}
```

```
begin {main program }
        {get ready to output to files 1 and 2}
        rewrite(file1);
        rewrite(file2);
        done := false;
        {sort in blocks of ten onto files 1 and 2 in turn}
        repeat
                sort(length,file1);
                if length >= maxstore
                        then sort(length,file2)
        until length < maxstore;
        {final block will be less than ten items. All other blocks will be exactly
        ten long }
        {now to start the merge from files 1 and 2 to files 3 and 4}
        reset(file1);
        reset(file2);
        rewrite(file3);
        rewrite(file4);
        repeat
                mergepairs(file1,file2,file3,file4);
                {having merged onto files 3 and 4 merge back onto 1 and 2}
                reset(file3);
                reset(file4);
                rewrite(file1);
                rewrite(file2);
                if not eof(file4) then
                begin
                        mergepairs(file3,file4,file1,file2);
                        reset(file1);
                        reset(file2);
                        rewrite(file3);
                        rewrite(file4);
                        done := eof(file2)
                end
                else done := true
        until done;
        while not eof(file1) do
        begin
                writeln(file1^);
                get(file1)
        end;
        while not eof(file2) do
        begin
                writeln(file2^);
                get(file2)
        end;
```

```
        while not eof(file3) do
        begin
                writeln(file3^);
                get(file3)
        end;
        while not eof(file4) do
        begin
                writeln(file4^);
                get(file4)
        end
end. {------------------------------------------------------------------------}
```

RESULTS

The original data input were
67
45
67
98
34
12
78
45
99
34
79
123
165
775
45
987
35
87
234
678
123
67
23
5
656
45
98
46
678
34
57
23
56

76
23
456
68
34
23
56
8
45
23
43
65
667
35
56
7
23

The output from the program was

5
7
8
12
23
23
23
23
23
23
34
34
34
34
35
35
43
45
45
45
45
45
46
56
56
56
57
65

67
67
67
68
76
78
79
87
98
98
99
123
123
165
234
456
656
667
678
678
775
987
−1

DISCUSSION

Once the principle of merging tapes has been mastered, the coding of this problem is fairly straightforward. One point to note is the use of −1 as a block separator. On actual tapes a number of files would be used instead of blocks and end-of-file would be the separator. Although the solution offered is based on sorting positive integers, it is interesting to see how little code would have to be changed if some other form of data was to be sorted. Obviously the definition of the file type would have to be changed, and a suitable interblock value selected. Other than that, the only change would be to ensure that the comparison operators (<, >, = etc.) work on the new data type.

Much of programming is tedious once the initial design is sorted out — beware of the boredom that leads to errors

PROBLEM STATEMENT 28 THE LIBRARY REVISITED

TOPICS COVERED	An amalgam of previous points
	Combining ideas
	Using variant records

This is the last exercise based on the computerisation of a library. Two text-files are provided. The first contains a list of up to 50 books sorted according to author. Books in the library fall into one of two categories: reference books which may not be borrowed, and borrowable books that may be borrowed for up to three weeks. The file contains records in the following format:

Author's surname (max 15 char), initials (max 3),
title (max length 35), R or B

The R or B indicates whether or not the book is a reference book or a borrowable book. The second file contains a maximum of 50 names of borrowers. This file is also sorted. The format for this file is

Surname (max 15 chars), initials (max 3), title (Mr, Mrs, Miss, Ms)

The first task is to read in these text-files and create two structured files, representing the books and the borrowers. Having created these structured files we need to write a program which will maintain them, and at the same time allow the user to perform a number of tasks.

1) Allow a user to borrow a book.
2) Allow a user to return a book.

Users should be asked for their surnames, and the system should then check that it has found the right person by printing out the name with title and initials.

Books should be referred to either by title or by author. Again the system should confirm that it has found the right book. Books are borrowed for a period of 3 weeks. Each borrower is allowed a maximum of 4 books out at any one time. If a borrower has an overdue book (s)he is not allowed to borrow any more.

3) Allow a book to be either added to or deleted from the stock of the library.
4) Allow a borrower to be added to or deleted from the membership list.
5) Print out a list of books borrowed by a given person.
6) Print who (if anybody) has borrowed a certain book.

The system on starting should ask for the date; it should then update the list of people who have overdue books, and print out a list of overdue books with the names of their borrowers. Whilst the program is running it may be more efficient to store indexes to the files (say names of borrowers, authors, and titles) in arrays. You should not, however, attempt to store all the information in core.

PROGRAM(S)

The first program creates structured files from text-files.

```
program create(input,output,bookstext,borrowerstext,books,borrowers);
{program to read text files containing lists of books and borrowers and
create structured files}
const  maxsurname  = 15;
       maxinitials = 3;
       maxbooktitle = 35;
       maxborrowed= 4;
       maxentry    = 50;
type   surnamestep  = 1..maxsurname;
       initialsstep = 1..maxinitials;
       booktitlestep = 1..maxbooktitle;
       borrowedstep= 1..maxborrowed;
       entryindex   = 0..maxentry;
       title        = (mr,mrs,miss,ms);
       booktype     = (borrowable,reference);
       bookstatus   = (loaned,shelved);
       name         = packed array[surnamestep] of char;
       initials     = packed array[initialsstep] of char;
       booktitle    = packed array[booktitlestep] of char;
       date         = record day : 1..31;
                             month : 1..12;
                             year : 0..99
       end;
       person       =     record
                          surname     : name;
                          inits       : initials;
                          status      : title;
                          borrowed    : array[borrowedstep] of
                                        entryindex;
                          overdue     : boolean;
                          memberno    : entryindex
       end;
       book         =     record
                          catalogno   : entryindex;
                          authorname  : name;
                          authorinits : initials;
                          bktitle     : booktitle;
                          case bktype : booktype of
                               borrowable : (case available :
                               bookstatus of
                               loaned : (borrower :
                                    entryindex;
                                    duedate : date );
                               shelved : ()
                          );
```

```
                        reference : ()
        end;
var     bookstext, borrowerstext   : text;
        books                      : file of book;
        borrowers                  : file of person;
        currmember, currbook       : entryindex;
{-------------------------------------------------------------------}
procedure readname(var from : text; var this : name);
{read a surname from a text-file}
var     ch      : char;
        i       : 0..maxsurname;
begin
        for i:=1 to maxsurname do
                this[i] := ' ';
        i := 0;
        read(from,ch);
        while (ch <> ',') and (i < maxsurname) do
        begin
                i := i + 1;
                this[i] := ch;
                read(from,ch)
        end;
        while ch <> ',' do
                read(from,ch)
end;
{-------------------------------------------------------------------}
procedure readinits(var from : text; var this : initials);
{read initials from text-file}
var     ch      : char;
        i       : 0..maxinitials;
begin
        for i := 1 to maxinitials do
                this[i] := ' ';
        i := 0;
        read(from,ch);
        while (ch <> ',') and (i < maxinitials) do
        begin
                i := i + 1;
                this[i] := ch;
                read(from,ch)
        end;
        while ch <> ',' do
                read(from,ch)
end; {readinits}
{-------------------------------------------------------------------}
```

```
procedure readperson (var from : text; var this : person;
                    var currmember : entryindex);
{read details of person from text-file}
var     ch      : char;
        i       : borrowedstep;
        {------------------------------------------------------------}
        procedure readstatus(var from : text; var this : title);
        {procedure to read title of person}
        var     titlearray : packed array[1..4]of char;
                i,j       : integer;
        begin
                i := 1;
                while (not eoln(from)) and (i <= 4) do
                begin
                        read(from,titlearray[i]);
                        i := i + 1
                end;
                readln(from);
                for j:=i to 4 do
                        titlearray[j] := ' ';
                if titlearray = 'Mr  ' then
                        this := mr
                else if titlearray = 'Mrs ' then
                        this := mrs
                        else if titlearray = 'Miss' then
                                this := miss
                                else if titlearray = 'Ms  ' then
                                        this := ms
                                        else begin
                                                write('error detected in reading
                                                title : ');
                                                for j:=1 to 4 do
                                                        write(titlearray[j]);
                                                writeln;
                                                this := mr
                                        end
        end; {readstatus}
        {------------------------------------------------------------}
begin
        with this do
        begin
                readname(from,surname);
                read(from,ch);     {skip space}
                readinits(from,inits);
                read(from,ch);     {skip space}
                readstatus(from,status);
                for i := 1 to maxborrowed do
                        borrowed[i] := 0;
                overdue := false;
```

```
              memberno := currmember;
              currmember := currmember + 1
         end
end; { readperson}
{-----------------------------------------------------------------------}
procedure readbook(var from : text; var this : book;
                   var currbook : entryindex);
{read book from text-file}
var      ch : char;
         {-------------------------------------------------------}
         procedure readbooktitle(var from : text; var this : booktitle);
         {read book title from text file}
         var      ch       : char;
                  i        : 0..maxbooktitle;
         begin
                  for i := 1 to maxbooktitle do
                           this[i] := ' ';
                  i := 0;
                  read(from,ch);
                  while (ch <> ',') and ( i < maxbooktitle) do
                  begin
                           i := i + 1;
                           this[i] := ch;
                           read(from,ch)
                  end;
                  while ch <> ',' do
                           read(from,ch)
         end; {readbooktitle}
         {-------------------------------------------------------}
begin
         with this do
         begin
                  readname(from,authorname);
                  read(from,ch);     {skip space}
                  readinits(from,authorinits);
                  read(from,ch);     {skip space}
                  readbooktitle(from,bktitle);
                  read(from,ch);     {skip space}
                  read(from,ch);
                  if ch = 'R' then
                           bktype := reference
                           else if ch = 'B' then
                                    begin
                                             bktype := borrowable;
                                             available := shelved
                                    end
                                    else begin
```

```
                              bktype := reference;
                              write('invalid book type —')
                              writeln('reference assumed')
                          end;
            readln(from);
            catalogno := currbook;
            currbook := currbook + 1
        end
end; {readbook}
{---------------------------------------------------------------------}
begin {main program}
        currmember := 1;
        reset(borrowerstext);
        rewrite(borrowers);
        while not eof(borrowerstext) do
        begin
            readperson(borrowerstext,borrowers^,currmember);
            put(borrowers)
        end;
        currbook := 1;
        reset(bookstext);
        rewrite(books);
        while not eof(bookstext) do
        begin
            readbook(bookstext,books^,currbook);
            put(books)
        end
end.
```

PROGRAM (2)

The second program performs the interactive maintenance.

```
program library(input,output,books,borrowers);
{library program allows interactive maintenance of files on books and
borrowers}
const   maxsurname   = 15;
        maxinitials   = 3;
        maxbooktitle = 35;
        maxborrowed= 4;
        maxentry      = 50;
type    surnamestep  = 1..maxsurname;
        initialstep    = 1..maxinitials;
        booktitlestep = 1..maxbooktitle;
        borrowedstep= 1..maxborrowed;
        entryindex    = 0..maxentry;
        title             = (mr,mrs,miss,ms);
```

```
         booktype      = (borrowable,reference);
         bookstatus    = (loaned,shelved);
         name          = packed array[surnamestep] of char;
         initials      = packed array[initialstep] of char;
         booktitle     = packed array[booktitlestep] of char;

         date          =      record day : 1..31;
                                     month : 1..12;
                                     year : 0..99
         end;
         person        =      record surname      : name;
                                     inits        : initials;
                                     status       : title;
                                     borrowed     : array[borrowedstep] of
                                                    entryindex;
                                     overdue      : boolean;
                                     memberno     : entryindex
         end;
         book          =      record catalogno          : entryindex;
                                     authorname         : name;
                                     authorinits        : initials;
                                     bktitle            : booktitle;
                                     case bktype        : booktype of
                                       borrowable : (case available :
                                                     bookstatus of
                                                     loaned : (borrower :
                                                               entryindex;
                                                               duedate : date
                                                               );
                                                     shelved : ()
                                                    );
                                     reference : ()
         end;
         bookfile      = file of book;
         borrowerfile  = file of person;
         namerec       = record      sname       : name;
                                     number      : entryindex
         end;
         namearray     = array[entryindex]of namerec;
         titlerec      = record         btitle   : booktitle;
                                        catno    : entryindex
         end;
         titlearray    =array[entryindex]of titlerec;

var      books          : bookfile;
         borrowers     : borrowerfile;
         noborrowers,
         nobooks       : entryindex;
         borrowbyname,
```

```
        booksbyauthor   : namearray;
        booksbytitle    : titlearray;
        today           : date;
{------------------------------------------------------------------}
procedure readname(var from : text; var this : name);
{read a surname from a text file}
var     ch      : char;
        i       : 0..maxsurname;
begin
        for i:=1 to maxsurname do
                this[i] := ' ';
        i := 0;
        read(from,ch);
        while (not eoln(from)) and (i < maxsurname) do begin
                i := i + 1;
                this[i] := ch;
                read(from,ch)
        end;
        if eoln(from) and (i < maxsurname) then
                this[i+1] := ch;
        readln(from)
end; {readname}
{------------------------------------------------------------------}
procedure readdate(var today : date);
{read date in format dd/mm/yy}
var     ch              : char;
        dy,mn,yr        : integer;
        daysinmonth     : 28..31;
        valid           : boolean;
begin
        repeat
                writeln('Please type in to-day''s date in form dd/mm/yy');
                repeat
                        read(ch)
                until ch <> ' ';
                dy := ord(ch) - ord('0');
                read(ch);
                while ch <> '/' do
                begin
                        dy := dy * 10 + ord(ch) - ord('0');
                        read(ch)
                end;
                read(ch);
                mn := ord(ch) - ord('0');
                read(ch);
```

```
            while ch <> '/' do
            begin
                mn := mn * 10 + ord(ch) - ord('0');
                read(ch)
            end;
            read(ch);
            yr := ord(ch) - ord('0');
            while not eoln do
            begin
                read(ch);
                yr := yr * 10 + ord(ch) - ord('0')
            end;
            readln;
            if (dy >= 1) and (dy <= 31) and (mn >= 1) and
            (mn <= 12) and (yr >= 0) and (yr <= 99) then
                {check for correct number of days in month}
                begin case mn of
                        1,3,5,7,8,10,12   : daysinmonth := 31;
                        4,6,9,11          : daysinmonth := 30;
                        2                 : if (yr < 0) and
                                            (((yr div 4) * 4) = yr) then
                                              daysinmonth := 29
                                              else daysinmonth := 28
                        end;
                        if dy <= daysinmonth then
                        begin
                            valid := true;
                            with today do
                            begin
                                day := dy;
                                month := mn;
                                year := yr
                            end
                        end
                        else valid := false
                end
                else valid := false;
                if not valid then
                writeln('invalid date')
        until valid
end; {readdate}
{----------------------------------------------------------------}
function createborrowerarray(var borrowers : borrowerfile;
                        var borrowbyname : namearray):entryindex;
var     index : entryindex;
begin
        reset(borrowers);
        index := 1;
        while not eof(borrowers) do
```

```
        begin
                borrowbyname[index].sname := borrowers^.surname;
                borrowbyname[index].number := borrowers^.memberno;
                index := index + 1;
                get(borrowers)
        end;
        createborrowerarray := index - 1
end; {createborrowerarray}
{----------------------------------------------------------------}
function createbooksbyauthor(var books : bookfile;
                        var booksbyauthor : namearray):entryindex;
var     index : entryindex;
begin
        reset(books);
        index := 1;
        while not eof(books) do
        begin
                booksbyauthor[index].sname := books^.authorname;
                booksbyauthor[index].number := books^.catalogno;
                index := index + 1;
                get(books)
        end;
        createbooksbyauthor := index - 1
end;{createbooksbyauthor}
{----------------------------------------------------------------}
function createbooksbytitle(var books : bookfile;
                        var booksbytitle : titlearray):entryindex;
var     index : entryindex;
begin
        reset(books);
        index := 1;
        while not eof(books) do
        begin
                booksbytitle[index].btitle := books^.bktitle;
                booksbytitle[index].catno := books^.catalogno;
                index := index + 1;
                get(books)
        end;
        createbooksbytitle := index - 1
end; {createbooksbytitle}
{----------------------------------------------------------------}
procedure sortbyname(var given : namearray; size : integer);
var     pass, step      : integer;
        temp            : namerec;
begin
        for pass := size downto 2 do
                for step := 1 to pass - 1 do
                        if given[step].sname > given[step + 1].sname then
```

```
                    begin
                        temp := given[step];
                        given[step] := given[step + 1];
                        given[step + 1] := temp
                    end
end; {sortbyname}
{------------------------------------------------------------------}
procedure sortbytitle(var given : titlearray; size : integer);
var     pass, step      : integer;
        temp            : titlerec;
begin
            for pass := size downto 2 do
                for step := 1 to pass - 1 do
                    if given[step].btitle > given[step + 1].btitle then
                        begin
                            temp := given[step];
                            given[step] := given[step + 1];
                            given[step + 1] := temp
                        end
end; {sortbytitle}
{------------------------------------------------------------------}
function after(var due, today : date):boolean;
begin
        if due.year < today.year then
            after := true
            else if due.year = today.year then
                if due.month < today.month then
                    after := true
                    else if due.month = today.month then
                        after := due.day < today.day
                        else after := false
                else after := false
end; {after}
{------------------------------------------------------------------}
procedure writebook(var abook : book);
var     i       : booktitlestep;
        j       : initialstep;
        k       : surnamestep;
begin
        for i := 1 to maxbooktitle do
            write(abook.bktitle[i]);
        write(' by ');
        for j := 1 to maxinitials do
            write(abook.authorinits[j]);
        write(' ');
        for k := 1 to maxsurname do
            write(abook.authorname[k])
end; {writebook}
```

```
{----------------------------------------------------------------------}
procedure writedate(var adate : date);
begin
        write(adate.day:2,'/',adate.month:2,'/',adate.year:2)
end; {writedate}
{----------------------------------------------------------------------}
procedure writename(var aborrower : person);
var     i : initialstep;
        j : surnamestep;
begin
        case aborrower.status of
                mr      : write('Mr ');
                mrs     : write('Mrs ');
                miss    : write('Miss ');
                ms      : write('Ms ')
        end;
        for i := 1 to maxinitials do
                write(aborrower.inits[i]);
        write(' ');
        for j := 1 to maxsurname do
                write(aborrower.surname[j])
end; {writename}
{----------------------------------------------------------------------}
procedure copypeopleto(var one,two : borrowerfile; length : entryindex)
; var
        i : entryindex;
begin
        reset(one);
        rewrite(two);
        for i := 1 to length - 1 do
        begin
                two^ := one^;
                put(two);
                get(one)
        end
end; {copypeopleto}
{----------------------------------------------------------------------}
procedure copybooksto(var one,two : bookfile; length : entryindex);
var     i : entryindex;
begin
        reset(one);
        rewrite(two);
        for i := 1 to length - 1 do
        begin
                two^ := one^;
                put(two);
```

```
            get(one)
        end
end; {copypbooksto}
{-------------------------------------------------------------------}
procedure copyrestpeople(var one, two : borrowerfile);
begin
        while not eof(one) do
        begin
            two^ := one^;
            put(two);
            get(one)
        end
end; {copyrestpeople}
{-------------------------------------------------------------------}
procedure copyrestbooks(var one, two : bookfile);
begin
        while not eof(one) do
        begin
            two^ := one^;
            put(two);
            get(one)
        end
end; {copyrestbooks}
{-------------------------------------------------------------------}
procedure copyallpeople(var one, two : borrowerfile);
begin
        reset(one);
        rewrite(two);
        while not eof(one) do
        begin
            two^ := one^;
            put(two);
            get(one)
        end
end; {copyallpeople}
{-------------------------------------------------------------------}
procedure copyallbooks(var one, two : bookfile);
begin
        reset(one);
        rewrite(two);
        while not eof(one) do
        begin
            two^ := one^;
            put(two);
            get(one)
        end
end; {copyallbooks}
```

```
{-----------------------------------------------------------------------}
procedure overdueborrower(var borrowers : borrowerfile;
                          var aborrower : entryindex);
var     tempborrower : borrowerfile;
begin
        copypeopleto(borrowers, tempborrower, aborrower);
        writename(borrowers^);
        borrowers^.overdue := true;
        tempborrower := borrowers^;
        put(tempborrower);
        get(borrowers);
        copyrestpeople(borrowers, tempborrower);
        copyallpeople(tempborrower, borrowers)
end; {overdueborrower}
{-----------------------------------------------------------------------}
procedure findoverdue(var books : bookfile; var borrowers : borrowerfile;
today : date);
begin
        reset(books);
        writeln('overdue books');
        writeln;
        while not eof(books) do
        begin
                if books^.bktype = borrowable then
                if books^.available = loaned then
                        if after(books^.duedate,today) then
                                begin
                                        writebook(books^);
                                        writeln;
                                        write(' was due back on ');
                                        writedate(books^.duedate);
                                        writeln;
                                        write(' borrowed by ');
                                        overdueborrower(borrowers,
                                        books^.borrower);
                                        writeln
                                end;
                get(books)
        end
end; {findoverdue}
{-----------------------------------------------------------------------}
function searchname(var given : namearray; var howmany : entryindex;
        var inname : name; var borrowindex : entryindex): boolean;
var     low, mid, high entryindex;
        found           : boolean;
```

```
begin
        found := false;
        low := 1;
        high := howmany;
        repeat
                mid := (low + high) div 2;
                if given[mid].sname = inname then
                        found := true
                        else if given[mid].sname > inname then
                                high := mid - 1
                                else low := mid + 1
        until found or (low > high);
        if not found then
                borrowindex := 0
                else begin
                        while given[mid - 1].sname = inname do
                                mid := mid - 1;
                        {mid now points to first person with given surname}
                        borrowindex := mid
                end;
        searchname := found
end; {searchname}
{--------------------------------------------------------------------}
function searchtitle(var given : titlearray; var howmany : entryindex;
        var intitle : booktitle; var bookindex : entryindex): boolean;
var     low, mid, high entryindex;
found                   : boolean;
begin
        found := false;
        low := 1;
        high := howmany;
        repeat
                mid := (low + high) div 2;
                if given[mid].btitle = intitle then
                        found := true
                        else if given[mid].btitle > intitle then
                                high := mid - 1
                                else low := mid + 1
        until found or (low > high);
        if not found then
                bookindex := 0
                else begin
                        while given[mid - 1].btitle = intitle do
                                mid := mid - 1;
                        {mid now points to first book with given title}
                        bookindex := mid
                end;
                searchtitle := found
end; {searchtitle}
```

```
{-----------------------------------------------------------------------}
function findname(var borrowers, tempborrowers : borrowerfile;
                  var borrowersbyname : namearray;
                  var noborrowers : entryindex;
                  var borrowindex : entryindex):boolean;
var    inname: name;
       found  : boolean;
       {-----------------------------------------------------------------------}
       function checkname(var borrowers : borrowerfile; inname : name;
                  var found : boolean):boolean;
       var    ans : char;
       begin
              found := true;
              if borrowers^.surname = inname then
              begin
                     write('Are you');
                     writename(borrowers^);
                     write('?');
                     readln(ans)
              end
              else found := false;
              checkname := (ans <> 'y') and (ans <> 'Y') and found
       end; {checkname}
       {-----------------------------------------------------------------------}
begin
       writeln('Please type in your name (surname only)');
       readname(input, inname);
       if not searchname(borrowersbyname, noborrowers, inname,
       borrowindex)
       then begin
              writeln('Sorry no-one of that name on file');
              findname := false
            end
            else begin
              copypeopleto(borrowers, tempborrowers,
              borrowersbyname[borrowindex].number);
              while checkname(borrowers,inname,found) do
              begin
                     tempborrowers^ := borrowers^;
                     put(tempborrowers);
                     get(borrowers)
              end;
              findname := found;
              if not found then
              begin
                     writeln('Sorry — person not on file');
                     reset(borrowers)
```

```
            end
            else borrowindex := borrowers^.memberno
        end
end; {findname}
{-------------------------------------------------------------------}
procedure readtitle(var from : text; var this : booktitle);
{read book title from text-file}
var     ch      : char;
        i       : 0..maxbooktitle;
begin
        writeln('Please type in the title then');
        for i := 1 to maxbooktitle do
            this[i] := ' ';
        i := 0;
        read(from,ch);
        while (not eoln(from)) and ( i < maxbooktitle) do
        begin
            i := i + 1;
            this[i] := ch;
            read(from,ch)
        end;
        if eoln(from) and ( i < maxbooktitle) then
            this[i+1] := ch;
            readln(from)
end; {readtitle}
{-------------------------------------------------------------------}
function findbook(var books, tempbooks : bookfile; var booksbyauthor :
            namearray;
        var booksbytitle : titlearray; var nobooks : entryindex;
        var bookindex : entryindex):boolean;
var     inname      : name;
        intitle     : booktitle;
        found       : boolean;
        ans         : char;
        {-----------------------------------------------------------}
        function checkauthor(var books : bookfile; inname : name;
                                var found : boolean):boolean;
        var     ans : char;
        begin
            found := true;
            if books^.authorname = inname then
            begin
                write('Is it ');
                writebook(books^);
                write('?');
                readln(ans)
            end
```

```
        else found := false;
        checkauthor := (ans <> 'y') and (ans <> 'Y') and found
    end; {checkauthor}
    {---------------------------------------------------------------------}
    function checktitle(var books : bookfile; intitle : booktitle;
                        var found : boolean):boolean;
    var     ans : char;
    begin
        found := true;
        if books^.bktitle = intitle then
        begin
            write('Is it ');
            writebook(books^);
            write('?');
            readln(ans)
        end
        else found := false;
        checktitle := (ans <> 'y') and (ans <> 'Y') and found
    end; {checktitle}
    {---------------------------------------------------------------------}
begin
    found := false;
    write('Do you know the title of the book?');
     readln(ans);
    if (ans = 'y') or (ans = ' Y') then
    begin
        readtitle(input, intitle);
        if searchtitle(booksbytitle,nobooks,intitle,bookindex) then
        begin
            copybooksto(books, tempbooks,
            booksbytitle[bookindex].catno);
            found := true;
            while checktitle(books,intitle,found) do
            begin
                tempbooks^ := books^;
                put(tempbooks);
                get(books)
            end
        end
    end
    else begin
        writeln('please type in name of the author then');
    readname(input, inname);
    if searchname(booksbyauthor,nobooks,inname,bookindex) then
    begin
            copybooksto(books, tempbooks,
            booksbyauthor[bookindex].number);
```

```
                    found := true;
                    while checkauthor(books,inname,found) do
                    begin
                              tempbooks^ := books^;
                              put(tempbooks);
                              get(books)
                    end
          end
       end;
     if not found then
     begin
          writeln('Sorry no such book on file');
          reset(books)
     end
     else bookindex := books^.catalogno;
     findbook := found
end; {findbook}
{-------------------------------------------------------------------------------}
procedure setreturndate(var return, today : date);
var    daysinmonth : 28..31;
begin
     {borrow books for 3 weeks}
     case today.month of
          1,3,5,7,8,10,12      : daysinmonth := 31;
          4,6,9,11             : daysinmonth := 30;
          2         : if (today.year < 0) and ((today.year mod 4 ) = 0)
          then daysinmonth := 29
          else daysinmonth := 28
     end;
     if (today.day + 21) daysinmonth then
          return.day := (today.day + 21) mod daysinmonth
     else return.day := today.day + 21;
     if return.day < today.day then
          if today.month = 12 then
          begin
                    return.month := 1;
                    return.year := today.year + 1
          end
          else    begin
                              return.month := today.month + 1;
                              return.year := today.year
                    end
          else    begin
                              return.month := today.month;
                              return.year := today.year
                    end;
```

```
        write('book due back on ');
        writedate(return);
        writeln
end; {setreturndate}
{-----------------------------------------------------------------------}
procedure borrowbook(var abook : book; var aborrower : person;
                        bookindex, borrowindex : entryindex; today : date);
var     i : borrowedstep;
begin
        if abook.bktype = reference then
                writeln('Sorry book is for reference only')
        else if abook.available = loaned then
                writeln('Sorry book already out on loan')
        else if aborrower.overdue then
        begin
                writeln('Sorry all overdue books must be returned before');
                writeln('new books can be borrowed')
        end
        else if aborrower.borrowed[maxborrowed] <> 0 then
                writeln('You have already borrowed the maximum number of
                books')
        else    begin
                        abook.available := loaned;
                        abook.borrower := borrowindex;
                        setreturndate(abook.duedate,today);
                        i := 1;
                        while aborrower.borrowed[i] <> 0 do
                                i := i + 1;
                        aborrower.borrowed[i] := bookindex
                end
end; {borrowbook}
{-----------------------------------------------------------------------}
procedure borrow(var books : bookfile; var borrowers : borrowerfile;
                 var borrowersbyname,booksbyauthor : namearray;
                 var booksbytitle : titlearray; var noborrowers, nobooks :
                 entryindex; today : date);
var     tempbooks               : bookfile;
        tempborrowers           : borrowerfile;
        bookindex, borrowindex  : entryindex;
begin
        if findname(borrowers,tempborrowers,borrowersbyname,
                noborrowers,borrowindex) then
        if findbook(books,tempbooks,booksbyauthor,booksbytitle,
                nobooks,bookindex) then
        begin   borrowbook(books^,borrowers^,bookindex,borrowindex,
                today);
                copyrestbooks(books, tempbooks);
```

```
            copyallbooks(tempbooks,books);
            copyrestpeople(borrowers, tempborrowers);
            copyallpeople(tempborrowers, borrowers)
        end
end; {borrow}
{-----------------------------------------------------------------------}
procedure returnbook(var abook : book; var aborrower : person;
            bookindex : entryindex;
            var books, tempbooks : bookfile; today : date);
var     i, j            : 0..maxborrowed;
        found, moreoverdue: boolean;
begin
        i := 0;
        found := false;
        while (not found) and (i <maxborrowed) do
        begin
            i := i + 1;
            found := aborrower.borrowed[i] = bookindex
        end;
        if not found then
            writeln('Book not borrowed by that person')
        else    begin
                    aborrower.borrowed[i] := 0;
                    for j := i to maxborrowed - 1 do
                    aborrower.borrowed[j]:=aborrower.borrowed[j+1];
                    aborrower.borrowed[maxborrowed] := 0;
                    abook.available := shelved;
                    copyrestbooks(books,tempbooks);
                    copyallbooks(tempbooks,books);
                    {We can now reset the borrower's overdue flag
                      provided that no other books are overdue}
                    moreoverdue := false;
                    j := 1;
                    while(aborrower.borrowed[j]<>0)and
                    (j<maxborrowed) do
                    begin
                        copybooksto(books,tempbooks,
                                aborrower.borrowed[j]);
                        moreoverdue := after(books^.duedate,today);
                        if moreoverdue then
                            {no point checking any more}
                                j := maxborrowed
                        else j := j + 1
                    end;
                    if not moreoverdue then
                        aborrower.overdue := false
                end
end; {returnbook}
```

```
{---------------------------------------------------------------------}
procedure return(var books : bookfile; var borrowers : borrowerfile;
                 var borrowersbyname,booksbyauthor : namearray;
                 var booksbytitle : titlearray; var noborrowers, nobooks :
                     entryindex;
                 today : date);
var     tempbooks                 bookfile;
        tempborrower            : borrowerfile;
        bookindex, borrowindex : entryindex;
begin
        if findname(borrowers,tempborrowers,borrowersbyname,
              noborrowers,borrowindex) then
        if findbook(books,tempbooks,booksbyauthor,booksbytitle,
              nobooks,bookindex) then
        begin
              returnbook(books^,borrowers^,bookindex,books,
                    tempbooks,today);
              copyrestpeople(borrowers, tempborrowers);
              copyallpeople(tempborrowers, borrowers)
        end
end; {return}
{---------------------------------------------------------------------}
procedure printloaned(var books : bookfile; var borrowers : borrowerfile;
        var borrowbyname : namearray; var noborrowers : entryindex);
var     tempborrowers : borrowerfile;
        tempbooks     : bookfile;
        i             : borrowedstep;
        borrowindex   : entryindex;
begin
        if findname(borrowers,tempborrowers,borrowbyname,
              noborrowers, borrowindex) then
        begin if borrowers^.borrowed[1] = 0 {no books borrowed} then
                    writeln('You have not borrowed any books')
              else  for i:=1 to maxborrowed do
                    begin
                          if borrowers^.borrowed[i] < 0 then
                          begin
                                copybooksto(books,tempbooks,
                                      borrowers^.borrowed[i]);
                                writebook(books^);
                                write( 'due back on ');
                                writedate(books^.duedate);
                                writeln

                          end

                    end;

        end
end; {printloaned}
```

```
{----------------------------------------------------------------------}
procedure findborrower(var books : bookfile; var borrowers : borrowerfile;
        var booksbyauthor : namearray; var booksbytitle : titlearray;
        var nobooks : entryindex);
var     tempbooks : bookfile;
        tempborrow : borrowerfile;
        borrowindex : entryindex;
begin
        if findbook(books,tempbooks,booksbyauthor,booksbytitle,
                nobooks, borrowindex) then
        begin if books^.bktype = reference then
                        writeln('book is reference only')
                else    if books^.available = shelved then
                                writeln('book not on loan')
                        else    begin
                                        copypeopleto(borrowers,tempborrow,
                                                books^.borrower);
                                        writename(borrowers^)
                                end
        end
        else    writeln('book not found')
end; {findborrower}
{----------------------------------------------------------------------}
function terminate:boolean;
begin
        writeln('Thank you for using the library — Good Bye');
        terminate := true
end; {terminate}
{----------------------------------------------------------------------}
procedure notimplemented;
begin
        write('Sorry, the feature you have ');
        writeln('requested is not yet implemented');
        writeln('Please refer to librarian')
end; {notimplemented}
{----------------------------------------------------------------------}
function menu(var books : bookfile; var borrowers : borrowerfile;
var booksbyauthor, borrowersbyname : namearray; var booksbytitle :
titlearray; var noborrowers, nobooks : entryindex;
today : date): boolean;
var ch : char;
    valid : set of char;
{----------------------------------------------------------------------}
        procedure display;
        begin
                writeln;
                writeln;
```

```
        writeln('Welcome to the library — what facility do you wish to
use?');
                writeln;
                writeln('Borrow a book —                          type b');
                writeln('Return a book —                          type r');
                writeln('Add a book to the library —              type a');
                writeln('Delete a book from the library —         type d');
                writeln('Join the library —                       type j');
                writeln('Leave the library —                      type l');
                writeln('Print out books on loan —                type p');
                writeln('Find who has a borrowed a book —         type f');
                writeln('Terminate using the library —            type t')
        end;
        {-----------------------------------------------}
begin
        valid:=['b','r','a','d','j','l','p','f','t',
                'B','R','A','D','J','L','P','F','T'];
        repeat
                display;
                readln(ch);
        until ch in valid;
        menu := false;
        case ch of
                'b','B' : borrow(books,borrowers,borrowersbyname,
                                booksbyauthor, booksbytitle,noborrowers,
                                nobooks,today);
                'r','R' : return(books,borrowers,borrowersbyname,
                                booksbyauthor, booksbytitle,noborrowers,
                                nobooks,today);
                'a','A','d','D','j','J','l','L' : notimplemented;
                'p','P' : printloaned(books,borrowers,borrowersbyname,
                                noborrowers);
                'f','F' : findborrower(books,borrowers,booksbyauthor,
                                booksbytitle,nobooks);
                't','T' : menu := terminate
        end
end; {menu}
{--------------------------------------------------------------------------}
begin   {main program}
        {find out today's date}
        readdate(today);
        {The files are ordered in terms of memberno and catalogno. We wish
        to create index arrays which are sorted according to surname of
        borrower, author, and title. To do this we shall read the files and
        create the index arrays and then sort them. }
        noborrowers := createborrowerarray(borrowers,borrowbyname);
```

```
        nobooks := createbooksbyauthor(books,booksbyauthor);
        nobooks := createbooksbytitle(books,booksbytitle);
        sortbyname(borrowbyname,noborrowers);
        sortbyname(booksbyauthor,nobooks);
        sortbytitle(booksbytitle,nobooks);
        {We now need to find, and list, the overdue books}
        findoverdue(books,borrowers,today);
        {Now the interactive maintainance of the system}
        while not menu(books,borrowers,booksbyauthor, borrowbyname,
                       booksbytitle, noborrowers,nobooks,today) do
end.
```

RESULTS

First here are the contents of the file ***bookstext*** read by the file creation program.

Sharp, JA, Data Flow Computing,
B Moseley, LG, Pascal for Beginners, B
Meek, BL, Guide to Good Programming Practice, B
Harland, DM, Polymorphic Programming Languages, R
Young, S J, Real Time Languages, B
Guru, A, A Guide to Unix, R
Wizard, U, A Guide to Unix, B
Other, A N, Basic for Everybody, B
Other, A N, Pascal for Everybody, B
Burns, A, New Information Technology, R

Next we have the contents of the file ***borrowerstext***

Sharp, JA, Mr
Moseley, LG, Mr
Salenieks, P, Mr
Jones, D, Mr
Jones, D, Miss
Nightingale, F, Miss
Leggett, M, Mrs
Winsdor, E, Ms
Ferguson, S, Miss

If we run the file creation program we get two structured files ***books*** and ***borrowers*** which cannot be simply listed by the usual means. After giving some example runs of the program we will take a look at parts of these files to see how they are updated.

```
Please type in to-day's date in form dd/mm/yy
21/7/86

overdue books

Welcome to the library — what facility do you wish to use?

Borrow a book —                           type b
Return a book —                           type r
Add a book to the library —               type a
Delete a book from the library —          type d
Join the library —                        type j
Leave the library —                       type l
Print out books on loan —                 type p
Find who has a borrowed a book —          type f
Terminate using the library —             type t
b
Please type in your name (surname only)
Sharp
Are you Mr JA Sharp       ?y
Do you know the title of the book?
y
Please type in the title then
Pascal for Beginners
Is it Pascal for Beginners        by LG Moseley        ?y
book due back on 11/ 8/86
Welcome to the library — what facility do you wish to use?


Borrow a book —                           type b
Return a book —                           type r
Add a book to the library —               type a
Delete a book from the library —          type d
Join the library —                        type j
Leave the library —                       type l
Print out books on loan —                 type p
Find who has a borrowed a book —          type f
Terminate using the library —             type t
B
Please type in your name (surname only)
Sharp
Are you Mr JA Sharp         ?Y
Do you know the title of the book?
N
please type in name of the author then
Harland
Is it Polymorphic Programming Languages     by DM Harland        ?y
Sorry book is for reference only
Welcome to the library — what facility do you wish to use?
```

```
Borrow a book —                          type b
Return a book —                          type r
Add a book to the library —              type a
Delete a book from the library —         type d
Join the library —                       type j
Leave the library —                      type l
Print out books on loan —                type p
Find who has a borrowed a book —         type f
Terminate using the library —            type t
b
Please type in your name (surname only)
Sharp
Are you Mr JA Sharp          ?y
Do you know the title of the book?
n
please type in name of the author then
Other
Is it Basic for Everybody    by A N Other        ?N
Is it Pascal for Everybody   by A N Other        ?Y
book due back on 11/ 8/86
Welcome to the library — what facility do you wish to use?

Borrow a book —                          type b
Return a book —                          type r
Add a book to the library —              type a
Delete a book from the library —         type d
Join the library —                       type j
Leave the library —                      type l
Print out books on loan —                type p
Find who has a borrowed a book —         type f
terminate using the library —            type t
b
Please type in your name (surname only)
Sharp Are you Mr JA Sharp          ?y
Do you know the title of the book?
y
Please type in the title then
A Guide to Unix
Is it A Guide to Unix        by A Guru    ?n
Is it A Guide to Unix        by U Wizard  ?y
book due back on 11/ 8/86
Welcome to the library — what facility do you wish to use?

Borrow a book —                          type b
Return a book —                          type r
Add a book to the library —              type a
```

```
Delete a book from the library —         type d
Join the library —                       type j
Leave the library —                      type l
Print out books on loan —                type p
Find who has a borrowed a book —         type f
Terminate using the library —            type t
b
Please type in your name (surname only)
Sharp Are you Mr JA Sharp          ?y
Do you know the title of the book?
y
Please type in the title then
Guide to Good Programming Practice
Is it Guide to Good Programming Practice by BL Meek      ?y
book due back on 11/ 8/86
Welcome to the library — what facility do you wish to use?
Borrow a book —                          type b
Return a book —                          type r
Add a book to the library —              type a
Delete a book from the library —         type d
Join the library —                       type j
Leave the library —                      type l
Print out books on loan —                type p
Find who has a borrowed a book —         type f
Terminate using the library —            type t
b
Please type in your name (surname only)
Sharp
Are you Mr JA Sharp          ?y
Do you know the title of the book?
n
please type in name of the author then
Other
Is it Basic for Everybody          by A N Other          ?y
You have already borrowed the maximum number of books
Welcome to the library — what facility do you wish to use?

Borrow a book —                          type b
Return a book —                          type r
Add a book to the library —              type a
Delete a book from the library —         type d
Join the library —                       type j
Leave the library —                      type l
Print out books on loan —                type p
Find who has a borrowed a book -         type f
Terminate using the library —            type t
p
Please type in your name (surname only)
```

```
Sharp
Are you Mr JA Sharp          ?y
Pascal for Beginners                       by LG Moseley  due back on 11/ 8/86
Pascal for Everybody                       by A N Other   due back on 11/ 8/86
A Guide to Unix                            by U Wizard    due back on 11/ 8/86
Guide to Good Programming Practice         by BL Meek     due back on 11/ 8/86
Welcome to the library — what facility do you wish to use?

Borrow a book —                        type b
Return a book —                        type r
Add a book to the library —            type a
Delete a book from the library —       type d
Join the library —                     type j
Leave the library —                    type l
Print out books on loan —              type p
Find who has a borrowed a book —       type f
Terminate using the library —          type t
t
Thank you for using the library — Good Bye
```

Now we will run the program again giving a date to ensure that some books will be overdue.

```
Please type in to-day's date in form dd/mm/yy
32/7/86
invalid date
Please type in to-day's date in form dd/mm/yy
21/8/86
overdue books
Pascal for Beginners                  by LG Moseley
was due back on 11/ 8/86
borrowed by Mr JA Sharp
Guide to Good Programming Practice by BL Meek
was due back on 11/ 8/86
borrowed by Mr JA Sharp
A Guide to Unix                  by U Wizard
was due back on 11/ 8/86
borrowed by Mr JA Sharp
Pascal for Everybody                  by A N Other
was due back on 11/ 8/86
borrowed by Mr JA Sharp
Welcome to the library — what facility do you wish to use?

Borrow a book —                        type b
Return a book —                        type r
Add a book to the library —            type a
```

```
Delete a book from the library —          type d
Join the library —                        type j
Leave the library —                       type l
Print out books on loan —                 type p
Find who has a borrowed a book —          type f
Terminate using the library —             type t
r
Please type in your name (surname only)
Sharp
Are you Mr JA Sharp       ?y
Do you know the title of the book?
n
please type in name of the author then
Young
Is it Real Time Languages by S J Young         ?y
Book not borrowed by that person
Welcome to the library — what facility do you wish to use?

Borrow a book —                           type b
Return a book —                           type r
Add a book to the library —               type a
Delete a book from the library —          type d
Join the library —                        type j
Leave the library —                       type l
Print out books on loan —                 type p
Find who has a borrowed a book —          type f
Terminate using the library —             type t
r
Please type in your name (surname only)
Sharp
Are you Mr JA Sharp       ?y
Do you know the title of the book?
n
please type in name of the author then
Mosel;
Sorry no such book on file
Welcome to the library — what facility do you wish to use?

Borrow a book —                           type b
Return a book —                           type r
Add a book to the library —               type a
Delete a book from the library —          type d
Join the library —                        type j
Leave the library —                       type l
Print out books on loan —                 type p
Find who has a borrowed a book —          type f
Terminate using the library —             type t
```

```
r
Please type in your name (surname only)
Sharp
Are you Mr JA Sharp          ?y
Do you know the title of the book?
n
please type in name of the author then
Moseley
Is it Pascal for Beginners              by LG Moseley        ?y
Welcome to the library — what facility do you wish to use?

Borrow a book —                          type b
Return a book —                          type r
Add a book to the library —              type a
Delete a book from the library —         type d
Join the library —                       type j
Leave the library —                      type l
Print out books on loan —                type p
Find who has a borrowed a book —         type f
Terminate using the library —            type t
p
Please type in your name (surname only)
Sharp
Are you Mr JA Sharp          ?y
Pascal for Everybody                 by A N Other
due back on 11/ 8/86
A Guide to Unix              by U Wizard
due back on 11/ 8/86
Guide to Good Programming Practice by BL Meek
due back on 11/ 8/86
Welcome to the library — what facility do you wish to use?

Borrow a book —                          type b
Return a book —                          type r
Add a book to the library —              type a
Delete a book from the library —         type d
Join the library —                       type j
Leave the library —                      type l
Print out books on loan —                type p
Find who has a borrowed a book —         type f
Terminate using the library —            type t
b
Please type in your name (surname only)
Sharp
Are you Mr JA Sharp          ?y
Do you know the title of the book?
n
```

```
please type in name of the author then
Other
Is it Basic for Everybody             by A N Other        ?y
Sorry all overdue books must be returned before new books can be
borrowed
Welcome to the library — what facility do you wish to use?

Borrow a book —                       type b
Return a book —                       type r
Add a book to the library —           type a
Delete a book from the library —      type d
Join the library —                    type j
Leave the library —                   type l
Print out books on loan —             type p
Find who has a borrowed a book —      type f
Terminate using the library —         type t
b
Please type in your name (surname only)
Jones
Are you Mr D Jones          ?n
Are you Miss D Jones        ?y
Do you know the title of the book?
n
please type in name of the author then
Meek
Is it Guide to Good Programming Practice by BL Meek       ?y
Sorry book already out on loan
Welcome to the library — what facility do you wish to use?

Borrow a book —                       type b
Return a book —                       type r
Add a book to the library —           type a
Delete a book from the library —      type d
Join the library —                    type j
Leave the library —                   type l
Print out books on loan —             type p
Find who has a borrowed a book —      type f
Terminate using the library —         type t
b
Please type in your name (surname only)
Jones
Are you Mr D Jones          ?y
Do you know the title of the book?
n
please type in name of the author then
Sharp
Is it Data Flow Computing             by JA Sharp         ?y
```

```
book due back on 11/ 9/86
Welcome to the library — what facility do you wish to use?

Borrow a book —                         type b
Return a book —                         type r
Add a book to the library —             type a
Delete a book from the library —        type d
Join the library —                      type j
Leave the library —                     type l
Print out books on loan —               type p
Find who has a borrowed a book —        type f
Terminate using the library —           type t
t
Thank you for using the library — Good Bye

Yet another run of the program

Please type in to-day's date in form dd/mm/yy
21/9/86
overdue books

Data Flow Computing by                  JA Sharp
was due back on 11/ 9/86
borrowed by Mr D Jones
Guide to Good Programming Practice by BL Meek
was due back on 11/ 8/86
borrowed by Mr JA Sharp
A Guide to Unix by                  U Wizard
was due back on 11/ 8/86
borrowed by Mr JA Sharp
Pascal for Everybody                by A N Other
was due back on 11/ 8/86 borrowed
by Mr JA Sharp
Welcome to the library — what facility do you wish to use?

Borrow a book —                         type b
Return a book —                         type r
Add a book to the library —             type a
Delete a book from the library —        type d
Join the library —                      type j
Leave the library —                     type l
Print out books on loan —               type p
Find who has a borrowed a book —        type f
Terminate using the library —           type t
b
Please type in your name (surname only)
Jones
```

```
Are you Mr D Jones          ?y
Do you know the title of the book?
n
please type in name of the author then
Moseley
Is it Pascal for Beginners                by LG Moseley      ?y
Sorry all overdue books must be returned before new books can be
borrowed
Welcome to the library — what facility do you wish to use?

Borrow a book —                           type b
Return a book —                           type r
Add a book to the library —               type a
Delete a book from the library —          type d
Join the library —                        type j
Leave the library —                       type l
Print out books on loan —                 type p
Find who has a borrowed a book —          type f
Terminate using the library —             type t
r
Please type in your name (surname only)
Jones
Are you Mr D Jones          ?y
Do you know the title of the book?
y
Please type in the title then
Pascal for Beginners
Is it Pascal for Beginners                by LG Moseley      ?y
Book not borrowed by that person
Welcome to the library — what facility do you wish to use?

Borrow a book —                           type b
Return a book —                           type r
Add a book to the library —               type a
Delete a book from the library —          type d
Join the library —                        type j
Leave the library —                       type l
Print out books on loan —                 type p
Find who has a borrowed a book —          type f
Terminate using the library —             type t
r
Please type in your name (surname only)
Jones
Are you Mr D Jones          ?y
Do you know the title of the book?
n
```

```
please type in name of the author then
Sharp
Is it Data Flow Computing            by JA Sharp        ?y
Welcome to the library — what facility do you wish to use?

Borrow a book —                      type b
Return a book —                      type r
Add a book to the library —          type a
Delete a book from the library —     type d
Join the library —                   type j
Leave the library —                  type l
Print out books on loan —            type p
Find who has a borrowed a book —     type f
Terminate using the library —        type t
b
Please type in your name (surname only)
Smith
Sorry no-one of that name on file
Welcome to the library — what facility do you wish to use?

Borrow a book —                      type b
Return a book —                      type r
Add a book to the library —          type a
Delete a book from the library —     type d
Join the library —                   type j
Leave the library —                  type l
Print out books on loan —            type p
Find who has a borrowed a book —     type f
Terminate using the library —        type t
b
Please type in your name (surname only)
Jones
Are you Mr D Jones       ?y
Do you know the title of the book?
y
Please type in the title then
Pascal for Beginners
Is it Pascal for Beginners          by LG Moseley        ?y
book due back on 12/10/86
Welcome to the library — what facility do you wish to use?

Borrow a book —                      type b
Return a book —                      type r
Add a book to the library —          type a
Delete a book from the library —     type d
Join the library —                   type j
Leave the library —                  type l
```

```
Print out books on loan —                 type p
Find who has a borrowed a book —          type f
Terminate using the library —             type t
f
Do you know the title of the book?
y
Please type in the title then
Data Flow Computing
Is it Data Flow Computing                 by JA Sharp        ?y
book not on loan
Welcome to the library — what facility do you wish to use?

Borrow a book —                           type b
Return a book —                           type r
Add a book to the library —               type a
Delete a book from the library —          type d
Join the library —                        type j
Leave the library —                       type l
Print out books on loan —                 type p
Find who has a borrowed a book —          type f
Terminate using the library —             type t
f
Do you know the title of the book?
n
please type in name of the author then
Other
Is it Basic for Everybody               by A N Other        ?y
book not on loan
Welcome to the library — what facility do you wish to use?

Borrow a book —                           type b
Return a book —                           type r
Add a book to the library —               type a
Delete a book from the library —          type d
Join the library —                        type j
Leave the library —                       type l
Print out books on loan —                 type p
Find who has a borrowed a book —          type f
Terminate using the library —             type t
f
Do you know the title of the book?
n
please type in name of the author then
Other
Is it Basic for Everybody      by A N Other        ?y
Is it Pascal for Everybody     by A N Other        ?y
Mr JA Sharp
```

```
Welcome to the library — what facility do you wish to use?

Borrow a book —                          type b
Return a book —                          type r
Add a book to the library —              type a
Delete a book from the library —         type d
Join the library —                       type j
Leave the library —                      type l
Print out books on loan —                type p
Find who has a borrowed a book —         type f
Terminate using the library —            type t
f
Do you know the title of the book?
n
please type in name of the author then
Guru
Is it A Guide to Unix                by A Guru         ?y
book is reference only
Welcome to the library — what facility do you wish to use?

Borrow a book —                          type b
Return a book —                          type r
Add a book to the library —              type a
Delete a book from the library —         type d
Join the library —                       type j
Leave the library —                      type l
Print out books on loan —                type p
Find who has a borrowed a book —         type f
Terminate using the library —            type t
p
Please type in your name (surname only)
Sharp
Are you Mr JA Sharp          ?y
Pascal for Everybody                 by A N Other
due back on 11/ 8/86
A Guide to Unix              by U Wizard
due back on 11/ 8/86
Guide to Good Programming Practice             by BL Meek
due back on 11/ 8/86
Welcome to the library — what facility do you wish to use?

Borrow a book —                          type b
Return a book —                          type r
Add a book to the library —              type a
Delete a book from the library —         type d
Join the library —                       type j
Leave the library —                      type l
```

```
Print out books on loan —           type p
Find who has a borrowed a book —    type f
Terminate using the library —       type t
p
Please type in your name (surname only)
Jones
Are you Mr D Jones        ?y
Pascal for Beginners          by LG Moseley
due back on 12/10/86
Welcome to the library — what facility do you wish to use?

Borrow a book —                     type b
Return a book —                     type r
Add a book to the library —         type a
Delete a book from the library —    type d
Join the library —                  type j
Leave the library —                 type l
Print out books on loan —           type p
Find who has a borrowed a book —    type f
Terminate using the library —       type t
a
Sorry the feature you have requested is not yet implemented
Please refer to librarian
Welcome to the library — what facility do you wish to use?

Borrow a book —                     type b
Return a book —                     type r
Add a book to the library —         type a
Delete a book from the library —    type d
Join the library —                  type j
Leave the library —                 type l
Print out books on loan —           type p
Find who has a borrowed a book —    type f
Terminate using the library —       type t
l
Sorry the feature you have requested is not yet implemented
Please refer to librarian
Welcome to the library — what facility do you wish to use?

Borrow a book —                     type b
Return a book —                     type r
Add a book to the library —         type a
Delete a book from the library —    type d
Join the library —                  type j
Leave the library —                 type l
Print out books on loan —           type p
Find who has a borrowed a book —    type f
```

```
Terminate using the library —             type t
t
Thank you for using the library — Good Bye
```

To examine the structured files we use an octal dump facility that reads the files byte by byte giving us their octal values, and a character interpretation where possible. Looking at the initial state of the record for the first book in the structured file ***books*** we can identify some of the fields.

```
catalog  noauthorname
001      123 150 141 162 160 040 040 040 040 040 040 040 040 040 040 001
          S   h   a   r   p

authorinits
112 101 040
 J   A
bktitle
 104 141 164 141 040 106 154 157 167 040 103 157 155 160 165 164 151 156 147 040
  D   a   t   a       F   l   o   w       C   o   m   p   u   t   i   n   g ..

bktype=borrowable, and available=shelved 000 001 000 000 000 000 \0 001 \0 \0 \0 \0
```

If we look at one of the reference books we can see a difference

```
catalog  noauthorname
006      107 165 162 165 040 040 040 040 040 040 040 040 040 040 040006
          G   u   r   u

authorinits
101 040 040
 A
bktitle
 101 040 107 165 151 144 145 040 164 157 040 125 156 151 170 040 040
  A       G   u   i   d   e       t   o       U   n   i   x ...
bktype = reference 001 001 000 000 000 000 001 001 \0 \0 \0 \0
```

We can do the same for a borrower. We will take as an example Mr D Jones.

```
surname                                                                inits
112 157 156 145 163 040 040 040 040 040 040 040 040 040 040         104 040 040
 J   o   n   e   s                                                    D
borrowed[1..4], overdue = False
memberno 000 000 000 000 000 000          004 \0 \0 \0 \0 \0 \0004
```

After Mr Jones has borrowed the book by Sharp, his entry becomes:

```
surname                                                        inits
112 157 156 145 163 040 040 040 040 040 040 040 040 040 040    104 040 040
 J   o   n   e   s                                              D
borrowed[1..4], overdue = False
memberno 000 001 000 000 000 000          004 \0 001 \0 \0 \0 \0        004
```

The record of the book by Sharp is also changed to record the fact that it has been borrowed.

```
catalog  noauthorname
001      123 150 141 162 160 040 040 040 040 040 040 040 040 040 040 001
          S   h   a   r   p
authorinits
112 101 040
 J   A
bktitle
 104 141 164 141 040 106 154 157 167 040 103 157 155 160 165 164 151 156 147 040
  D   a   t   a       F   l   o   w       C   o   m   p   u   t   i   n   g  ...
bktype=borrowable, available=loaned, borrower=4, duedate=11/9/86 000 000
                                         004         013 011 126 \0 \0
                                         004         013 —t V
```

DISCUSSION

1. Two programs have been written to solve this problem. The first creates structured files from the original text-files. The reasons for using structured files are that they should be more economical in storage, and also easier to manipulate in the main program. The advantage of retaining text files would be the possibility of using standard facilities such as the editor to perform unusual searches or manipulations.

The second program interactively maintains the library database. It could be argued that a suite of programs should have been used to do this with a menu program actually calling the other programs. This is indeed the way we would expect a real system to work. The advantage is that each program can be developed and maintained separately. Unfortunately the Pascal standard does not specify how we might link programs together in this way so we have adopted a monolithic program approach to avoid system specific features.

2. The file creation program should be self evident by this stage. It uses standard techniques to read records and enumerated types. It is, however, necessary to consider the record structures to be used. We have separated the surname, initials and title (Mr, Mrs etc) into separate fields. This means that we can search for named people more easily, using their surname alone as the key which is being sought.

Design a data structure to make operations on it as simple and straightforward as possible

3. As an alternative to using files we could have designed this program so that all the information was stored in main memory and not on files held on backing store. This would have made the task easier as we could have used pointers to link a reader with the books(s) he has borrowed and vice versa.

In a realistic library system with many thousands of books and borrowers such an approach would be impossible to implement because of the amount of storage required. The problem specification, therefore, sensibly required the use of files. Pointer values saved in a file would have no reliable meaning when read back in since they are essentially memory addresses. A simple array is therefore used to maintain index values to refer to the books borrowed. These integer index values are really pointers which are maintained and interpreted by the programmer rather than by the system.

In designing the record structure for the books we have used variant records. It is necessary to record whether or not a book has been borrowed only if it is not a reference book. Similarly only if a book has been loaned out do we need to store details of the date due back, and who has borrowed it. We once again use an index value here rather than a pointer. All this information could have been stored using a standard record type without any variant parts. There are two main advantages to using variant records.

Firstly there is no need to invent spurious data to fill fields which are not required. These fields could be left undefined but it is always dangerous to have undefined variables. Furthermore if a record is updated (say a book is returned) it would be tempting to update only the field indicating if the book has been borrowed and not the details of who had borrowed it. Consider a program which in order to print out lists of borrowers merely looked at the borrower field of book records. Such a program could appear to work perfectly yet produce incorrect results if we had been lazy in updating a record structure which always had the same fields. Thus by using variant records we prevent accidental reference to invalid fields.

Secondly, by using variant records, an optimising compiler can often reduce the amount of space required to store a record by overlapping alternative fields. This is not the case in this example because in each set of variant parts only one alternative actually contains any extra fields.

The moral here is to try to design data structures in such a way as to minimise the chances of invalid values being obtained

4. We will now turn to the main program which interactively updates the database. This program also contains a number of procedures to read information from the terminal. These are similar in structure to those used in the creation program. Procedures to write out the records are also fairly straightforward. We have included a simple date reading routine, but this

could be made more elaborate alone the lines of the exercise in chapter seven.

The index arrays which we decided to use are created by the three functions ***createborrowerarray***, ***createbooksbyauthor***, and ***createbooksbytitle***. The functions return the length of the arrays which is a necessary value for use in later manipulations. We have written simple bubble sort routines to sort these arrays, but more efficient algorithms could have been used (see chapter three).

5. Before examining in more detail the workings of the program it is worth looking at the principles upon which it is based.

Unless the principles underlying a program are clear it is unlikely that a working program can be written

6. We are limited to strictly sequential files (according to the Pascal standard). A more efficient implementation could have been achieved using direct access files, but again this would introduce system dependent features. Whatever operation is required we follow the same basic process. First of all the index arrays are searched using a binary search to find out which record on a file we are interested in (book or person). All records up to, but not including, that one are then copied onto a temporary file. That record is then manipulated as required and written onto the temporary file. The rest of the original file is then copied onto the temporary file, and finally the temporary file is copied back onto the original to produce the updated file.

The same basic process can be re-used for clarity

7. Once we have got a clear idea idea of how each of the required operations is to be carried out the actual implementation is straightforward, but rather longwinded, simply because very similar routines have to be written for both types of file (book and person). The processes of borrowing and returning books follow much the same pattern but require slightly different checks. In order to make the operation of the program clearer we will look at what happens when someone wishes to borrow a book.

In order to borrow a book the user selects option b. This causes the procedure ***borrow*** to be called. This procedure is given a number of parameters:

the name of the book file — books
the name of the file of borrowers — borrowers
the various index files — borrowersbyname, booksbyauthor, booksbytitle
the number of borrowers — noborrowers
the number of books — nobooks
the date (to check for overdue books) — today

The procedure ***borrow*** first of all asks for the name of the user. (It could be argued that this should be done when the user first sits down at a terminal and then all subsequent transactions assume that user's name until another user signs on. This alternative approach is left as an exercise for the reader.) A function ***findname*** is used to locate the user's name in the index file. It returns a value true or false depending upon whether the user name is found. The position of the borrower (if any) is returned via a var parameter ***borrowindex***. In order to find a borrower the procedure needs to have access to

the name of the file of borrowers
the index to the borrowers (borrowersbyname)
the number of borrowers

In addition a temporary file is required so that the file can be updated by the method outlined earlier. The parameter ***tempborrowers*** is this file.

In some ways this function is a very bad function in that it has a number of side effects:

(1) it returns a result via one of its parameters (borrowindex)
(2) it reads part way through one file (borrowers)
(3) it partially creates a second file (tempborrowers).

It is, however, difficult to see how such behaviour can easily and efficiently be avoided.

Remember that functions and procedures with side effects should be used with care and should always be clearly commented

8. Let us now look at the procedure ***findname*** in more detail. It is also called by a number of other procedures which need to locate a user's name.

The procedure ***checkname***, which is defined within ***findname***, compares a name on the file with the name input from the terminal (***inname***) and asks if this is the right person. The main body of ***findname*** has a number of stages. Firstly it reads a name from the terminal using the procedure ***readname*** which is similar to the one used in the file creation program. This procedure has been made very general by including as a parameter the input file. The function ***searchname*** looks the name up in the index file ***borrowersbyname*** using a simple binary search algorithm. A value of 0 is returned if the name is not found. Note that all comparisons are based only on surname.

Assuming that the surname is found, the procedure ***copypeopleto*** copies all the records preceding the one to be looked at onto the file ***tempborrowers***. The function ***checkname*** returns a false value when the correct person is found and is used to control the WHILE loop in the main body of ***findname***. This loop is repeated until either the correct person is found or all people with that surname are exhausted. Individual records are copied across from the file ***borrowers*** to the file ***tempborrowers***. If the user's name has been found the function ***findname*** terminates with the required record being the one currently accessible on the file ***borrowers***. That is the record pointed at by the buffer variable ***borrowers^*** is the record that needs to be modified. Otherwise it tidies things up by resetting the file ***borrowers***.

Control will now pass back to the procedure ***borrow***. A similar procedure is followed to find the correct book record. One difference is that we can search for a book either by title or by author. Should we be successful in finding the appropriate person and book the procedure ***borrowbook*** is called with a particular person and a particular book as parameters. The other parameters are the catalogue number of the book, the membership number of the reader and today's date.

A number of checks need to be made including whether the book is a reference book. We also check whether the book has already been loaned. The final check made is whether the borrower is to be permitted to borrow the book. The record for a borrower contains a flag indicating whether (s)he has any overdue books. Further borrowing is not permitted if (s)he has. Furthermore each borrower is limited to the number of books (s)he is permitted to borrow.

It might be argued that these checks could be made before actually looking for the book but then the borrowing process becomes more disjoint. It is usually better to keep related actions together in one procedure or function. The final action of the procedure ***borrowbook*** is to update the records of the borrower and of the book including setting the date due back (procedure ***setreturndate***).

The final tidying up is left to the procedure ***borrow*** which copies the rest of the borrower and book files to the temporary versions and then copies the updated versions back.

A serious program rarely does just one thing !

9. The original problem specification suggested that books and people may be added to and deleted from the lists. Adding records is fairly easy. They would just be appended to the files, and the index files updated accordingly. Deleting records is harder, as the index file relies on the position of records in the files to find them. It could be done by maintaining lists of deleted records and then when the program is terminated the files could be compacted to remove redundant records. We will leave these extensions as an exercise.

Plus ultra (look up the motto of the Royal Society)

10. It should be noted how the fully parameterised nature of the procedures in this program forces us to declare a large number of user-defined types in

order to permit us to pass information to and from those procedures. Here we have an example of the swings and roundabouts phenomenon. In order for the compiler to protect us against silly slips, we are forced to create a large number of user-defined types in order to be able to pass information from procedure to procedure via parameters. This is a healthy safeguard. The cost which we pay is that we have to have the ingenuity to think up a number of different names for objects which are in fact only slightly different.

An advantage of the fully parameterised approach we have taken is that it should be relatively straightforward for groups of procedures in this program to be compiled as separate modules. As we pointed out at the start of this discussion this is actually what would be done in any realistic system.

Costs and benefits go together. Consider the benefits

10

The use of pointers

PROBLEM STATEMENT 29 LINKED LISTS — DYNAMIC ALLOCATION

TOPICS COVERED
- Static v. dynamic allocation of memory
- Pointers
- The importance of the NIL pointer
- Creation of a list — stack insertion
- The logic of dynamic allocation
- NEW and DISPOSE
- Iteration and Recursion
- (While and If)

There is stored on disk, in a text-file called ***linkfile***, a list of names and telephone numbers. The task facing the programmer is a relatively simple one — to get these items from disk into the main memory of the computer, and then to print them out on the screen. Many people would automatically reach for an array as an appropriate data structure. If one has a compiler which permits the use of conformant arrays, this may be possible. As noted earlier, this may be available if the compiler reaches compliance level 1 of the international standard. At compliance level 0, unfortunately, an array must be of a fixed maximum size. The question is "What maximum size?" This involves several problems. Firstly, we have no idea how many cases there are on the file — 2, 2000, or 2 million. How do we decide what maximum size to use? If we make it too small, there will not be enough room to process all the cases, and we are likely to be trying to insert cases off the end of the array. If we declare our array to be 1000 long, and there are 1001 people on file, the program will quite simply fail — with an "array index out of range" error. What if we try to make the array large enough for any amount of data? This causes two difficulties. Supposing that we make the array 1000 long, and there are only 200 cases. In this instance, we shall have allocated 800 array elements which are never used. Note that though they are never used, they are still allocated to the task and are not available for other purposes. So we may very well not have enough room to do other things which we wish to do in our program.

The other difficulty is that we may quite simply not be able to declare an array large enough for our purposes. It is quite common for the array area to of the order of 64 kilobytes. On the machine which we use (which is a 5 megabyte machine) and with the compiler which we use most regularly, there is a stringent limit. For records of the kind used in this example — 2 strings, each of 30 characters (one for the name, the other for the phone number) — the largest array which the compiler permitted us to use was just under 1100 long. If our data-file had contained more than 1100 people, then we would have been trying to insert them into non-existent slots!

It is possible to overcome this problem, but it is fiddly. One has to re-use the array. That is, one would have to read in the first 1000 people, process them in some way (say, print out their details), and then set the array index back to 1 and use the space over again for the next 1000 .... and so on. This is a clumsy "fix"; it is not a natural way of proceeding. Also, if we needed all the people in memory at one time, say for sorting them into order, we would face further complications.

Fortunately, there is a way out of this difficulty. Rather than using STATIC allocation, which is what we have with an array (since we allocate the space when we declare the array, and it is fixed or static from then on), we can use DYNAMIC allocation. There are many ways of doing this. In the program used in this section we construct a linked list.

This, like most structures built using dynamic allocation, makes use of the data type ***pointer***. We declare a record which contains, in this case, two fields of information (name and phone number) and one field, called ***next***, which is a pointer to the next record in the list. Of course, for other applications we could have far more fields of information, and, if we so desired, many more pointers. For the moment, let us keep it simple.

PROGRAM

```
program linklist(input,output,linkfile);
const  stringlength=30;
type   string=packed array[1..stringlength] of char;
       ptr=^person;
       person=record
              name, phone : string;
              next : ptr;
       end;
var    linkfile :text;
       head, newone : ptr;
{-----------------------------------------------------------------------}
procedure readstring ( var subfile : text; var substring : string);
var     index : integer;
begin  for index:= 1 to stringlength do substring [index] := ' ';
       index := 0;
       while not eoln ( subfile ) and ( index < stringlength ) do
       begin  index := index + 1;
              read ( subfile, substring [index] )
       end;
       readln ( subfile )
end; {readstring}
```

```
{-----------------------------------------------------------------------}
procedure writestring (var subfile : text; substring : string; newline :
                              boolean);
var     index : integer;
begin
        for index := 1 to stringlength do write ( subfile, substring [index]);
        if newline then writeln ( subfile )
end; {writestring}
{-----------------------------------------------------------------------}
procedure create(var subfile:text; var subnew:ptr);
begin
        new(subnew);
        with subnew^ do
        begin
                readstring(subfile, name);
                readstring(subfile, phone);
                next :=nil
        end
end; {create}
{-----------------------------------------------------------------------}
procedure stackinsert(subnew:ptr;var subhead:ptr);
begin
        subnew^.next:=subhead;
        subhead:=subnew
end; {stackinsert}
{-----------------------------------------------------------------------}
procedure display(oneperson:ptr);
begin
        with oneperson^ do
        begin
                writestring(output,name,false);
                writestring(output,phone,true)
        end
end;
{display}
{-----------------------------------------------------------------------}

procedure itprint(subhead:ptr);
begin
        while subhead<>nil do
        begin
                display(subhead);
                subhead:=subhead^.next
        end
end; {itprint}
{-----------------------------------------------------------------------}
```

```
procedure recprint(subhead:ptr);
begin
        if subhead<>nil then
        begin
                recprint(subhead^.next);
                display(subhead)
        end
end; {recprint}
{--------------------------------------------------------------------------}
begin  {MAIN}
        head := nil;
        reset(linkfile);
        while not eof(linkfile) do
        begin
                create(linkfile,newone);
                stackinsert(newone,head)
        end;
        writeln('ITERATIVE');
        writeln;
        itprint(head);
        writeln;
        writeln('RECURSIVE');
        writeln;
        recprint(head)
end.
```

RESULTS

```
ITERATIVE

Bartlett, Melanie    0232-56129
McArthur, Douglas    021-346-8174
Williams, Jane       0876-65439
Ossigton, Al         01-543-9876
Bartlett, George     0232-56129
Anderson, Hans       098-321-5186
Lyon, Pierre         01-444-345681
Williams. Harry      0987-65127
Leggatt, M           0656-65456
Garrison, K          0101-215-6501
Matthews, Bill       01-765-8632
Jones, John          01-345-6789
```

RECURSIVE

```
Jones, John          01-345-6789
Matthews, Bill       01-765-8632
Garrison, K          0101-215-6501
Leggatt, M           0656-65456
```

Williams. Harry 0987-65127
Lyon, Pierre 01-444-345681
Anderson, Hans 098-321-5186
Bartlett, George 0232-56129
Ossigton, Al 01-543-9876
Williams, Jane 0876-65439
McArthur, Douglas 021-346-8174
Bartlett, Melanie 0232-56129

DISCUSSION

1. The first thing to note is that the order of declarations is rather unusual. Normally one is not permitted to mention an object until it has been declared. In the case of dynamic structures this creates a problem. It is common for one type to be a pointer to another. The second one is normally a record containing a field which is itself of the pointer type. We have a problem in that the pointer declaration must mention the record, while the record declaration must mention the pointer. Which should come first?

Pascal recognises this problem and relaxes its strict rules for this special case. Thus we are able to write:

```
ptr=^person;
```

even though ***person*** has not yet been declared. Of course, we do go on to declare it immediately afterwards, and naturally its declaration includes a reference to ***ptr***. This is of the form:

```
next : ptr;
```

When using pointers, one can mention an object before it is declared

2. Note also that although we have a record type ***person*** we have no variables of that type. The only way we can find a ***person*** is via a pointer to it. In fact, one common feature of programs containing dynamic structures is that they tend to have relatively few global variables. In the present example, we have only three — ***linkfile*** whence comes the data, ***head*** which is a variable telling us where to find the first record in the list, and ***newone*** which is only a temporary variable anyway and is constantly being re-used.

With dynamic pointer-constructed objects, few variables are needed

3. The general method for creating a list should be straightforward. It is in a ***while not eof*** loop. For each case encountered, i.e. two lines of the file, we firstly create a record, and then we insert that record in a list starting at ***head***. If there are more cases to be read, we create another record and

then insert that one in the list starting at ***head*** .... and so on. The general structure is:

```
while not eof (somefile) do
begin
        create a node from the file;
        insert that node in the list
end;
```

4. We hope that the logic of creating a node is clear. Recall that we are reading data from a file. We have defined a ***person*** to consist of ***name***, ***phone***, and ***next***. To make a node (which we have called a ***person***), we merely have a procedure to create one. As usual, we have given this procedure an obvious name — ***create***. This procedure will be called many times, once for each person in the list, in fact. It is, however, necessary to declare it only once. It does three things:

A. It allocates the space for the new record, using the statement:

```
new(subnew);
```

This finds enough memory locations to store a ***person*** and then makes a note of whereabouts in the computer these locations start. So, if a person is to be stored starting at location 42186, then the value stored in ***subnew*** will be 42186.

B. It reads a name and phone number into the relevant fields of the record at 42186.

C. It sets the value of the ***next*** field of the record to nil. This may seem surprising, but it is a form of initialisation. Almost all dynamic structures depend heavily upon nil values at some point in their life. If you are printing out a list, for example, you normally keep on doing it until you come to a nil pointer. If, for whatever reason, the machine never finds a nil pointer, i.e. a pointer field whose value is nil, strange things can happen. Sometimes the program just fails with a message such as "attempted access via nil pointer". This merely means that instead of trying to write out, say, ***42186^.name*** you have tried to write out ***nil^.name!*** Sometimes, records start to point back at themselves and you get a circular list printed out over and over again. Very many of these mysterious errors occur simply because you have failed to initialise a pointer to the value nil. A simple and obvious way of ensuring that this can never happen is to include one or more pointer initialisation statements inside the procedure which creates the node in the first place.

Having a separate *create* procedure saves a lot of work later

5. Note that the pointer parameter ***subnew*** is a var parameter. This is

because it MUST be passed back to the main program. The purpose of ***create*** is to allocate and fill a record somewhere in the machine's main memory. If we do not consciously make a note of where that somewhere is, it will be forgotten and we shall never again be able to find the record. So the address of the record is stored in ***subnew***. If this was a value parameter, it would lose this value as soon as the procedure was completed, i.e. before the record had been inserted in the list. Recall that the procedure is used with the call:

```
create( subfile, newone);
```

and ***newone*** will be inserted in the list starting at ***head***. This insertion takes place only after ***create*** has finished its work. So the value of ***subnew*** must be transferred to ***newone***. A var parameter is the safest mechanism for doing this.

Var parameters are essential if you wish to pass values back

6. There are at least three ways of inserting nodes into a linked list — at the top, at the bottom, and somewhere in the middle (say, in alphabetical order). All three are fairly simple. We have here used the simplest form, called stack insertion — hence the name of the procedure. This inserts each new record at the top of the list. This is sometimes difficult to visualise, but it merely means that the variable ***head*** always points to the most recent record read and inserted. That record in turn points to the next most recent, that to the next, and so on. This means that the first record which was read in has been pushed all the way down to the bottom. If we were to print out the list starting at ***head*** and continuing step by step, following each ***next*** pointer, the list would be printed out in reverse order to that in which it was originally read in. In fact, a stack is often called a LIFO structure, standing for Last In First Out. It has many applications in systems programming.

Stacks are very simple lists to build

7. The way in which the insertion works is also straightforward; indeed the only mysterious part is the insertion of the very first record. Note that the procedure contains only two statements:

```
subnew^.next := subhead;
subhead := subnew;
```

Recall that the actual parameters corresponding to these two were ***newone*** and ***head***. This means that the first step is to get the new record to point to the record which was previously at the top of the list. We do this by assigning the value of subhead (i.e. ***head***) to ***subnew^.next*** (i.e. ***newone^.next***). At this point we merely have two pointers to the old first record; we have not actually done the insertion. This is carried out by the next statement in which we give the value of subnew (***newone***) to subhead (***head***). This means that he head of the list is at long last pointing at the new record, the one which we have just read in using ***create***.

The point about the first record is as follows. The first record read in will eventually be at the bottom of the list. So its ***next*** field will need to be set to nil, otherwise later in the program we shall never know when we have got to the bottom. The code of this procedure does not need to be modified to take care of this special case. At the very beginning of the main body of the program we initialised ***head*** with the statement ***head := nil***. Hence, the very first time we try to insert a record (the one which will eventually be at the bottom) the statement ***subnew^.next := subhead*** ensures that this record's ***next*** field is nil, which is what it should be. This is yet another example of how sensible initialisation simplifies the coding considerably.

Finally, notice how simple and brief the code is. This procedure for inserting in a stack consists of only two statements. Such simplicity is the norm for well-written programs involving dynamic structures. Indeed, when one starts to handle such structures recursively, one often finds that one is using procedures which consist of only one statement much of the time!

Procedures for dynamic structures are commonly brief and simple

8. Note that ***subhead*** must be a var parameter, since it passes back a pointer value to ***head***. The other parameter, ***subnew***, does not need to be: it may be, indeed should be, a value parameter. This is because the address of the new record is not changed merely by it being inserted in the list. It is still in the same place in the machine's memory and thus its address should remain the same. In fact, if we changed it we might never find the record again. "But", one is tempted to ask, "we use the statement ***subnew^.next := subhead***". Does this not mean that ***subnew*** is changed and should be a var parameter? The answer is a resounding "No". What is stored in location 42186 (or wherever) has been changed — it is, however, still in location 42186. That value must not be changed; therefore, we need a value parameter.

Changing a field does not change where the record is stored

9. We use two procedures to print out the list. Both of them use a further procedure ***display*** to print out a single person. It is important to distinguish the two processes. Processing a list involves processing a single record many times; one merely processes a different record each time. Having a procedure to process a single record is frequently a means of making this clear. It also saves a lot of typing.

A procedure to process a single record helps in processing an entire list

10. The first printing procedure ***itprint*** uses a process called iteration.

This merely involves processing a record, forgetting it and going on to the next record, processing that, forgetting and going on to the next, and so on until one reaches the end of a list. With arrays this is normally done with one or more FOR loops. In arrays we normally know how many steps to take before we start. In the case of linked lists and other dynamic structures, it is usually the case that the number of records (and hence steps to be taken) is unknown. Indeed, it is this factor which often leads us to use a dynamic structure in the first place. So we cannot use a method which depends upon counting.

Instead, we take the view that we will process records until we come to one which has the pointer value nil. So the general method is:

```
while pointervariable<>nil do
begin
    process the record in pointervariable^
    go on to the next one
end;
```

Of course, the processing may be of any kind and of any degree of complexity. In our example, it is very simple, merely printing out a name and phone number. What you put in this step depends upon the application. Going on to the next record is, however, fairly standard. We merely write:

```
pointervariable := pointervariable^.next;
```

or, in our case:

```
subhead := subhead^.next;
```

This means that the next time round the loop, the new ***subhead*** with which we will be working will be the old ***subhead^.next***. If this new ***subhead*** has a meaningful value, then it will go on to perform the ***display*** operation using it. If this new ***subhead*** happens to be nil, then the ***while*** test will fail and it will not perform the loop any more, but will go on with whatever follows lower down the program. In our case this is a ***writeln***.

Iteration with pointers normally involves 2 steps:

```
process(x);
x := x^.next
```

11. Note that the loop has to be a ***while*** loop. A ***repeat*** would contain at least one major danger. What happens if we were processing a lot of lists and one or more of them happens to be empty, i.e. there is no one in it? Since our program involves initialising ***head*** to nil, if we insert nothing, ***head*** remains unchanged, and it will continue to have the value nil. This means that if we used a ***repeat*** loop (which of course is always entered at least once),

the machine would attempt to ***display (nil)***, which would give an error. You cannot print out something which isn't anywhere!

This could happen in practice if, say, we were processing orders for a large number of items. It is quite conceivable that on particular days, certain items are ordered by no-one at all. In that case there might be many lists whose head had the value nil. The use of a ***while*** loop safeguards us against disaster in such a case.

Of course, we could put in a test in all our procedures to ensure that any pointer parameter was not nil. This is somewhat cumbersome and very easy to overlook. Using the ***while*** loop form means that it is unnecessary. So why not do the safest and simplest thing?

Dynamic iteration is commonly performed using a <while> loop

12. The final procedure ***recprint*** uses a technique called recursion. This is quite different from iteration. It is more costly in machine resources, but has two compensating advantages:

(1) It oftens fits the problem more naturally and leads to clearer and simpler code which anyone can understand.

(2) It often does things which are difficult or impossible to do using iteration.

There are two crucial features of a recursive procedure. Firstly it must call itself. This means that if you have a procedure with the name ***recprint***, one of the statements INSIDE the procedure involves ***recprint*** itself. Thus you can have recprint calling recprint calling recprint calling recprint... and so on. Obviously, if it did this *ad infinitum*, you would quickly fill the machine with copies of ***recprint*** μ and its data. More important, logically the process would never end. Therefore, you need the second crucial feature. There must be some test inside the procedure which can effectively say "if some condition arises then DON'T call ***recprint*** again". This is called a terminating condition.

A recursive procedure has two crucial features:
a) it calls itself
b) it has a terminating condition

13. The normal structure is visually different from the structure of dynamic iteration. That, you will recall, normally had a ***while*** as the test for terminating it. Recursive procedures normally have an ***if*** as the test for a

terminating condition. When processing lists the normal recursive structure is:

```
if x <> nil then         OR   if x <> nil then
begin                         begin
        process (x)                   call itself
        call itself                   process (x)
end;                          end;
```

The outline on the left would process the list from the top downwards, i.e. it would do the processing and then go on to the next item. The output would be identical to that produced by iteration. In this case there would be little point in doing the job recursively, since it would involve additional costs, and would provide no benefit. By contrast, the one on the right works the other way round. The first thing it does is to go on to the second item, leaving the processing until it has finished with that second item. Within the second item, it would go on to the third item, leaving the processing of the second one until it has finished with the third. Eventually it will come to a pointer with a nil value. It will then have finished calling itself, but is left with all the processing to do. It will process the last meaningful item and will then be at the end of that call of the procedure. However, it will still be at the stage of the last-but-one item (which has called itself but not done any processing). So it processes the last-but-one, and has finished that recursive call. It is now on the last-but-two...... and so on, until the whole process has been unwound.

This means that the form on the left would print out the list from the head downwards (i.e. in reverse order to that in which it was read in — just like the iterative version). The one on the right would print it out from the bottom up, i.e. in the original order. All the printing out would be done INSIDE the first call — ***recprint(head)***. This procedure would start by calling itself — ***recprint (subhead^.next)*** — and would then wait until the whole list had been printed out, apart from the head node. Then, and only then, would it perform its own final action, that of printing out the name in the first node. Figure 1 perhaps shows more clearly than words can, just what is happening at each stage. The grey box shows the first call — ***recprint(head)***. This call remains in operation throughout and it does not finish, i.e. it does not ***display(head)*** until all the other calls have terminated. You can see how each call is like a card placed on top of a pile, or stack, of other cards. One first of all stacks the cards one on top of the other, and then one peels them off, performing the instructions which are revealed by this peeling-off operation.

Try it with an actual stack of cards. However, do it with a fairly short list

Our example uses a list of only four items, and that was quite difficult to fit

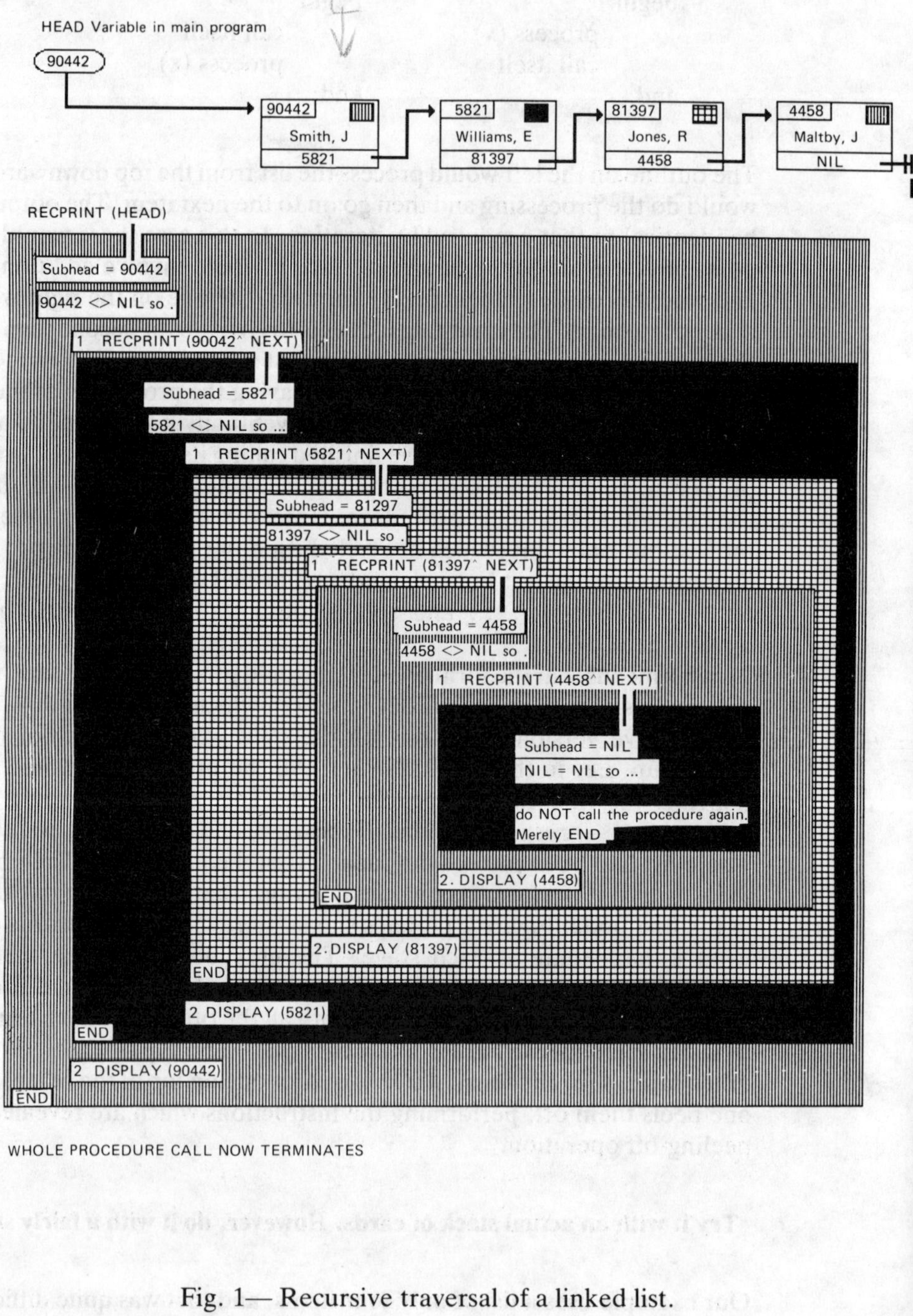

Fig. 1— Recursive traversal of a linked list.

onto a page. With longer lists, it becomes impossible to fit it within the confines of a single sheet of paper!

Recursion can go backwards more easily than can iteration

14. The purpose of using this dynamic structure in the first place was to allow us to handle data of unknown size. Recall that on our machine we were limited to arrays of about 1100 records. Could we actually get more using a dynamic linked list? When we tested the program above, we processed more than 90,000 records. In our case a different limitation came into force — our time limit was up. By altering the time limit, we were able to go far beyond this.

Dynamic structures can handle large numbers of data items

15. Of course, a computer is of a finite size, and eventually one will run out of memory, both real memory and virtual memory. This may not be until one has filled up several megabytes-worth (or even giga-bytes on some machines), but it will happen sooner or later. Thus there is a limitation even on dynamic structures which cannot be avoided if you need all your data at the same time. Of course, if you don't need them all at the same time, there is an operation ***dispose*** in Pascal which makes even more space available to you.

We do not have enough space in this book to discuss ***dispose*** fully, but to give you an idea of how it might work, here is a version of the ***itprint*** procedure which gives up a record when it has finished processing it. The memory space which had been used for the record, i.e. the locations starting at ***subhead***, will then be placed back on a list of free memory and can be used for other purposes.

```
{-----------------------------------------------------------------------}
procedure itprint(var subhead:ptr);
var     x:ptr;
begin
        while subhead<>nil do
        begin
                display(subhead);
                x:=subhead;
                subhead:=subhead^.next;
                dispose(x)
        end
end; {itprint}
{-----------------------------------------------------------------------}
```

Dynamic structures are powerful and flexible — learn to use them

PROBLEM STATEMENT 30 BINARY TREES — DYNAMIC ORDERING

TOPICS COVERED	Binary trees
	Logic of creation, insertion and traversal
	Recursive traversal
	Lexicographical ordering
	Run-time analysis — order (N) and (log N)

You have the same data, i.e. names and telephone numbers, as for the linked list exercise. However, on this occasion you have to store them in alphabetical order of the persons' names. Of course, you could do this with a linked list. The only problem would be that it would be a very time-consuming way of sorting them into order since on average you would need to go halfway through the list to insert a person each time (since the average person is in the middle of the alphabet). This means that insertion, deletion, or finding someone in the list can be time-consuming processes. As the list gets longer, the number of steps needed to insert someone in the right place increases proportionately. You may not mind taking 5 steps to insert someone in a list of 10 people, but you will probably object to taking 500 to insert someone in a list of 1000 people.

Fortunately there is a simple data-structure which can speed things up fairly dramatically. The linked list is proportional to the number of items in the list. This other structure is proportional to the logarithm (to the base 2) of the number of items in the list. The structure is called a binary tree. To give you an idea of the number of steps needed to insert a record in each structure, we give some typical figures below

	No. of steps needed	
No. of items to be stored	Linked list	Binary tree
10	5	3.3
100	50	6.6
1000	500	10.0
1000000	500000	20.0

As you can see, the larger the number of items, the greater the saving from using the binary tree. There are other storage methods more efficient still, and these are dealt with in a topic called Data Structures, but for the moment the sort of improvement outlined above will be sufficient for our purposes.

What, then, is a binary tree? It is made up of nodes (records) just like the linked list. Like the linked list, it has a single head. As it is a tree, this is often called the ***root***. Like the linked list, it is held together by pointers.

However, it differs from the linked list in the number of pointers needed. The list had only one pointer in each record, which we called ***next***. The tree, however, has two pointers, usually called ***left*** and ***right***.

Suppose that the tree is going to be maintained in alphabetical order. In the list, ***next*** pointed to the following record in the list. In the tree, we have two pointers. The ***left*** pointer points to a node whose ***name*** field comes before the current node's ***name*** in the alphabet. That does not mean that it is the immediately preceding name, merely that it is *A* preceding name. Similarly, the ***right*** pointer points to a record whose ***name*** field comes after the current record's ***name*** field. Thus, if the current node contained the name 'Thomas', its left pointer might indicate a node containing 'Martin', and its right pointer might indicate a node containing 'Victor'. Similarly, Martin's right son might be 'Peter'. Note that his right son could not be 'William'. If 'William' was put in the tree he would be to the RIGHT of 'Thomas'. If he was the right son of 'Martin' he would have to be to the LEFT of 'Thomas', which would violate the rules which make up the tree. Figure 2, page 257 shows this digrammatically.

This means that wherever you are in the tree, all the records alphabetically before the one you are currently visiting lie in the sub-tree pointed to by ***left*** and all the records alphabetically after the current one lie in the sub-tree pointed to by ***right***. This does not mean that they are necessarily in the very next record pointed to. It does mean, though, that if the person is in the list, that is where you have to start looking.

If the person you are looking for is not in that next record, treat it as the current record and do the same — look in ITS left or right sub-tree. You carry on doing this until either you find the person you are looking for or the sub-tree you are about to go into consists of a nil pointer. In this case, you can be sure that the person you are looking for is not actually in the tree.

That may sound complicated. It is in fact very simple, especially if you do it recursively. Here is one way of doing it.

PROGRAM

```
program tree(input,output,linkfile);
const  stringlength=30;
type
        string=packed array[1..stringlength] of char;
        ptr=^node;

        node=record
                name, phone :string;
                left, right      :ptr
        end;
var
        linkfile:text;
        head, newone :ptr;
```

```
{---------------------------------------------------------------------------}
procedure readstring ( var subfile : text; var substring : string);
var     index : integer;
begin   for index:= 1 to stringlength do substring [index] := ' ';
        index := 0;
        while not eoln ( subfile ) and ( index < stringlength ) do
        begin
                index := index + 1;
                read ( subfile, substring [index] )
        end;
        readln ( subfile )
end; {readstring}
{---------------------------------------------------------------------------}
procedure writestring (var subfile : text; substring : string; newline :
                        boolean);
var     index : integer;
begin
        for index := 1 to stringlength do write ( subfile, substring [index]);
        if newline then writeln ( subfile )
end; {writestring}
{---------------------------------------------------------------------------}
procedure create(var subfile:text; var subnew:ptr);
begin
        new(subnew);
        with subnew^ do
        begin   readstring(subfile,name);
                readstring(subfile,phone);
                left:=nil; right:=nil
        end
end; {create}
{---------------------------------------------------------------------------}
procedure insert(subnew:ptr; var subhead:ptr);
begin
if subhead=nil then subhead:=subnew else
if subnew^.name<subhead^.name then insert(subnew,subhead^.left)
   else insert(subnew,subhead^.right)
end; {insert}
{---------------------------------------------------------------------------}
procedure display(oneperson:ptr);
begin
        with oneperson^ do
        begin
                writestring(output,name,false);
                writestring(output,phone,true)
        end
end; {display}
{---------------------------------------------------------------------------}
```

```
procedure treeprint(subhead:ptr);
begin
      if subhead<>nil then
      begin
            treeprint(subhead^.left);
            display(subhead);
            treeprint(subhead^.right)
      end
end; {treeprint}
{------------------------------------------------------------------}
begin {MAIN}
      head:=nil;
      reset(linkfile);
      while not eof(linkfile) do
      begin create(linkfile,newone);
            insert(newone,head)
      end;
      writeln('LIST IN ORDER');
      writeln;
      treeprint(head)
end.
```

RESULTS

LIST IN ORDER

```
Anderson, Hans       098-321-5186
Bartlett, George     0232-56129
Bartlett, Melanie    0232-56129
Garrison, K          0101-215-6501
Jones, John          01-345-6789
Leggatt, M           0656-65456
Lyon, Pierre         01-444-345681
Matthews, Bill       01-765-8632
McArthur, Douglas    021-346-8174
Ossigton, Al         01-543-9876
Williams, Jane       0876-65439
Williams. Harry      0987-65127
```

DISCUSSION

1. Note that the program has apparently failed. Surely Harry Williams should come before Jane Williams; after all, H comes before J in the alphabet. That is true. However, if you look carefully you will see that the machine has done exactly what we told it to do.

What is the punctuation symbol between Williams and Jane? And what is the one between Williams and Harry ? In the case of Jane it is a comma (,) while for Harry it is a full-stop (.). This means that the strings of characters which it is comparing are <Williams,> (with a comma) and <Williams.> (with a full-stop). We have talked about alphabetical ordering, but really we should have called it lexicographical ordering. The system of characters used by the computer, most commonly the ASCII code, consists of a lot more than just letters. There are, for example, the digits from '0' to '9'. There are all sorts of symbols like '#' and our usual punctuation symbols, including ',' and '.'.

Humans are able to put letters and numbers into order. What, though, would we do if we were asked to put into order the three names below:

'!@#$%^&*()'
'−=&^%$++!'
'−=&^%$++~'

Of course, most of us would be baffled. We have in our heads a 'natural' ordering of letters and digits because they have been with us since our earliest days at school. We do not, though, have any sense of order for these special characters. The computer, however, must have such an order. That order is the one imposed by the underlying character set, usually ASCII. As you have probably guessed by now, in that character set the symbol ',' comes before '.' Therefore, the machine was quite correct in placing 'Williams, Jane' before 'Williams. Harry'. The fault lies not with the machine but with either the person who typed in the data or the programmer who did not go to the trouble to tell the machine to ignore things other than letters when making its comparisons ! In a real-life production system, the programmer ought to take such a precaution.

Apparent errors often provide instructive lessons

2. Note that the declarations are very similar to those for the linked list program. The only difference is that the record contains the two pointers, ***left*** and ***right***. Apart from that they are identical. The ***const***, the ***ptr***, the ***string***, even the variable names — they are all the same apart from that small difference of having two pointers instead of one. In fact, you can often copy a set of declarations and make slight modifications, thus saving on time and typing errors.

Dynamic structures have a family resemblance in their declarations

3. The logic of the process of building a tree is the same as that of building a list. As long as we are not at the end of the datafile we perform two operations — ***create*** and ***insert***. The details of what happens inside these two procedures is slightly different for a tree than it is for a list. The overall logic, however, is the same. We create a node, then we insert it.

Get the overall logic right, the details will follow naturally

4. Note also that the ***create*** procedure is almost identical with its

counterpart in the linked list program. Since there are two pointers, we must of course initialise them both. This we do by setting both of them to nil. Apart from that, the procedure to create a node is the same.

Initialisation matters, whether you have 1 pointer or 200

5. The most interesting feature of this program is the actual ***insert*** procedure. This can be done iteratively, although that is a somewhat cumbersome method. However, you should now be at a stage where you can start to think recursively, so we have included a recursive insert.

This procedure consists of only one statement. Yes, only one statement to implement the cumbersome description which we gave above. It is a single statement consisting of 2 IFs and 2 ELSEs. The logic is:

(1) If you have come to a nil pointer, this is where the new person should be located — so join them up ...... ELSE

(2) If the name of the person to be inserted is less than the name in the node which you are currently visiting you have to try to the left. So call ***insert*** using the current node's left son as the root of the new tree to try... ELSE

(3) The new person has got to find their home somewhere in the right subtree so try there. Call ***insert*** using the right son as the root of the new tree to try.

6. That logic reflects exactly the code written in the procedure. Suppose we were inserting the first person into an empty tree (with ***head*** of course initialised to nil). We would write:

```
insert(newone, head);
```

and inside the procedure ***newone*** would be matched with ***subnew*** and ***head*** would be matched with ***subhead***. Now, since ***head*** is nil, so will ***subhead*** be. Thus the first line of the procedure will fire and the action taken, at the very first call of the procedure will be to give the value of ***newone*** to ***subhead*** and thus, via the parameter passing — remember that ***subhead*** is a var parameter — ***head*** will take on the value of ***newone***. This is exactly what we want the first time.

Parameter passing takes care of the actual insertion

7. What, though, if we are inserting further down the tree after hundreds or thousands of other records have already been inserted. Remember that it is in the nature of the insertion process that we attach a new record only when we come across a nil pointer. That was true at the top of the tree, and is equally true no matter how deeply we descend within it. This is because we

are always trying to insert ***newone*** into a tree — albeit a sub-tree. Suppose that, 10 levels down in the tree, we are visiting a record whose pointer has the value 56422 and which is therefore to be found at memory location 56422. Now clearly 56422 is not equal to nil (since it is equal to 56422), so the machine has to make a comparison on the names in ***newone*** and in the record at 56422. Let us suppose that ***newone***'s name is Zacharias while 56422's name is Williams. Clearly we have to try to go right and the machine will make the recursive call:

```
insert(subnew, subhead^.right);
```

In plainer English this means "try to insert Zacharias's record in 56422's right sub-tree". In this call to the procedure ***subnew*** will match with ***subnew*** (!) while the new ***subhead*** will match with 56422^.right. If 56422^.right happens to be nil we will get the assignment:

```
subhead := subnew;
```

which passing back actually means:

```
56422^.right := Zacharias's record location
```

We suggest that you draw up a few diagrams like the one given in Figure 3 on page 260 and work through this. It sometimes takes a while to click, but when it does it is surprisingly simple. It is in the nature of recursive procedures, once you have mastered them, that you are always doing things in the right place. With iteration you will find that you are often one step past where you want to be before you realise that you have forgotten where you last were! That statement summarises a profound truth about pointer structures.

Recursion simplifies the process of keeping track of where you are

8. Printing out the tree in order is also much simpler than one would at first imagine. After all one must go arbitrarily as far left as possible, which might be 20 levels or none at all. One must then go up one level. One then has to go right for an unknown distance. At each point one has to do the same again. It all seems terribly confusing. In fact, it is simplicity itself as long as you realise that a tree is a recursively defined structure, and that at every point you are dealing, not with a single record, but with a tree. Let us look at what a binary tree can be. In fact, it can be one of only two things:

(1) A nil pointer
(2) A tree with two sub-trees.

Thus every node will be a tree. It may have two large sub-trees with hundreds of nodes in each. It may have two barren sons (which of course are trees each with two sub-trees, which gives us 4 trees below that, all of which

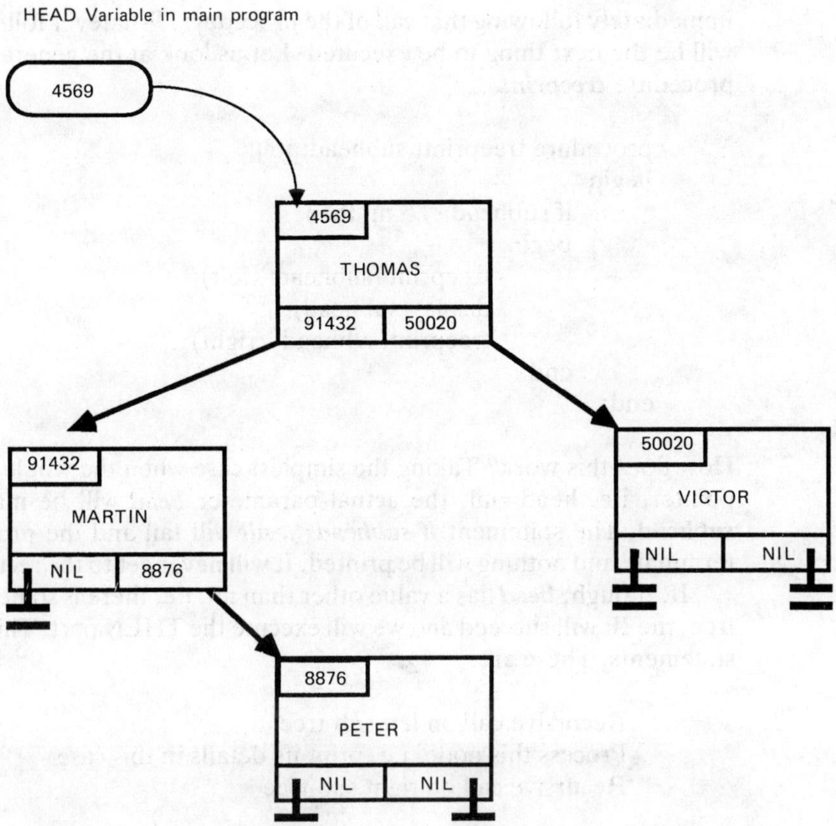

Fig. 2 — A very simple tree (which will be traversed in Figure 3).

are nil pointers). It may itself be a nil pointer. It should be apparent that this definition fits neatly into our paradigm of a recursive procedure. Point (1) is the terminating condition while point (2) is the recursive condition.

Thus, the nil pointer is fundamental to our operations. There will be many nil pointers — at least one at the end of every branch of the tree and two on the leaf nodes. It is fundamental because it represents the terminating condition. This is one of the reasons why we have to take great care with our initialisations. Failing to initialise one of the sons at, say, the ***create*** stage may show up at the insert stage, or perhaps only at the printing out stage. The origin of the error may be quite mysterious and difficult to trace.

Nil pointers really matter — pay attention to them

9. As usual with a recursive procedure the terminating condition is an IF (not a WHILE), with the test being for the current pointer being nil. If it is nil, nothing further is done in the procedure; it merely terminates since the only statement left is ***end;***. This leaves the program back at the point

immediately following that call of the procedure. Whatever follows that call will be the next thing to be executed. Let us look at the general method of procedure ***treeprint***.

```
procedure treeprint( subhead:ptr);
begin
        if subhead <> nil then
        begin
                treeprint (subhead^.left);
                display(subhead);
                treeprint(subhead^.right)
        end
end;
```

How does this work? Taking the simplest case when the whole tree is a nil pointer, i.e. head=nil, the actual parameter ***head*** will be matched with ***subhead***. The statement ***if subhead<>nil*** will fail and the procedure will terminate and nothing will be printed. It will never get to the recursive calls.

If, though, ***head*** has a value other than nil, i.e. there is something in the tree, the IF will succeed and we will execute the THEN part. This involves 3 statements. These are:

Recursive call on left sub-tree
Process this node, i.e. print its details in this case
Recursive call on right sub-tree

The recursive call on the left sub-tree will involve all of these actions, and each further call will involve them too. Thus the whole of ***head***'s left sub-tree will be traversed (and printed out) before this call to ***treeprint(head^.left)*** is finished. When it has finished, the first call to ***treeprint*** will have only finished this one statement. Thus, although the whole left sub-tree has been printed out (perhaps hundreds or thousands of names), this was done with only one statement at the level of ***head***. It has finished statement 1 at this level and of course will go remorselessly on to statement 2. That asks it to print out ***head***'s details. Note that it does this only after the entire left sub-tree has been processed, so it will be in the correct order. Having done this there is only one more statement (at this level) to execute. This is the call to traverse the right sub-tree. This may be as (or even more) complicated as the traversal of the left sub-tree. Even though it is only one statement at this level, it generates many statements lower down the tree.

The analysis of what happens at the ***head*** node is true of what happens at every other meaningful node.

An ordered tree traversal is the same for every sub-tree

10. In the linked list example above we tried to clarify matters with a

diagram. Let us try it again. The diagrams (Figures 2 and 3) are very similar. The only difference is is that instead of having a two-step procedure, we have a three-step one. Instead of:

```
        if x<>nil then
        begin
                CALL    NEXT
                DISPLAY
        end
```

we have:

```
        if x<>nil then
        begin
                CALL LEFT
                DISPLAY
                CALL RIGHT
        end
```

In terms of visualising what is happening one might well try to imagine cards being stacked up. With a linked list, each card had ONE other card piled onto it, and that had one on top of it. In the case of a binary tree, each card has TWO other cards stacked on top of it. Work through the diagram in Figure 3 on page 260.

PROBLEM STATEMENT 31 PALINDROMES REVISITED

TOPICS COVERED: Manipulation of strings as linked lists
Creation, Reversal, Comparison, Modifying
Comparison with packed arrays

In chapter seven we presented a problem on palindromes using strings stored as packed arrays of char. In this chapter we are going to repeat the exercise (more or less) but using a linked list representation. We require functions/procedures to do the following:

1) read a string of characters terminated by either space or end-of-line
2) write a string of characters
3) find the length of a string of characters
4) delete a string
5) reverse a string
6) encode a string by rotating the characters by a given factor (If we assumed that we only used the letters a–z then if we rotated by a factor of 5 then every a would be replaced by f, b by g, c by h, and so on. At the end of the alphabet z would be replaced by e — in other words we wrap round the end of the sequence. The same principle can be extended to the set of ASCII characters.)
7) decode a string which was encoded by the above procedure
8) check if a string is a palindrome

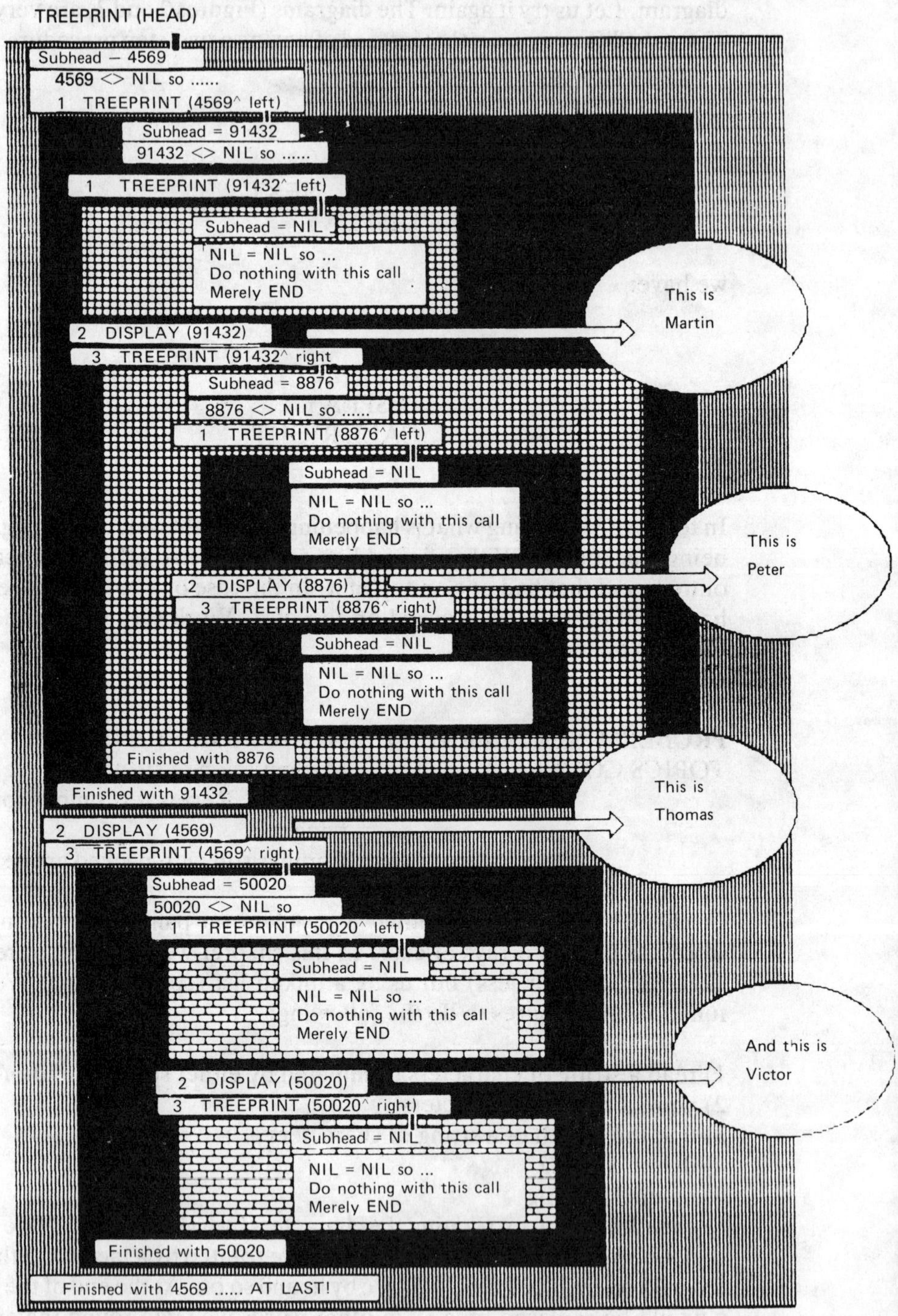
TREEPRINT (HEAD)
Subhead – 4569
4569 <> NIL so ......
1 TREEPRINT (4569^ left)
Subhead = 91432
91432 <> NIL so ......
1 TREEPRINT (91432^ left)
Subhead = NIL
NIL = NIL so ...
Do nothing with this call
Merely END
2 DISPLAY (91432)
This is
Martin
3 TREEPRINT (91432^ right
Subhead = 8876
8876 <> NIL so ......
1 TREEPRINT (8876^ left)
Subhead = NIL
NIL = NIL so ...
Do nothing with this call
Merely END
2 DISPLAY (8876)
This is
Peter
3 TREEPRINT (8876^ right)
Subhead = NIL
NIL = NIL so ...
Do nothing with this call
Merely END
Finished with 8876
Finished with 91432
This is
Thomas
2 DISPLAY (4569)
3 TREEPRINT (4569^ right)
Subhead = 50020
50020 <> NIL so
1 TREEPRINT (50020^ left)
Subhead = NIL
NIL = NIL so ...
Do nothing with this call
Merely END
And this is
Victor
2 DISPLAY (50020)
3 TREEPRINT (50020^ right)
Subhead = NIL
NIL = NIL so ...
Do nothing with this call
Merely END
Finished with 50020
Finished with 4569 ...... AT LAST!

Fig. 3

The above procedures/functions should be checked by writing a program which will read in a sentence from a text-file, find the first palindrome, and encode the sentence by rotating it by the length of the first palindrome. Sentences which contain no palindromes should be rotated by a factor of 10. A second program should decode sentences encoded by the first. Sentences will consist of a sequence of words separated by single spaces, and without punctuation. For ease of programming we will terminate sentences by end-of- file not by a full-stop, and the end-of-file marker may be assumed to occur after an end-of-line.

PROGRAM

```
program encrypt(straight,coded);
{program to encrypt sentences (containing no punctuation)
by rotating letters by the length of the first palindrome. The uncoded
sentence will be on a file called straight, and the coded sentence will be
output to a file called coded }
const  defaultrot = 10;          linelength = 80;

type   pstring= ^string;
       string  = record
                   this : char;
                   next : pstring
       end;
var    rotator                 : integer;
       found                   : boolean;
       word, codedword         : pstring;
       linecount               : integer;
       straight, coded         : text;

{--------------------------------------}

procedure readstring(var source : text; var result : pstring);
{procedure to read up to first space or end-of-line}
var    ch               : char;
       current, last    : pstring;
begin
       new(result);
       current := result;
       read(source,ch);
       while (not eoln(source)) and (ch <> ' ') do
       begin
              current^.this := ch;
              last := current;
              new(current^.next);
```

```
                current := current^.next;
                read(source,ch)
        end;
        if eoln(source) then
        begin
                current^.this := ch;
                current^.next := nil;
                readln(source)
        end else
        begin
                last^.next := nil;
                dispose(current)
        end
end; {readstring}
{---------------------------------------}

function length(given : pstring):integer;
{function returns length of string}
var     i : integer;
begin   i := 1;
        while given^.next <> nil do
        begin
                i := i + 1;
                given := given^.next
        end;
        length := i
end; {length}
{---------------------------------------}

procedure writestring(var dest : text; given : pstring);
{procedure to write a string}
begin
        while given <> nil do
        begin
                write(dest,given^.this);
                given := given^.next
        end
end; {writestring}
{---------------------------------------}

procedure reverse(fwd : pstring; var backward : pstring);
{procedure to reverse the string given in fwd and place it in background}
var
        current, last       : pstring;
begin
        new(current);
        current^.next := nil;
```

```
        while fwd <> nil do
        begin
                current^.this := fwd^.this;
                new(last)
                last^.next := current;
                current := last;
                fwd := fwd^.next
        end;
        backward := last^.next;
        dispose(current)
end; {reverse}
{--------------------------------------}
procedure encode(plain : pstring; var coded : pstring; rotfactor : integer);
{procedure to encode string plain into string coded by rotation by rotfactor}
var     current, last       : pstring;
begin
        new(coded)
        current := coded;
        while plain <> nil do
        begin
                current^.this := chr(ord(plain^.this)+rotfactor);
                new(current^.next);
                last := current;
                current := current^.next;
                plain := plain^.next
        end;
        last^.next := nil;
        dispose(current)
end; {encode}
{--------------------------------------}
function compare(given1,given2 : pstring):boolean;
{function to compare two strings and return value true iff they are identical}
var     equal : boolean;
begin   equal := true;
        while (given1 <> nil) and (given2 <> nil) and equal do
        begin
                equal := given1^.this = given2^.this;
                given1 := given1^.next;
                given2 := given2^.next
        end;
        if equal then compare := (given1 = nil) or (given2 = nil)
            else compare := false
end; {compare}
{--------------------------------------}
```

```
function palindrome(given : pstring):boolean;
{returns value true or false depending upon whether given string is palin-
drome or not}
var
        temp : pstring;
begin
        reverse(given,temp);
        palindrome := compare(given,temp)
end; {palindrome}
{----------------------------------------}
begin  {MAIN PROGRAM}
        reset(straight);
        repeat
                readstring(straight,word);
                found := palindrome(word)
        until found or eof(straight);
        if not found then rotator := defaultrot else rotator := length(word);
        reset(straight);
        rewrite(coded);
        linecount := 0;
        repeat
                readstring(straight,word);
                linecount := linecount + length(word);
                if linecount > linelength then
                begin
                        writeln(coded);
                        linecount := length(word)
                end;

                encode(word,codedword,rotator);
                writestring(coded,codedword);
                write(coded,' ')
        until eof(straight);
        writeln(coded)
end.
```

SAMPLE RESULTS

Here is the original uncoded file ***straight***.

the quick brown fox jumped over the lazy dog no palindromes yet madam

The resulting file ***coded*** produced by the program contains:

ymj vznhp gwt<s kt} ozruji t{jw ymj qf ~itl st ufqnsiwtrjx ~jy rfifr

The following is an octal dump of this file where bytes are interpreted as characters.

```
0000000   171 155 152 040 166 172 156 160 040 147 167 164 174 163 040
            y   m   j       v   z   n   h   p       g   w   t   |   s
0000020   153 164 175 040 157 172 162 165 152 151 040 164 173 152 167 04
            k   t   }           q       f 177   ~           i   t   l       s   t
0000060   165 146 161 156 163 151 167 164 162 152 170 040 176 152 171 04
            u   f   q   n   s   i   w   t   r   j   x           ~   j   y
0000100   162 146 151 146 162 040 012
            r   f   i   f   r      \n
0000107
```

The decoding program is the same as the encoding program except that th rotation factor is negated. Running this program gives us the following file:

the quick brown fox jumps over the lazy dog no palindromes yet madam.

DISCUSSION

1. The basic structure of the solution is the same as in the earlier example. Indeed the only change made in the main program is the name of the input procedure ***combinedread*** to ***readstring***. Obviously the changes are in the procedures because of the changed method of storing strings

A well-structured program is at an abstract level independent of the data structures used to implement it

2. In reading a string we have to create space for every character read. Similarly when encoding or reversing strings space has to be created. The advantage of this method is that strings of any length can be stored. The disadvantages are the increased storage required for short strings (each character has a pointer associated with it), and the need to write a specific comparison routine. An intermediate solution that is sometimes proposed to solve this problem of whether to use packed arrays or linked lists is to mix them. That is because it is wasteful of space to store a link for every character. Each node in the linked list is allowed to contain a number of characters, say 8. This solution retains the advantage of allowing strings of any length, whilst reducing the storage required. The price paid is an increasing complexity in the program.

All problem solutions have advantages and disadvantages

3. During the reading of the strings the algorithm we used caused an additional storage location to be created which we did not use in the end. We therefore used the standard procedure ***dispose*** to delete it. There is a

great danger in using linked lists that unwanted storage locations will be left around with no links left pointing to them.

Always be tidy and dispose of unwanted storage

11

CODA

This book has tried to give some advice to the beginning programmer on how to go about this most fascinating and challenging enterprise. We hope that it may also be of use to those who already have some experience, especially if that experience involves using a less structured language than Pascal. Most of our major points have been summarised in the form of an aphorism during the discussion of the pieces of code offered. However, we would wish to stress that, at the moment, programming still has a major element of art and creativity and these aphorisms are just that; they are not hard and fast rules. We believe that if you follow them you will find the process of creating programs less stressful and more rewarding than would otherwise be the case. However, you will gradually develop your own style — and probably your own aphorisms!

We lay considerable stress on the need to solve the problem first and then, and only then, to try to express your solution in Pascal. This is because the first instinct of many programmers is to rush to a terminal and to try to hack together something which will work. This instinct will frequently lead to disaster and unnecessary labour later.

This does not mean that you should not go near a terminal until you have every last detail worked out. That can be a frustrating process too. We have all had the experience of designing the perfect program, the only fault of which is that it will not work. No, there is an interplay between thought and action. Get a general solution and then try a preliminary coded version on the machine. Try it out with a variety of data sets, especially those which will test it beyond endurance. If you do not, some ham-fisted user will find a really nasty data set the first day they use it.

This will throw up all sorts of problems, both computing and substantive, which you hadn't thought of before, and you will go away and refine your ideas and then try them out on the machine again. It is often the case that it is easier to write a program which doesn't work and then write one which does, than to write one which does. This is why we talk most of the time, not about just writing programs, but about developing them.

One needs ideas when trying to solve problems. You can get these ideas from anywhere. They may come from your head; you need, however, to realise that people have been trying to find useful solutions to programming problems for many years, and one can learn from other people's experience. If you are going to do any serious programming you should have on your bookshelf, preferably within arm's reach, at least one good book on algorithms and at least one on data structures. There are so many aspects of computer science in which one feels that the problem is a mystery, but when one reads someone else's solution, you kick yourself and say ''Now, why didn't I think of that''. Thus, although programming is in many ways an individual, indeed at times a solitary venture, there is a large programming community which can add to it a social dimension, even if only through the printed word. By reading their books, you can cooperate with some of the profoundest thinkers in the subject.

There is a social dimension on a smaller scale, too. Often one has a difficulty in visualising how to solve a problem, or even one has a program which contains a mysterious and hard-to-trace bug. It is possible to sit for hours and hours and make no progress. In this case, discussion with friends or colleagues (one hopes that most colleagues are both) can often break the log-jam. Sometimes they make a helpful suggestion. More often, much more often in our experience, what happens is that, even if they are not of much help, the fact that you have had to explain it so someone else clarifies the problem so much in your own mind that the solution appears as if by magic. Again, one has the ''Why didn't I think of that (before)'' phenomenon.

Above all, we would recommend you to develop a style. By this we mean that you know where to look in your own programs when problems arise or modifications are needed. You are able to tell at a glance what are parameters and what are local variables. You are probably able to tell very quickly which parts of program were written by you and which by someone else. It is very likely that colleagues will be able to look at a piece of code and say ''Oh, that is Brenda's'' or ''That looks as though Jim had a hand in it''.

The style does not need to be that of someone else. Obviously there will be influences from friends, teachers, textbooks and so on. However, these other people are not you, and do not think exactly like you. So their style, although it may have similarities to your way of thinking, will not be your style. In writing this book, the three authors, all experienced programmers, have consciously tried to make their style more similar than it would otherwise be. However, we would be surprised if professionals who read the book are unable to tell which program examples were created by different members of the writing team. If we, working together, cannot be clones, how can we expect other people to be so.

Above all, when writing programs, try to write programs which do not just work, and work efficiently. That is, of course, essential. Try to write programs which people can use. A program which an experienced scientific engineeer can use may be very different from one which is to be used by nurses, for example, at least in the user-interface. Also, remember that writing the program in the first place is not the major part of the task. Very few programs are written and then stay fixed like tablets of stone for all time. Most need to revised. Bugs are found. Even standard programs, used by thousands of people, have bug reports weekly. The requirements change. Instead of processing hundreds of cases, the company has to process thousands or millions, and they suddenly find that the disk access is too frequent and is slowing the job down intolerably. The program has to be modified to take account of this. Even more common is that the user finds that the problem has changed. To begin with, they find the computer of great assistance in doing more efficiently what they did by hand before. Then suddenly they realise that that they can in fact do things differently, or do more things, and they in effect rewrite the program specification AFTER the programming has been running for a year or two.

This means that your programs must above all be modifiable. This means that they must be crystal clear to you in a year's time, and to other people at anytime. Estimates in the industry vary, but it seems to be generally agreed that program maintenance and modification now accounts for well over half the total cost of software provision. The original program creation is a declining factor in the costs and effort expended. This does not mean that the original program creation is less important. Indeed, we would argue that it is more important. If you have to write your programs so that they can be quickly and easily modified in some unspecifiable way at some unspecifiable time in the future by some unspecifiable programmer, then you, as the original author, or member of a team of authors, have a heavier responsibility than falls on someone who just has to get a program working somehow or other. Therefore, our final aphorism is appropriate in more than one sense:

When you develop a program, think of other people

Appendix

STANDARD PASCAL TERMS

abs	**and**	arctan	**array**
begin	*boolean*	**case**	*char*
chr	**const**	cos	dispose
div	**do**	**downto**	eof
eoln	exp	*false*	**function**
get	**goto**	**if**	**in**
input	*integer*	**label**	ln
maxint	**mod**	new	**nil**
not	odd	**of**	**or**
ord	*output*	pack	**packed**
pred	**procedure**	**program**	put
read	readln	*record*	**repeat**
reset	rewrite	round	**set**
sin	sqr	sqrt	succ
text	**then**	**to**	*true*
trunc	**type**	unpack	**until**
var	**while**	**with**	write
writeln			

Reserved words are in boldface

Pre-defined functions and procedures are in plain text

Other pre-defined standard identifiers are in italic

THE ASCII PRINTABLE CHARACTER SET

Final digit of character code

Initial digits of character code	0	1	2	3	4	5	6	7	8	9
0	Control characters (Non-printable)									
1										
2										
3			blank space	!	"	#	$	%	&	'
4	(	)	*	+	,	-	.	/	0	1
5	2	3	4	5	6	7	8	9	:	;
6	<	=	>	?	@	A	B	C	D	E
7	F	G	H	I	J	K	L	M	N	O
8	P	Q	R	S	T	U	V	W	X	Y
9	Z	[	\	]	^	_	`	a	b	c
10	d	e	f	g	h	i	j	k	l	m
11	n	o	p	q	r	s	t	u	v	w
12	x	y	z	{	|	}	~			

Thus 6 5 is the code for 'A'
9 0 is the code for 'Z'
12 2 is the code for 'z'
12 5 is the code for '}'
3 2 is the code for ' ' i.e. a blank space
2 8 is a non-printable character

Index